"What a splendid book! It reads so well and with so much interesting history, I didn't want to put it down."

Margaret Hayes
Former President, Rima Publications Ltd.

"Jerrine Weigand has written about modern China through the eyes of an average Canadian visiting a whole new world ... but Chen Yu Hua is not the average obedient Chinese daughter dominated by ancient traditions. Whoever reads this story will have a greater understanding of modern China and its people."

Florence Whyard, CM
Longtime journalist, editor and biographer in Yukon and Northwest Territories.

To Jerrine Weigand – Knowing Miss Chen
"I read your book twice with much laughing and tearing. It is very educational, informative and amusing. I am amazed how clearly you describe in detail Chen Yu Hua's past and how accurate you present the emotional settings. I like your analysis of the Chinese way of thinking and habits. It helped me understand myself even better. I think this is a wonderful book. Both interesting for Westerners and Chinese. I would encourage you to translate it into Chinese where you will have many readers."

Xiu-Mei (Sue May) Zhang, MD, Dr. TCM
Whitehorse, Yukon

Knowing Miss Chen
Living with the Chinese

Jerrine R Weigand
Trafford Publishing
Victoria, BC

Disclaimer
Whenever I considered it necessary in Chen Yu Hua's young life story I have created certain fictitious characters, some dialogue and events as might have happened at that time in history during The Cultural Revolution and the 1989 Tiananmen Incident.

Editing and production: Gillian (Jill) Veitch. Kelowna, BC
This book is typeset in Garamond.

© Copyright 2006 Jerrine R. Weigand.
All rights reserved. No part of this publication may be reproduced, stored in a retrieval system, or transmitted, in any form or by any means, electronic, mechanical, photocopying, recording, or otherwise, without the written prior permission of the author.

Note for Librarians: A cataloguing record for this book is available from Library and Archives Canada at www.collectionscanada.ca/amicus/index-e.html
ISBN 1-4120-8125-4

Printed in Victoria, BC, Canada. Printed on paper with minimum 30% recycled fibre. Trafford's print shop runs on "green energy" from solar, wind and other environmentally-friendly power sources.

TRAFFORD
PUBLISHING
Offices in Canada, USA, Ireland and UK

Book sales for North America and international:
Trafford Publishing, 6E–2333 Government St.,
Victoria, BC V8T 4P4 CANADA
phone 250 383 6864 (toll-free 1 888 232 4444)
fax 250 383 6804; email to orders@trafford.com
Book sales in Europe:
Trafford Publishing (UK) Limited, 9 Park End Street, 2nd Floor
Oxford, UK OX1 1HH UNITED KINGDOM
phone +44 (0)1865 722 113 (local rate 0845 230 9601)
facsimile +44 (0)1865 722 868; info.uk@trafford.com
Order online at:
trafford.com/05-3122

10 9 8 7 6 5 4 3 2

My love to Bill, who lived every moment of this story with me, and without whom, I could never have finished this book.

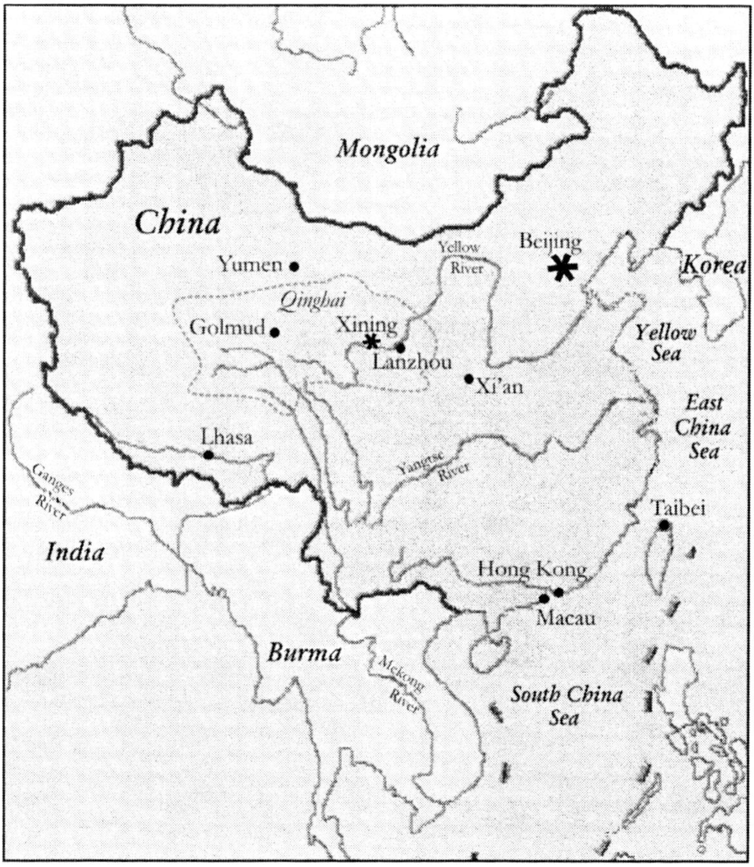
Mongolia
China
Yellow
River
Beijing
Korea
Yumen
Qinghai
Golmud
Xining
Lanzhou
Yellow
Sea
Xi'an
East
China
Sea
Lhasa
Ganges
River
Yangtse
River
Taibei
India
Hong Kong
Macau
Burma
Mekong
River
South China
Sea

The essence of mind is like the sky
Sometimes it is shadowed by the clouds of thought-flow
Then the wind of the Guru's inner teaching
Blows away the drifting clouds
Yet the thought-flow itself is the elimination
The experience is as natural as sun and moonlight
Yet it is beyond both space and time

Song by Milarepa,
Tibet

Acknowledgments

My first appreciation must go to the late Pierre Berton. Arriving home from China in 1997, I met Mr. Berton at a Northern Circumpolar Conference at Yukon College in Whitehorse. As we chatted about my China experience I explained that I was about to write my first book, a promise I had made to a young Chinese lady. When I asked him how I should start my manuscript, he smiled and said, "The best advice I can give you is to write your book like you were writing a letter to a friend."

My thanks to my editor, Jill Veitch, for her enthusiasm and humor and believing in my story. Bringing a new author through the mine field of a first book has to be a challenging task.

And to The Hon. Audrey McLaughlin, Norman Ross, Shirley and Bill Read, Lynda and Murray Adams and Jill Gillett (my first unofficial editor) who made the long journey to visit us on the Tibetan Plateau, I thank them all.

To the people who took time out of their busy lives to read my story and offer advice and encouragement: Sue May Zhang, Darlene George, Rusty and Bob Erlam, Leslie Leibel, Rolf and Marg Hougen, Edi Cousins, Sandra Pearson, Missy Follwell, Doug Winkley, Colin and Rosemary Cook, Kay Bartlett, Sharon Edwards, Dawn Weigand, Rose Fowler, Connie Como, Jeff Como, Kate Hume, Vern and Sheila Weigand, Dorothy and Ernie Brisco, Victoria Chen, Amelia Hu and Gary Chen, Alma Selig, Verna Goddard, Giselle Hahn and Enid Holloway.

And to Professor Stephen Brown, Simon Fraser University, who offered many valuable suggestions and resolved my concerns about blending two personal stories. Thank you.

There are people who jolted me out of my writing doldrums: Maxine Gunoff, phoning me long distance to ask, "Are you writing today?" Every time I felt sorry for myself and set my writing aside, my old friend, Florence Whyard, would say "Get busy! Quit being such a reluctant author." When I used the same words on my author friend, Margaret Hayes, she would ignore me with "It's good. Just get the darn thing published."

Much inspiration came to me while attending forums at the CBC Studio One Book Club hosted by Sheryl MacKay with John Burns from *The Georgia Straight*. They create the perfect atmosphere for new writers to meet published Canadian and international authors.

My love and thanks to my family for always believing in me and understanding my dream to write this book.

To the Chinese people who were a part of our adventure, I must thank them for their patience and incredible understanding of two naïve Canadians living and working in their country.

Above all, to Miss Chen Yu Hua, who said, "It was fate that we met." This is our story.

From Candace Paris, Hospital Administrator,
Niagara, Ontario, Canada—2006

It was my pleasure and good fortune to meet Chen Yu Hua in the fall of 2004, when she was assigned to be my official translator for lectures I was giving at the First Peoples Municipal Hospital in Xining City, Qinghai Province, China. As a volunteer adviser with the Canadian Executive Services Organization, I had been invited to the hospital to provide training in cost accounting and contemporary management practices. From the onset, Chen Yu Hua and I became friends, and so I was genuinely honored when she discreetly asked me if I would like to read a draft of the book being written about her life by a friend in Canada. Her story immediately captivated me. In my journal I noted that this was an important story that needed to be told, and needed to be heard. The extraordinary challenges this young woman faced in order to achieve her dream as an educated professional woman makes this a page-turner. I could not put it down! My esteem for this quiet, charming, and determined lady rose to even higher heights.

Before leaving Xining City, Chen Yu Hua invited me to spend an evening with her and her family (her husband and teen-aged daughter) at her home and visiting a night market. We chatted long into the evening, and once again I was fascinated by the lessons I was learning and delighted with the warm hospitality extended to me.

As one reads this story, one must take into account the social and political period in which the character of the young Miss Chen was molded. It makes her successes all the more admirable.

Pronunciation

In the Chinese language the letter 'X' is pronounced something similar to 'sh':

Xining is pronounced *Shin-ning*
Xunhua is *Shoon Wha*

The letter 'Q' is pronounced 'ch':

Qinghai is *Ching-high*
Qipao is *Chi-pow*

Nihao is the Chinese greeting, and is pronounced *Nee How*.

Main character names & pronunciation:

Chen Yu Hua	*Chen You Wha*
Miss Wei	*Miss Way*
Mr. Cheng	*Mr. Chong*
Mayor Yang	*Mayor Young*
Mr. Liu	*Mr. Leo*
Driver Zhang	*Driver Zhong*
Si Xian	*Sue Shee An*
Liu Hao	*Leo How*
Li	*Lee*
Mi	*Mee*

Chen Yu Hua    Miss Wei    Mr. Cheng

Mayor Yang    Boss Liu    Driver Zhang

Bill and Jerrine Weigand

Knowing Miss Chen
Living With The Chinese

Chen Yu Hua was born in 1960. A tumultuous time in China: the same year the Soviet Union withdrew its resources and experts; one year after the disastrous floods of 1959; one year after the failure of the Great Leap Forward when more than 25 million people reportedly starved to death; three years after the incarceration of 300 thousand intellectuals during Chairman Mao's "Letting a Hundred Flowers Bloom."

These were turbulent times and a prelude to ten years (1966-76) of the brutal onslaught known as The Great Proletarian Cultural Revolution, when the people of China were at the mercy of the Red Guards. These idealistic, inexperienced youths were driven to heights of revolutionary frenzy. They burned books, and destroyed ancient relics and works of art. They humiliated, beat harshly or murdered anyone with an alleged bourgeois taint. No one was safe. No intellectual or successful merchant or landowner. No one associated with a foreign corporation.

China was in chaos. The reign of terror by the PLA (People's Liberation Army) came next, with the Campaign to Purify Class Ranks, and again no one went unscathed, not even high government officials or army officers. Thousands were sent from their homes to camps and schools in the countryside to study and combine hard labor with self-criticism.

By 1976, the years of unrest and mass movement were drawing to a close with the death of the popular Zhou Enlai in January, the Qing Ming Demonstrations and the Tiananmen Incident in March and April of the same year. Three more events in 1976: the death of one of China's greatest revolutionary heroes, Marshall Zhu De on July 7th, followed by the powerful Tangshan earthquake, which claimed over 250,000 lives on July 26th, and the death of Chairman Mao Zedong on September 9th, ended this violent cycle in Chinese history.

These were the formative years of Chen Yu Hua's childhood in Xunhua, Northwest China.

one

中国

She was thinking about her father. She must not be late getting home from school; yesterday she received a sharp cuff to the back of her head for being a few minutes late, bringing tears to her eyes.

She loved her father but was fearful of him. Years later Chen Jian Pin would tell her he was sorry for being so strict, so severe with the family, and she would understand then, but not now. She clutched Mao's Little Red Book close to her heart and hurried along dusty lanes flanked by high dusty clay walls, to the safety of her home, and to her father. A slight, undernourished seven-year-old Chinese girl in the county of Xunhua in Qinghai province, she was fanatically obedient.

The loud speakers blasted out the repetitious slogans of Chairman Mao as the little girl opened the old wooden gate to her home. Wet clothes hung on rope lines in the courtyard. Grandma was washing, or was it her mother? They must be back from the fields early today, tired and irritable as always, not accustomed to working like peasants. Her mother had been a grade school teacher and her father was once Dean of Gandu Normal School, a prestigious position in the 1950s as there were only two normal schools in all Qinghai Province. But that was a lifetime ago. After being demoted in the Anti-Rightist Movement, he was sent to his former home in Xunhua Salar Autonomous County where, in grinding poverty, he and his wife worked in the fields with the peasant-farmers. It was a never-ending struggle to feed and clothe their family; a struggle that stretched out for sixteen miserable years.

"Chen Yu Hua," called her father. "Come in here at once."

He was in a small room leading off the kitchen area, an airless, gloomy space just big enough for a chair, a stool and a wooden bench carved with motifs, stretching along one wall. A faded piece of printed yellow silk, used as a curtain, was pulled to one side of a narrow window wedged tightly up to the corner of the other wall. The window appeared awkward and out of place, as if it had been cut in half.

Her father was home too early today. Chen Yu Hua would not be able to climb the narrow ladder to the loft and sit alone for a few minutes. Adults never went up to the secret room where sometimes she and her sisters sang or played hide and seek or simply talked. Of course these play times were rare; there was always work after school, carrying water, carrying wood or searching for food. Often Chen Yu Hua and her brothers and sisters would raid the neighboring farmers' gardens for carrots and tomatoes. They slipped into the orchards and picked fruit from the trees: pears, apples or walnuts. Once they even stole watermelons, but never again. They were too frightened. The Watcher might grab them. He would turn his dog on them, beat them with a willow branch and drag them home to their parents where more harsh discipline was waiting. Today she was so hungry. If she was lucky, her mother might have left buns in the wooden steam boxes or under the linen cover on the kneading board. But with her father calling, there was no time to look for food.

Her father drew the thin silk cloth across the window, shading out the sun, making sure no one could see into the room. Chen Yu Hua studied the ancient scenes on the curtain. She squinted her large brown eyes. Three beautiful ladies wearing traditional *qipao* were standing on a curved stone bridge, umbrellas pressed close to the backs of their heads where orange blossoms clasped smooth black hair. Or were they chrysanthemums? It was hard to tell. Every time she came to this room she wondered about the flowers. Dirty fingerprints and endless tugging of the old cloth had paled the colors and distorted the pictures.

"Chen Yu Hua." His quiet voice was tired. A ray of light squeezed through frayed edges of the curtain and crossed his sober face. She thought he was very handsome. "You will thank me one day for this." His voice hardened, became demanding. "You know you must learn more than what you are being taught in school ... more than the words of Chairman Mao's Little Red Book. You must be educated properly and someday I want you to go to university in Beijing ... to be a teacher ... you must be educated."

He gave a great sorrowful sigh, feeling perhaps his next words would be shameless lies. He had to lie. To pretend to never let go of the hope that reason would soon return to his country. He straightened his slightly-bowed shoulders and, with an emotional voice, said slowly, "I know this much ... these times will not last forever. It cannot be long before life will be good again ... we must be ready. Now let us begin ... we only have a few minutes."

Chen Yu Hua knew all too well her father would be severely punished if anyone heard him talking like this, or if he was caught teaching his children thoughts other than the "thoughts of Chairman Mao." So the obedient little Chinese girl became her father's student. She sat on the small brown wooden stool in front of him, and opened one of the old musty smelling schoolbooks that had been banned and hidden, at great risk, for years.

She began to read for him.

It was April 1994 in Yukon, northern Canada. My husband, Bill, was the mayor of the territory's capital city, Whitehorse, and we were giving a party in our home for a visiting delegation of Chinese. The group had come all the way from Northwest China, from the city of Xining in the province of Qinghai, to observe our part of the world, considering it to be geographically similar to their own. They were looking for advice and information on northern transportation and communications systems as well as economic development opportunities for their own northern regions. This was part of the new Chinese Opening to the West policy. Mayors and senior cadres (government officials) were sent out from their country to gain exposure to North America and the rest of the world.

Chen Yu Hua was standing in our living room the first time I saw her, and when I asked, "Who is that lady," I was told she was the interpreter for the delegation. I thought she was tall for a Chinese lady. Her thick black hair was partly held back by a metal clasp, giving her a youthful, sophisticated appearance. She wore a simple black dress with a patterned burgundy shawl draped stylishly over her shoulders. It was not only her pretty face that caught my attention, but also the straight and confident way she carried herself. I assumed Chen Yu Hua was quite worldly, but later discovered this was her first trip out of China and her first visit to a Western home. She was puzzled by our unfamiliar foreign customs, like standing nose to nose at the cocktail party, drinking red wine from long-stemmed glasses and using fingers to eat strange hors d'oeuvres. Little toast points of ham and cheese were bizarre, especially the cheese. There was no cheese in China. The buffet was even stranger to her. The idea of picking up food from a table, and then finding somewhere to sit and eat it with cold metal knives and forks, seemed clumsy and intimidating. Later, in China, she told me how she feared making any mistakes so she never ate or drank at our home.

The next evening, a special farewell dinner honoring our visitors was held at a local restaurant. Mayor Yang Qi Lian watched curiously as the pretty server created a Caesar salad at our table. When the raw egg yolk and olive oil dressing had been drizzled over the romaine lettuce and the last of the anchovies, croutons and Parmesan cheese were added, she asked if he would like to do the mixing. He was delighted. Everyone cheered as he tossed the salad as though he knew what he was doing. No Caesar salads in Qinghai.

I knew enough about Chinese food to wonder what they thought when the steaks were put before them; a chunk of rare meat seared on both sides, sitting on a big plate beside a steaming baked potato gushing with sour cream, butter, bacon pieces and green chives. Several months later my husband asked Mayor Yang what his favorite food had been when he visited Canada. He thought for a long time. "Hot dogs," he said. So much for the New York steaks marinated in fine brandy and grilled to perfection.

At the table that evening I sat next to Chen Yu Hua. I learned she was a teacher before joining the Foreign Trade Bureau, she was thirty-four years old, married to a teacher by the name of Liu Hao and had a little girl. "I miss her," she smiled, "her name is Si Xian." We chatted about her life in Xining as I watched Director Liu Li Xun and our guests toying with their dessert. Nudging creamy chocolate Black Forest cake glazed with maraschino cherries and Kirsch around their plates, it was obvious sweets were not very appetizing for the Chinese. Then, making things worse, coffee was served. By then they must have been dying for a cup of green tea. What would I do if I had to face a table of food so unfamiliar and disagreeable to me that I couldn't eat it?

The dinner was coming to an end and, if they didn't enjoy the food, they found the beer and Canadian Club very much to their liking.

Director Liu leaned across the table towards me, eagerly asking a question. I turned to Chen Yu Hua. "Mr. Liu asks if you and Mr. Weigand would like to be volunteer Foreign Experts. We could invite you to come to Xining and work with us. We have a lot to learn about the West and perhaps you and Mr. Weigand could help us."

I nodded my head. "I think that's a great idea!" I said, "Yes ... we can go to Xining. But only after my husband has finished his term as mayor."

"Mr. Liu asks would you stay for one year."

"Yes, we could stay for one year."

She looked surprised. "Without asking your husband first?" Chen Yu Hua's translation of my answers to Director Liu made him laugh. But everyone agreed, including Bill, it was an excellent opportunity for a retired business couple to spend a year in China.

It all sounded so easy. Someone in the crowd suggested it would be a great adventure to explore a new culture and Mayor Yang raised his glass, "See you in Xining," he said.

It was a full year later before we received the formal written invitation.

The Qinghai Provincial Government and the Xining Municipal Government invite Mr. William Weigand and Mrs. Jerrine Weigand to work for one year with the Xining Bureau of Foreign Trade and Economic Cooperation.

The details of the invitation explained that, as volunteer Foreign Experts (a title relating to foreigners invited to work in China), our airfare and accommodation would be provided by the Chinese Government.

Before we left for China, we had some doubts and fears. We were leaving our comfortable home, family and friends, and our familiar way of life. What did we know about China? Were we too old for such a trip?

"You're neither too young, nor too old," a friend assured us. "You should go."

And we did.

two

中国

Chen Yu Hua's mother saw her reflection in the chrome wheel of her sewing machine; a tiny distorted vision of her face. She sat staring at the precious machine with the famous Chinese brand name *Feiren* (Flying Man) stamped on a burnished oval disk riveted to the front.

It was morning and the family had gathered for breakfast, only this morning there would be no breakfast. There were times when the children left for school having eaten a meager handful of dried peas or a ration of plain flour fried in hot black cooking oil or yak butter. Often, like today, they ate nothing. Although the parents worked on the Farm Production Team for the entire year, when autumn came and the crops were gathered, they were given only enough wheat to feed themselves for three months. The rest of the year was spent scrounging for food and money. It was a life of making-do, making-over and trying to survive. The two or three months prior to harvest were the cruelest months of all. Desperation forced them to borrow food from relatives or The Team. The vegetables they grew on their half-mu of land were soon consumed or used for trading and now the family of nine needed money urgently to buy wheat flour or highland barley flour, or they would starve.

Jia Ying sighed and covered the sad image on the wheel with her frail, callused hand. Tears of despair poured from her hollow eyes. She didn't want to cry in front of her family but she could not help herself. It was shameful to show a weak spirit to the children.

Jian Pin studied his wife and for the first time he noticed how gaunt her face had become; how the distinct little white streaks, like fine lines drawn by schoolroom chalk, threaded their way through her short black hair. Dark olive skin under her eyes added years to her age and he knew she was exhausted. He also knew she was feeding the family her measure of limited food, never keeping enough nourishment for herself. He hoped she wouldn't fall ill. A dreadful thought jolted through him. She could get sick and die!

"I can't sell the sewing machine," she wept. "What will we do for clothes?"

As it was, they had few enough clothes to wear. In the hot summer she would make them shirts and trousers, but there was never enough material to sew more than one set each. When the clothes became dirty they were washed at bedtime, dried overnight and worn again the next day. In the cooler days of spring and autumn she made the family cotton vests; for winter, a heavy padded jacket and a loose-fitting coat. She was continually cutting down old jackets to make new ones for the younger children. Chen Yu Hua considered herself lucky; being the oldest daughter, she always had new clothes while her younger sisters got the re-designed hand-me-downs. Jia Ying also made shoes. When the last pair of shoes was finished for her big family she started making new ones all over again.

A lifetime ago she was a pretty young girl married to a handsome school teacher, happy to face a bright future in the new free China after the revolution of 1949. But something went terribly wrong and here they were in 1967 exhausted and starving.

To make extra money she sewed clothes for neighbors. Sometimes she would not accept payment if the family were poorer than her own family. She worked at night in secret by the light of an oil lamp. Owning a small free enterprise business was not allowed. It was against all the rules of the Communist Party, and if she were found out the family would be branded as Capitalist Roaders, a punishable crime.

With the little money she made from her sewing venture or marketing pork meat and pig entrails (from the one and only pig they could afford to raise each year), she could usually feed and clothe her family. But now there was no more money. No more food. They had already sold anything of value, including their fur coats, wristwatches, satin brocade-lined camel hair coats, even the cherished large bronze cloisonné vase that had been in the Chen family for decades. The only precious possession left was the Feiren, the Flying Man sewing machine, and they must sell it or starve.

The Chen children witnessed for the first time two unusual and poignant moments that morning. While their mother wept, their father, who rarely demonstrated affection for his wife in their presence, calmly rested his hand on her shoulder. He told her they would never sell the sewing machine and promised he would find money for food somewhere.

"Perhaps I could sell the desk," he said.

"Not the desk … not the sewing machine," Jia Ying objected in a flat voice, "there has to be some other way."

Chen Yu Hua looked quizzically around the sparsely furnished house. What desk? She wondered.

Chen Jian Pin was not a religious man. He was too pragmatic for that. Like most Chinese he shaped his life on the philosophy of Confucius, holding deep respect for family and ancestor worship, but this conflicted dangerously with the ideas of Chairman Mao Zedong. He was also interested in Buddhism, and wisely cemented his relationship with the devoutly Buddhist Tibetan people who formed a large part of Xunhua. They were mostly poor farmers, with little love for politics, and Chen Jian Pin trusted them. "You must always respect the Tibetans," he would say. "You can trade with them or sell them goods and you can buy mutton or oil from them or yak butter."

Each morning he prayed to a Being of his choice and the words were always the same, "I must stay alive today. I must not get ill today. Help me to look after my family the best I can."

Luck would have it that Chen Jian Pin heard about the annual Communist Three-Level Cadre meeting being held in Xunhua by the county government. This meant that some of his Tibetan friends, who were community leaders in their villages, would be in town attending the sessions. He went to them, inquiring if they needed new clothes. His wife was a good seamstress, he told them.

He could not give them a written price list ... that would be capitalistic, but he could quote from memory:

one padded coat	3.0	yuan
one shirt	2.5	yuan
one overcoat	5.0	yuan
one short-sleeved shirt	2.0	yuan
one pair underpants	1.5	yuan
one pair trousers	2.0	yuan

The Tibetans were delighted. Yes, of course, they told him. Yes, they needed a good seamstress. He took the men to his home where Jia Ying designed and produced new trousers and shirts for them, colorful blouses and long black skirts for their wives and daughters, jackets and pants for their sons. The Flying Man (which should have been named Flying Woman) hummed in response and the little reflection on the chrome wheel was smiling. Jia Ying's small business enterprise would yield her dozens of yuan to buy new cloth to make clothes for her family and neighbors. And she knew her secret would be safe with the Tibetans.

She would buy food, and perhaps a little meat and Western medicine on the black market, like Aspirin for headaches, tetracycline for fighting bacteria, Mercurochrome for cuts. She was happy and, if she was careful the money would last for a while ... at least until the next harvest.

Our old Tupolev plane touched down in Xining. We had drifted across layers upon layers of uneven parallel lines of soft blues and purples, ochres and umbers. Below us lay the barren, treeless land of the Tibetan Plateau scored by China's great rivers and, far to the west, towered the great white Himalayas. If we stared hard enough, long enough, we could see the pinnacles, or so we imagined. This is the way I will always remember Qinghai Province that clear day on

Knowing Miss Chen

June 20, 1995.

Six days earlier we had landed in China.
There was not the mass confusion and bedlam we expected at the Beijing airport when we arrived. The customs man just stared at the luggage. Six large black suitcases, two small ones, and a cardboard box of books, carry-ons, and a stuffed duty-free shopping bag. He looked at the endless baggage then tapped the box with a long stick.
"What's in here?"
"Books," I answered.
He leaned wearily on the counter and motioned for us to go through. It all looked too formidable for him to start any serious questioning.
Chen Yu Hua was at the gate, waving her arms above her head. We were suddenly in the noisy crowd and she was hugging us tightly like old friends. She introduced us to Cheng Tang Xian. "Mr. Cheng is your immediate boss and has been sent by the office in Xining to greet you officially," she said, "and this is our driver, Mr. Wong." Mr. Wong was smiling until he saw the two carts piled high with our luggage.
They counted … "yi .. er .. san .. si .. wu .."
"You have eleven pieces," Chen Yu Hua said, her voice mildly accusing, "I've never seen so much luggage."
It was fourteen months since we saw Chen Yu Hua in Canada. Our correspondence had been mainly business and short messages by fax, letters and phone, but now we were here with her in China. She would be our interpreter and we would work in the same office, speak English with her every day and learn about her life and how to live with the Chinese people.
The next six days were a wonderful blur of the sights and sounds of Beijing. Our life revolved around 5000 years of Chinese history, bottled water, mad driving, weaving through a sea of bicycles and getting our ears accustomed to the tones of the Chinese language.
Mr. Cheng was a muscular man with strong shoulders and a handsome square jaw. He was in his early fifties and reminded me

of an athlete or a movie star from Hong Kong. He talked a lot, was witty and kept Driver Wong and Chen Yu Hua laughing. Sometimes she would translate what he said and we would all laugh. He was also a lover of Beijing Opera, or *piaoyou*, an ancient Chinese musical drama with splendid, exaggerated costumes and ornate *goulian* (face painting). Sitting in the front seat of the car as we moved along the hectic streets, he would close his eyes and burst into song, reaching the high notes with considerable ease and, for a few minutes, be passionately swept up in his own little musical world. We always applauded when he finished and he always said thank you, which sounded to our ears a bit like *sank you*. This was the other English saying he knew besides *hello* and *okay*.

We learned that twelve million people called Beijing home. Modern apartment blocks were replacing the old tenements of the 50s and 60s and glass skyscrapers belonging to giant Western corporations bordered broad new boulevards. Several ring roads helped to move the crush of automobiles, trucks, buses, bicycles and horse-drawn carts. Rush hour was the same nightmare as in any large city.

Beijing, they told us, was not reflective of China, but was one of the wealthy modern golden coast cities lacing their way from glittering Hong Kong north to prosperous Dalian. The bright cities of Shenzhen, Guangzhou, Shanghai, and Tianjin beckoned businessmen and tourists from all over the world, as well as peasant-farmers and poor young men seeking a better life. The cities bulged with illegal transients, alarming leaders of the possible social consequences of over-crowded conditions and unemployment.

"A person must carry a Resident Permit Card to be able to move from one part of our country to another," explained an official. "You can imagine the chaos if we allowed our citizens to move randomly to the cities like they do in Canada ... there are too many of them. Even now there are an estimated three million itinerant workers living in the Beijing area."

We trooped around the larger-than-life Tiananmen Square, "Soul of China", where a huge portrait of Chairman Mao was suspended prominently above Tiananmen Gate. Our minds raced back to the many publicized scenes from 1989: the student defying the tanks, the toppling of the Goddess of Democracy, the guns, the noise and the condemnation by the West.

"What would you like to see first?" asked Mr. Cheng.

Out of the blue, and a lucky guess for us, we said, "I think Chairman Mao's tomb." Later we would be praised many times for wanting to view Chairman Mao first before going to any other location.

The crowd inside the tomb was hushed and the mood was a mixture of reverence and curiosity, with perhaps more reverence from the older Chinese. Guards cautioned us to be quiet and asked the men to remove their headgear. The room was dark except for the illuminated glass catafalque. There lay the cold, wax-like figure of the Great Helmsman, the once foremost leader of a billion people.

Mao Zedong was the man who liberated China from the controlling tentacles of warlords and the corrupt reign of Chiang Kai-shek's Kuomintang government. He was a forceful man who rallied poverty-stricken peasant-farmers for the Long March and made soldiers out of them; whose slogan was "political power grows out of the barrel of a gun."

Mao fought the invasion by the Japanese and united China; it was clear that he made the country a better place in which to live. But the great leader fell victim to the old adage, "absolute power corrupts absolutely." He was responsible for more deaths and more chaos than any world war, but to the old men who remembered China before the Liberation of 1949, he was their savior. He may not have been a saint; after all, he was human and certainly had many weaknesses, but he was the greatest leader in their memory.

We made our way to the balcony and stood where Chairman Mao once stood overlooking Tiananmen Square. Thirty-year-old images of black and white newsreels scurried through my mind and I couldn't help but study the faces of our three companions.

Were they remembering too?

Chen Yu Hua never saw Chairman Mao, she was too young. But Mr. Cheng and Driver Wong may have witnessed that August day in 1966 when thousands of students who called themselves Red

Guards crowded the Square. They came from every part of China. From every province, city, village and farm, mostly on trains, traveling for hours or days in overcrowded coaches. They slept everywhere, under the seats and in the aisles, cramming doorways and toilets and, when the train stopped at stations, they crawled in and out of the windows. It was dirty and uncomfortable. In their revolutionary zeal they did not mind the hardships, for in a few days they would behold their hero in Beijing.

And soon they did. Tiananmen Square teemed with tens of thousands of tired but enthusiastic Red Guards dressed in army fatigues, proudly displaying their symbolic revolutionary red armbands. Although the day was intolerably hot and people fainted from lack of food and water, an electric energy rippled through the crowd as rumors spread that the great man was coming.

At last, Chairman Mao appeared on the balcony. He stood straight and commanding in his army uniform; god-like in the rays of the golden sun, or so he appeared to the awestruck young Red Guards. At first the crowd couldn't believe it was really him. Suddenly great roars and cheering exploded through the air, "Long live Chairman Mao! Long live Chairman Mao! Long live the glorious Chinese Communist Party!" Mao waved. More cheers. Everyone was sobbing. How fortunate they were to see the Great Helmsman. They would remember this moment all their lives.

Was Mr. Cheng remembering? Driver Wong?

three

中国

It was blistering hot in the fields of Xunhua County that summer of 1969.

Young Chen Yu Hua adjusted the month old baby on her back as she started the long trek to find her mother for the noon nursing. It was school holidays and another baby had arrived into her impoverished family. Chairman Mao would be proud of them. He encouraged his people to have many children, to rebuild the New China, regardless of whether or not his people could feed them. She now had two younger brothers and two younger sisters, and the burden of part-time parenting fell on her undeserving nine-year-old shoulders. The adults were always away working; even her grandma had endless chores of her own, leaving the frail little girl to watch over her siblings. She was depressed, although she had no idea what the word meant, and she was tired. The long walk to the fields exhausted her. She never got enough sleep at night, or enough food to eat, and never had free time for herself.

Along the way she sat down on ledges or stones to rest and to comfort the crying baby. It seemed there was always a crying baby or a hungry miserable child to mind. She would sing to them, make funny faces, dance around the room, rock them in her arms, or lift them up to see their reflections in a small mirror that hung on the kitchen wall. She did everything to keep them entertained until her mother and father came home from work.

Today the squirming bundle was not about to be comforted and, like a heavy stone, she felt hammered down with every step.

Nearing the fields, Chen Yu Hua stopped to listen to the frantic chatter of women. Something must have happened. Her mother was bent over a young woman clutching her stomach and writhing in the soft-turned earth. She ran towards her, bouncing the unhappy baby; his wide-open mouth the source of pitiful screams.

"Chen Yu Hua," Jia Ying called to her daughter. "Come here quickly. Give me the baby and run to the next field and get Aunty Ma Lin. Tell her to come at once. We have trouble. Hurry! Hurry!"

"Mamma, what's the matter?"

"Go! Go!"

The little girl ran, scared and confused, her legs like rubber. She ran across the short stalks of harvested barley, cutting her bare feet; through the tall, golden barley that stabbed her body with a thousand needles, and came to a group of women hoeing the soil. "Aunty Ma Lin," she panted, "Mamma needs you," and fell to her knees.

Ma Lin, in her late forties, had been the village midwife since her youth. She had no formal training and learned the calling from her mother, acquiring bits and pieces of knowledge from the many births she attended. She knew only about healthy births, not about detecting early problems that could occur in pregnancy, not about Caesarean section or post-partum depression. Her birthing kit was hopelessly inadequate. It contained a small basin, a ball of string, a pair of dull scissors, some Mercurochrome and a dusty roll of bandage. But Aunty Ma Lin was a trusted, kind and caring person and she came directly to attend the hysterical woman.

Several more women came running from neighboring fields. A few curious men also turned up, eager to know what the fuss was all about, but hastily disappeared when they realized there was no place for them in women's business.

Chen Yu Hua was frightened when she returned.

"What's happening, mamma?" But she was ignored.

"Take the baby," is all her mother would say, and someone plunked the small baby back into Chen Yu Hua's thin arms.

Midwife Aunty Ma Lin was examining the woman's stomach and pelvic area with grimy hands and nails clogged with old dirt that simply could not be washed away. She asked the crying woman, "How long have you been pregnant?"

"Not long," came the sobbing reply.

"Bring some water ... she's having a miscarriage!" Jia Ying called out. She wiped the sweaty forehead of the crying woman with a small rag and spoke soft reassuring words to her.

It was too late for water. Aunty Ma Lin pressed on the woman's abdomen while massaging her pelvis with dirty hands smeared with bright red blood.

Chen Yu Hua had never seen so much blood. She could hardly stand it. The hungry baby in her arms was squirming and screaming. The pregnant woman was screaming. The panic-stricken voices of the other women created an unbelievable din ... and the sun ... the hot sun. She had a light feeling in her head when suddenly the ground came up to meet her. She twisted her body at the last conscious second to fall on her back, protecting her baby brother, who momentarily became too surprised to scream anymore.

Chen Yu Hua opened her eyes. Something was shading her face. It was the piece of cloth Jia Ying had used to wipe away the sweat from the forehead of the pregnant woman. The noise and commotion had all but gone and she heard her mother's voice soothing the baby.

"Are you all right?" She asked her daughter.

"Where is the lady?"

"She's gone ... Aunty Ma Lin took her away."

"Is she going to live?"

"Yes. She lost her baby but she'll be fine."

"Did the baby die?"

"Yes."

There was so much Chen Yu Hua wanted to know. She wanted her mother to explain what happened, where did all the blood come from, why and how did the pregnant lady lose her new baby before it was big like her little brother? Could this happen to her someday? But Jia Ying was not a talker; she was a doer, and the explaining would have to come from someone else.

Jia Ying gave her daughter one steamed bun and a piece of dried fruit and helped strap the sleeping baby to her back. Clouds drifted across the sky, cooling the heat of the afternoon as the little nine-year old girl began her long walk home. She was a little more worldly but not any wiser. Perhaps some day she would understand.

Years later Chen Yu Hua heard the story being retold about the miscarriage of the twenty-five-year-old worker, and how she had developed a severe life-threatening infection and almost died. Unfortunately the lady could never have any more children, but believed she was lucky to be alive, considering the circumstances of that hot July day in the barley fields of Xunhua County.

We had set aside one day, not nearly enough time, to explore the collection of well-restored buildings in the center of Beijing known as the Forbidden City. Between 1406 and 1420, Emperor Yong Li made use of over one million laborers to build the city and the wall behind which it stood. The result was an intricate complex of marble bridges, pavilions, temples, throne-halls, parks and gardens, stone statues and the Palace of Eternal Harmony where the emperors of old ascended the Dragon Throne. For more than 500 years these premises were off-limits to all commoners. It meant death to be found inside the gates and even being close to the gates without a good reason was dangerous.

In past times, when the Emperor wished to journey outside the walls of the Forbidden City, the chosen route would first be dusted with golden sand and fragrant flower petals. His elaborate entourage would take hours to cross the Moat Bridge, where luminous pink lotus blossoms swayed on the water surrounding the city. Ordinary citizens would be warned by conscientious armed guards to hide their faces when the Emperor passed and to never look upon the *palanquin*, its windows draped in heavy yellow brocade, bearing Heaven's Son.

The Forbidden City was destroyed and re-built several times in its long history. In 1664, the Manchus took advantage of the weakened state of the Ming Dynasty, burning the palace and destroying irreplaceable books, calligraphy and paintings. The

Japanese looted the palace during their occupation from 1937 to 1945, but by far the most significant removal of precious treasures and relics came in 1949 when the defeated Chiang Kai-shek and his Kuomintang government left China for the Island of Formosa (Taiwan), taking crates of China's history with them.

We drove a few miles north from the center of Beijing to the magnificent Summer Palace set in the immense park that was once the royal gardens. After the Ming Dynasty collapsed, the Summer Palace and grounds fell into miserable disrepair. In 1888 Empress Dowager CiXi began reconstruction of the palace and the great park with funds originally appropriated to build new ships. At the time, it wasn't very prudent of her, but the ships would be gone by now, rotted away by time, sea, and wind, whereas the Summer Palace lives on for the world to enjoy.

After walking through the Long Corridor and studying the ornately carved cross braces painted with hundreds of mythical scenes, I needed a rest. We had been out most of the day when I said to Chen Yu Hua, "Do you suppose we could find a toilet?"

"You need a toilet?"

Did I hear a gasp? Did she say in Chinese, where in the world will we find a toilet for the foreigners? Mr. Cheng and Driver Wong promptly disappeared.

I didn't think it was such an unreasonable request.

The two men returned and the usual discussion followed. "Is there something the matter?" I asked.

"Mr. Cheng wants me to go and inspect the facilities to make sure they're clean enough," said Chen Yu Hua. "You wait here."

It was the first time we realized what a terrible problem it was for the Chinese to direct a foreigner to a public toilet. Usually they were non-existent and if you would be lucky enough to find one, it was likely dirty, disgusting and shrouded in a choking odor; enough to send any visitor into a coughing fit. There was little serious effort put into building public washrooms, even at historical attractions and famous parks, which was terribly embarrassing for guides and interpreters.

Eventually we found the elusive toilets. It was easy to spot the Chinese character sign for women, 'look for the lady with her legs crossed' was the way it was described to me. Mr. Cheng paid the fee of fifty fen each for the foreigners and we were handed a couple of pieces of toilet paper.

Water had been splashed on the floor and the squat Asian toilets had constant noisy torrents of water rushing through them. It was wet but very clean. One thing I was thankful for: these stalls had doors. I found that many public toilets in China, even those in modern airports, lacked doors for privacy. Just out from Canada, and a little uptight, it always unnerved me to have a line-up of women patiently watching and waiting for me to finish my very personal nature call. But this day there was a door, though of course there was no lock. I kept it shut with one hand, trying not to drop my precious paper or soak my jeans while doing a balancing act over the unfamiliar porcelain fixture under me.

As I left the comfort station (more like a cold Turkish bath), I noticed a tap pouring icy water into a large wooden barrel. The smiling attendant nodded towards it, indicating I could wash my hands and, for another fee, she would give me a paper towel.

"Are you alright, Mrs. Weigand?" called Chen Yu Hua from the warm sunlight, "Was it clean enough?"

"Yes, thank you. It was very clean," I said, and meant it.

It was too hot and steep for me to wander up Longevity Hill. I decided to stay with Chen Yu Hua in a small park while Bill and the others climbed to the Buddhist Sea of Wisdom Temple.

"Do you mind if I call you Miss Chen?" I said as we sat together on a stone bench waiting for the men. I knew that married women in China were never called 'Mrs.' and had heard British teachers in Chinese classrooms were addressed as 'Miss'. To me this sounded better than twisting my foreign tongue around 'Chen Yu Hua'.

"No, of course not," she laughed. "That's a bit formal but you can call me whatever you want. I know foreigners have trouble pronouncing Chinese names."

"What does your name mean in English?"

"My name is Jade Flower ... Yu is Chinese for Jade."

"Jade Flower, Chen Jade Flower ... very pretty."

"You can call me Miss Chen if you like," she said, then added an after thought, "When I was young I was Teacher Chen."

As we both traced the small figures climbing the steps high above us she gave me the first of many lessons about China.

"Names are very important to us," she explained, "and the history of Chinese names is particularly interesting. Surnames have been around for thousands of years. They are composed of one word or syllable such as *Chen* and, unlike western countries, the surname is always written first. Given names, or what you refer to as Christian names, are usually two words and written last ... you know, when a woman marries she will keep her father's family name but her children will take the family name of her husband."

"Makes sense," I said, thinking about the women in my country who challenged the norm and faced ridicule for keeping their maiden name.

"The men are coming. We must go now." She used a term I would hear her say over and over again. Never ... let *us* go or we *should* go ... but always we *must* go.

We watched the men walking towards us. From a distance they seemed to be speaking with one another, friendly smiles, hand signals and all.

"You would think Mr. Weigand knows how to speak Chinese," she said, laughing.

The famous Marble Boat on Kunming Lake had been described as rather ugly. We didn't find it so; we thought it unique. Obviously it was built to float, but when the heavy marble blocks were put in place during construction, it settled straight away to the bottom of the lake and there it rested in shallow water. Near the entrance to the boat was a small bustling business and for a couple of yuan, we could rent period costumes and have pictures taken wearing them. Miss Chen and I opted to be Empresses from the Qing dynasty.

"These costumes are very dirty," grumbled Miss Chen, emphasizing the "T" in dirty. "You should have these things cleaned." She was grousing in English, more for my benefit than the smiling assistant who was oblivious to her complaints. We slipped into the long royal robes and heavy ostentatious headdresses piled high with beads and dangling silk tassels were placed on our heads.

Miss Chen then folded her arms into the satin sleeves, held her body just so and firmed her jaw. She sat on the pretend throne like she was born to it, looking every inch an Empress. Although the robe was faded and in need of cleaning, it was still a beautiful pale blue, embroidered with gray cranes and leaves the shade of an autumn maple. Later, in Chinese shops, I was overwhelmed by the abundance of exotic fabrics; filmy brilliantly colored silks as well as equally lovely synthetic materials, and heavy brocades embossed with gold and silver threads in detailed patterns of dragons, peacocks or flowers.

"Mr. Cheng wants to know if you would like to go to McDonald's for lunch," Miss Chen asked as we packed into our Russian-made car. Bill and I looked at one another, the truth being, we were thinking of trying some new Chinese cuisine.

"Have you ever been to McDonald's?" we asked.

"Driver Wong has ... once," said Miss Chen.

McDonald's in Xidan was the largest McDonald's restaurant we had ever seen. The line-ups were enormous but we were pushed through quickly. Mr. Cheng and Driver Wong ordered two of everything ... two Big Macs, two large Cokes, two large Fries and we were amused as they chomped down, after close examination, two hot Apple Pies.

"Mr. Cheng says they're very good," said Miss Chen, "very tasty."

Xidan is one of the most famous shopping districts in Beijing, and Xtian Department store is where we went to buy a CD player. Before heading up to the third floor, where the electronics were sold, I spotted the most gorgeous silk blouses in every color. Bill and the others waited while I fingered through each one of them looking for my correct size.

"The saleslady wants to know what size you're looking for," said Miss Chen, "she's not sure she has any to fit you."

"I know ... they're all very small," I said, feeling like an elephant. Three more sales clerks hovered over us. One of them had a long tape measure hanging around her neck. Then came the strangers to have a look, including eight shoppers who designated themselves as helpers, as well as Cheng, Miss Chen and Bill. As they searched through the lovely blouses to find an XXXL, Mr. Cheng suddenly held up an ugly, red-striped mustard-colored, revolting-looking *blouse-thing* high in the air.

"I found it!" He called triumphantly, like a gold miner finding the mother load.

"Not my color!"

"Perhaps you don't take an XXXL," offered Miss Chen. "The sales lady wants to measure your ... " She paused and made a circular motion around her bust line. "She says she thinks you don't need such a big blouse ... you only look like you do."

By now the helpers were holding up all sorts of blouses ... reds, blues, some with polka dots, and some from other racks. None of them resembled the one I wanted.

The sales lady, waving the menacing tape and making large circles in the air with her arms, was closing in for the kill.

"I really don't need a blouse," I said to anyone who spoke English, which limited this remark to Bill and Miss Chen. I bolted for the escalator, leaving the crowd of helpers still searching for an XXXL and the "Tape Lady" wondering why the foreigner was so sensitive about having her bust measured.

The third floor was even more fun. Mr. Cheng was in his element; he got the best service, tried every CD player, played lots of music, asked pointed questions and all the while we waited ... and waited. It was obvious we weren't going any place until Mr. Cheng was absolutely satisfied with the player he thought was the best buy.

One of the over-friendly clerks motioned for me to have a seat. I looked around for the chair but she pointed to a four-inch ledge on the floor, so I sat on the floor and, within minutes, a lot of people were happily sitting on the floor with me. We smiled at one another as Mr. Cheng, with Bill agreeing, decided on a Sony single CD player with two powerful speakers.

"Chinese people are very interested in Western foreigners," said Miss Chen, "I hope you don't mind all the attention."

four

中国

After school, her constant companion was a basket. She carried it everywhere, no matter the season. No matter the weather.

Chen Yu Hua spent time each day searching for anything of value for her basket: twigs and branches from trees, hay, stalks of wheat and barley, stubble, other types of grasses or pieces of coal that fell from the coal carts. And she was always on the lookout for food of any kind: bruised windfall apples, wild berries, wild herbs and cabbage. Sometimes she found large round cakes of cattle manure, not quite solid, but firm enough to stack in her basket. This pleased her mother, who dried it for burning. It was Jia Ying's duty as a housewife to keep the fires blazing in the *kang* boxes, and if she failed to make a warm house for her family she would surely be scolded.

The kang was a large bed approximately eight feet long by six feet wide, situated in the house along an outside wall and enclosed on all but one side. Depending on the size of the house and family there could be several *kangs* in a row (like small rooms, each with three walls) offering a degree of privacy for the sleepers. Chen Jian Pin and Jia Ying always shared their kang with the youngest child. The rest of the children shared the other rooms. The fireboxes, built under the beds and used only in winter, were made from bricks and sand with the openings facing the courtyard on the outside walls of the house. The boxes could easily be stoked with fuel to heat the beds and give reasonable warmth to the house. During long winters the kangs also provided a cozy gathering place to play cards and games, to talk and visit and eat meals.

Chen Yu Hua and her sisters slept in their clothes. They snuggled together under thin cotton quilts in the warm middle part of the bed, knowing that in the night the kang fire would burn down, leaving the house cold and damp. She dreamed of the hot, dry days of summer when the evenings grew long and bright. She and the family would go down to the edge of the *Huang He* (Yellow River) and splash in the warm water. Their bodies and feet were always dirty. Her mother rubbed Vaseline on their tiny hands, so chapped and full of cracks that sometimes they bled. She washed their hair as often as the water supply allowed, but there were no baths. Late spring was the worst time of year, and Jia Ying was conserving fuel, resulting in the house being cold all the time.

It was especially clammy this morning and Chen Yu Hua could feel the dampness penetrating deep inside her bones. She rubbed her eyes and pulled herself out of the kang when she heard her father call to the family, "Come along ... get your baskets." This was the day they must clean the toilet. They walked in line to the corner of the *siheyuan*, the compound where small houses for cooking, washing, storage, as well as barns for animals belonging to the family, were built around a large open courtyard. There the whole family, down to the smallest child, chose a basket from the stack and obediently hoisted it to their shoulders.

The square toilet room had part of the roof open to the elements and a pit filled with sand used for covering the waste. Her father and two older brothers, faces wrapped with handkerchiefs, placed a full shovel of saturated soil into each basket to be emptied in a pile outside the walls. The rank smell was stomach-churning but Chen Yu Hua, cold and miserable like her siblings, knew this had to be done. Later they shoveled the soil into a cart and, with her oldest brother Chen Yan pulling, sweat soaking the collar at the back of his neck, they pushed the heavy load over frozen ridges, ditches and stones to the fields half a mile away. Chilled and hungry, they stumbled home from the last trip just as the sun was piercing the gray mist. They made four such tiring trips that morning, all before breakfast.

"When will this terrible life end for us," sighed her oldest brother in complete despair. "What an awful job. What an awful day."

The day was not yet over.

Soggy clouds tinged with a pink glow from the sun hung low over the sepia-toned landscape. Chen Yu Hua wondered if it was going to snow. This time of year could bring a late snowfall, just enough to turn the courtyard into muck, sending the family scurrying again for padded winter jackets.

"Father! Father!" Second eldest brother was running up the path towards the house. He had been carrying water from the recently installed tap at the bottom of the lane and the buckets were still sloshing where he dropped them in his excitement.

"A man told me about some sheep ... hurry, he wants to see you!" Young Chen was almost choking on his words. Behind him, waving his arms and calling Chen Jian Pin's name over and over, ran a thin scarecrow of a man with mud-spattered pants too short for his long legs and jacket sleeves crunched to his elbows.

"Sheep! There's sheep at the foot of South Mountain," he babbled, taking great gulps of air with each word. "Lots of sheep."

Grinning widely and showing his few nicotine stained teeth, he told them how the sheep had been swept down from the mountain slopes in a flash flood and drowned in the last few hours. They were still lying in icy waters, keeping the meat fresh, but the men must hurry if they wanted them. Rumors spread like wildfire through the valley and if others found the sheep first they would soon disappear.

"We must go *now*," agreed Chen Jian Pin, "this is our good fortune. Gather the neighbor men ... we have to hurry."

Hours later, when the men brought home the packed carts, Chen Yu Hua counted the drowned sheep. There were eleven of them and three small lambs. She had never in her life tasted a baby sheep. No one ever slaughtered one; that would be a waste. It had to grow into a large animal, giving up its wool for many years before it was used for food.

The carcasses were butchered, the skins washed and hung to dry, later to be sold in the market for much needed yuan. Some of the meat was divided among family members and neighbors and the rest set aside for salting down and storing.

Jia Ying put mutton ribs into a large pot of water, adding wild vegetables, sage and the Chinese Four Spices (cinnamon, licorice, anise, cloves) she kept in the back of her small cupboard. It simmered all afternoon on the old black cooking stove, exhausting some of the precious coal she had been hoarding for the coldest days.

A wonderful spicy, meaty aroma filled the house, drifting through the courtyard and out across the colorless fields. The family could hardly wait for the evening meal ... so famished were they for the taste of tender mutton. It had been years, perhaps three or four years since they felt such joy, since they last savored these pleasant smells. It was so long ago that Chen Yu Hua could not remember; she only knew that her youngest sister, who had just turned four, had never tasted mutton.

Seated at the stained wooden table in the drab kitchen, their eyes followed every movement of the ladle as their tired mother spooned out platters of ribs and vegetables and bowls of hot soup. It could have been a twelve-course banquet for an emperor, it was so delicious; could have been shark fin soup, garlic chicken, steamed quail eggs, mushroom caps stuffed with prawns. And, watching from the grimy wall at the other end of the room, slightly out of view, Mao Zedong peered down sternly from his place on a large discolored poster. Not since Spring Festival, when they boiled a small piece of pork, did they feel such happiness. There would be enough meat to feed the family for at least two or three more months before going back to noodles and tasteless starch soup, which was the left-over boiled water from the noodles, and the same tiresome diet of cabbage, radish, celery, carrots and steamed buns.

This night would be memorable. What a lavish meal it was. Everyone laughed as mutton juices ran down their chins and younger brother ate so much he became ill and went to bed early with a stomach ache. Older brother thought the day turned out better than expected and father remarked how their good fortune was sadly some one else's bad fortune. "Somewhere far away," he said, "a Tibetan herder on the high plains, a stranger to our family, has lost many of his sheep this day."

Chen Yu Hua looked out the window into the dark night before going to the kang, where her young sisters were already asleep.

She noticed it didn't snow after all.

The Great Wall at Badaling was a wonder. It didn't matter to us that tourists were swarming everywhere or that the latest Western fast food eating spots had just opened around the base. A cable car had been installed to shorten the long trip to the top, leaving the cynics to worry about how things were changing and being spoiled by tourist conveniences like busses and T-shirt vendors.

"I never thought I would ever walk on the Great Wall," said Bill, but here we were nearing the top of the wall and being coaxed to struggle up the last few steep, almost vertical feet of polished flat stones, fittingly called Heroes Walk. It was hot and the cloudless summer sky, barely blue, was so unlike the smog we left in Beijing. We panted to the top, wiped our sweaty foreheads and bought T-shirts bragging in bold letters "I Climbed the Great Wall" and had our pictures taken in front of a large sign that warned "Beware of Pickpockets."

We read in a travel brochure that the Great Wall stretched roughly 1600 miles in disconnected sections from Beijing to the Gobi Desert and was built in various time periods by ancient warlords and emperors to keep the northern barbaric hordes at bay. During his reign, Emperor Qin Shih Huang (221-206 BC) rebuilt and added segments to the wall at a tremendous human toll. Lives were cheap. As well as bricks and mortar and tons of earth, bodies of dead laborers were buried in the wall. It seemed nothing was wasted.

It also said the wall never succeeded in doing what it was intended to do. Bribery was prevalent and, as Genghis Khan noted, "the strength of the wall depends upon the courage of those who defend it." It was easy to imagine how cold and distant the far reaches of China would seem to the young men who were sent to outpost garrisons.

"Mr. Cheng says there is a poem written about a brave soldier who came home after serving twenty years on the most desolate part of the Great Wall," said Miss Chen. She translated quickly the words of Mr. Cheng. "The poem is about a man who returned home and was dismayed to find that no one could remember his name. At first he rejoiced at seeing the green newly-planted fields, the young girls washing clothes in the streams and smoke curling up from the homes, but sadly he had been gone too long and now was a stranger in his own village. When he did find someone who vaguely recognized him he was saddened, for the man was ancient and bent, his hair had turned gray and he hobbled with a staff. The soldier lamented. 'I have grown old, too, robbed of my youth and the pleasures of life.' And he wept with sorrow to know what he had become."

Surrounding a small lake in one of the oldest parts of Beijing, sprawled the Hutongs. Saved from developers, this collection of ancient houses twisted and turned along back lanes and narrow winding streets. We chose to have our "farewell to Beijing" dinner in this lively area full of shops, restaurants and tourists. We were leaving the next day for Xining.

"Miss Chen, the Flower-girls would have lived here." I had just finished reading a book about China at the turn of the century and felt terribly knowledgeable about Chinese history.

"I'm sorry ... I don't know anything about Flower-girls."

"They lived in old Peking," I said, and told her about the high-class prostitutes called Flower-girls, chosen young women trained to be interesting and entertaining companions for men. They sang and danced traditional songs, performed tea ceremonies and played music on the four-stringed *pipa*, a pear-shaped lute-style instrument favored by court musicians. "Being a stunning beauty was not all-important," I added, "but rather these women had be witty, charming and above all, refined."

Miss Chen pretended not to hear me.

"Then there were the poor Drum-girls," I continued, "These

were countrywomen sold as children by their families to traveling Drum-troupes. They were forced to sing and dance on stage to the rhythm of drums in the most dreadful places full of smoke and leering men. You can only imagine the kind of *dancing* the girls did." I flinched slightly before finishing the story. "While each girl was performing, a madam would carry a large fan through the audience. On the front of the fan were the characters relating to her act, such as a poem or the meaning of her song ... and if a man was even slightly interested or if he appeared prosperous enough, the fan would be swiftly turned around by the greedy madam to show the name, age and price of the girl."

"You read very interesting things about China," said Miss Chen in a cool voice, ending my story sharply. The way she pursed her mouth and frowned at me, I knew she didn't want to hear anymore about the prostitutes of Old Peking; instead she pointed her finger to the ground in front of steps leading up to a restaurant searing the night sky with blazing neon lights.

"This place is renowned for its food. They say there has been a restaurant here for at least 800 years. Not this one of course. You know what I mean ... a place to eat."

"What a week this has been," said Bill on the way up the stairs, "Beijing is a great city."

"Ah ... but you must remember, tomorrow you are going to the real China," said Miss Chen, who was duty bound to remind us, "Xining is not Beijing."

But tomorrow was tomorrow and tonight no one cared. The compelling neon signs were calling us to dine on famous Peking Duck.

When we were settled in the restaurant among the hordes of noisy patrons, I casually asked how this famous dish was prepared. Within minutes, Miss Chen rounded up a busy waiter to explain the method. With the man flourishing his arms and Miss Chen mimicking every impressive gesture, we learned the recipe for Peking Duck: a fat juicy duck, force-fed with rich grains during its short life, was coated with molasses, honey and spices and hung to dry for many hours. Next it was slowly roasted over a fragrant wood fire until the skin became crisp, turning to a dark golden lacquer.

When the waiter had finished his little speech we clapped for him and he hurried away. He must have been puzzled. I don't think he had ever been requested to give instructions for preparing duck to Western patrons.

A cart with a starched white linen cloth pulled taut was rolled to our table; there the glorious brown duck sat whole on a silver platter. A woman wearing white gloves, wielding an impossibly sharp meat cleaver, began to skillfully cut the crisp skin in strips from the carcass, laying the pieces on small thin crepes with fresh scallions and a dollop of rich sweet sauce; the most delectable taste ever.

Our meal was an extravagant array of hot and cold dishes: lemon chicken, pork, beef and tomato, shrimp, white fish cooked whole with almonds, sliced duck meat and noodle dishes, white rice and bottles of ice-cold Tsingtao beer.

We finished dinner with the fragrant Eight Treasure tea. A steady-handed waiter stood behind our chairs and, over our nervous shoulders, poured boiling water through a long, thin curved spout from a copper kettle held high above our cups. The Eight Treasures were brought to life: chunks of rock sugar, tea, spices and a Chinese berry that resembled a pink cranberry were served in a covered decorative Mongolian teacup without a handle, that balanced on a small saucer. The trick was to drink the sweet tea by holding the saucer, using only one hand, and sipping from the cup with the lid slightly ajar, straining the ingredients.

"I know you think we Chinese have some strange table manners, like slurping our soup or eating rice by holding the bowl close to our mouths ... very different from you," said Miss Chen, "but you foreigners do something we consider very bad manners."

"Oh? What would that be?" I said absently, using the Peking Duck roll-ups as finger-food. I took a bite of the perfect meat dripping with syrupy black sauce.

"You are always licking your fingers when you eat. I've seen this in movies too. Chinese never do this. We never pick up food with our fingers ... we use chopsticks."

"I suppose most people would consider licking fingers rude," I mumbled weakly, downing the last of my duck with my favorite beer. "That's as impolite as talking with food in your mouth or elbows on the table ... very bad."

She smiled at me sideways. She always did that. She always sat very upright in her chair, which constantly made me square my shoulders.

"Yes, very bad," I said. I wanted to lick the last sweet syrup from my fingers but thought better of it. Perhaps, unconsciously, I had already done this terrible deed and Miss Chen was witness to it.

five

中国

"Don't worry, Chen Yu Hua, you'll be fine. Don't be afraid of the men riding with you."

Chen Jian Pin took his ten-year-old daughter to find a seat for her long journey to Xining. The required seat was not in a bus but on top of an old blue stake truck loaded with supplies from the valley. Piled dangerously high between wooden slat sides were crates of fruit, a few live chickens and geese, bundles of timber and sacks of grain, and a limited supply of goods to be sold or exchanged for coal in these desperate times. A tattered brown tarpaulin was thrown over the cargo and tied down with coarse hemp rope. Open to the elements; rain, snow or sun, this was the transportation for her twelve-hour trip to the capital city.

Chen Yu Hua was nervous at the thought of leaving her family for the first time. She pulled her dark blue padded jacket closer around her thin shoulders, feeling in the pocket for the gray woolen scarf and gloves given to her by her young sister. "I know they're old," she had said, "but mother thinks you'll be needing them."

Jia Ying made a cloth bag for her daughter, packing it with a few clothes and some food for the trip: a handful of sunflower seeds, cold steamed buns, a little dried fruit, a jar of water and two apples; her valley was famous for apples. Before Chen Yu Hua left home earlier that day, her mother hugged her, tucked an extra pair of newly-made shoes into the bag and said, "Be good for your aunty."

Chen Yu Hua wanted to cry and say she was too young and fearful to go to the city alone, but she couldn't, and here she was standing with a group of men staring up at her father, who was beckoning from the top of the overloaded transport truck. She was hoisted up by one of the men, and Jian Pin, like a cat looking for a place to nest, rummaged around the tarpaulin until he found what he thought was the best seat.

"I've paid the driver extra money to look after you," he said, "so don't worry about anything. When you get to Xining your aunty will meet you."

He patted the canvas to make sure there were no hard lumps and smoothed out a hollow big enough for his daughter to snuggle into. When she was as comfortable as possible he knelt beside her.

"Obey your aunty and study hard. Do you understand?"

"Yes father," she said.

He did not hug her. He hardly looked at her as he hastily climbed down. If he was going to miss her he never once indicated it in any way. After all, he was happy just knowing she was getting a chance to better her education in a city school.

The truck started its lumbering, noisy pilgrimage along the dirt road. Chen Yu Hua clutched her cloth bag tightly to her chest and looked back towards her father. At least he was waving and, much to her shame, she began to cry softly. She didn't want to leave him; she was so scared. She felt very small surrounded by the crude grinning workers and poor peasant farmers who, like her, were probably on their first journey to the big city. One of them, an older man, tightened her jacket closer under her chin, letting his hand slowly trace a crease down her sleeve before he drew it away laughing. She caught her breath and stared at his large filthy hands with cracked, broken nails, not at all like her father's lean hands. He spoke in Salar dialect. The Salar people had lived in the valley for hundreds of years, since the area was part of the Tibetan world; long before the Han people arrived from China. She understood his language perfectly. He called her a beautiful little flower and his penetrating eyes made her squirm and feel uneasy.

"Don't do that!" scolded one of the younger men, "She doesn't want to be touched."

The two men locked glances briefly until the older one shrugged and maneuvered himself away on his hands and knees to find another spot on the uneven cargo.

"He won't bother you again."

Chen Yu Hua did not return the man's smile but leaned her head back against the tarpaulin and studied him. His young face was handsome and his eyes glinted when he smiled, but she noted the telltale signs of hunger: the dark circles, the hollow cheeks and the pallor of his skin. At ten years old she was well aware of the ravages of hunger and how it drives a person crazy, consuming them day and night with thoughts of food. The young man was wretchedly thin, his mended clothes were in shabby condition and he didn't have a proper overcoat to wear. A small knotted square of cloth lay beside him, perhaps holding sunflower seeds and a jar of water. He carried nothing else that she could see.

She closed her eyes for a moment. The cargo truck rattled through Xunhua County, taking her far away from the sunlit valley she knew so well. She was leaving everything familiar; her home, family and school, to go and live with strange relatives in a strange city.

She remembered the day when her father learned that his pregnant sister Chen Fugui was looking for a girl to live-in and help with the housework. It was very common for families to send young country girls to the city to be baby-sitters and housekeepers. Chen Yu Hua was on her way to the city but she would be lucky; Jian Pin had insisted that his daughter work in exchange for room and board *and* the chance to go to school. He knew most girls would spend five or six of their teenage years working full time with little or no schooling, only to be dismissed and deprived of formal education when they were no longer needed.

Warm early August breezes drifted through the green valley. Apple, peach and pear trees heavy with fruit stood in rows, and mauve flowers cascaded from mud walls that surrounded the farms. Chen Yu Hua wanted her eyes to take in every little detail but the thick gray-brown dust thrown up from the wheels of the truck clouded the air and blotted out the landscape.

The broad valley soon turned into Lamu Gorge. A spectacular rough narrow road scattered with chunks of granite rocks began its ascent up Qingsha Mountain. Ahead lay treacherous curves and steep grades edged with terrifying drop-offs. Guardrails were non-existent. The truck shuddered and moaned in low gear, spitting out gravel that plunged hundreds of feet to the river far below. The young girl had never been to this part of the country before and it would be a full year until she passed this way again. Craggy mountains, resembling castles, towered above. It was a beautiful world, spectacular and wild, that she never knew existed.

The truck rolled to a stop by the side of the road. Men tumbled down, bantering and stretching their legs, pulling cigarettes from their pockets. Chen Yu Hua watched as they wandered off in all directions, some drinking tea or water from jars or eating sunflower seeds and spitting husks on the dry gray road. One man hesitated. He was the young Salar man who had jumped to her defense. He held out his hands to her and she was surprised to see how fine they were; not dirty, perhaps rough and calloused from the hard farm labor, but not dirty.

She heard him asking if she wanted to get off the truck and stretch her legs. She could go behind the rocks and bushes to relieve herself. This may be the last stop for a few hours. Chen Yu Hua shook her head. She was not afraid of him, in fact she felt quite comfortable around him, but she was too shy and self-conscious to leave her place on the truck and join the men.

"No thank you," she said quietly in his dialect.

The drive to the top of Qingsha Pass was grueling. Similar trucks bulging with supplies trundled by, almost brushing the sides of their vehicle on the narrow road. Chen Yu Hua strained to see if there were any women or other young girls traveling on the passing trucks, but they were all men. Some of them called out and waved to her.

The air in the pass was getting much cooler and fog shrouded the mountains. Before long it was very cold. Snow was everywhere. She pulled the soft gray scarf and mittens from her pockets. Mother was right. She did need them. Now and then the truck, grinding along slowly, would slip back or skid to the edge of the road; heart-stopping moments for everyone. High above on rocky crags, colorful Tibetan prayer flags whipped on long poles in the strong cold wind. Chen Yu Hua watched them drift from her view, lost in the chilling mist. For a long time she could hear the crackle of the thin flags as she huddled down, disappearing into her jacket. She shivered and felt a sudden warm dampness under her. Oh no, she thought, she should have gone with the men at the last stop. She was embarrassed but knew if she did not move it would all be dry by the time she reached Xining. She snuggled deeper in her coat, drawing her scarf over her face and tried to sleep.

A bright moon followed the blue truck as it rumbled through the night across the great Tibetan plateau: ten impoverished men from the farms, two weary drivers and one drowsy little girl. Chen Yu Hua slept fitfully. Once she opened her eyes when she felt a loose fold of tarpaulin being pulled over her. It was the young Salar man.

"It's cold," he said simply and tucked the rough tarp around her head and shoulders.

The landscape became a maze of shadowy etchings: small streams, waterfalls, sheep, yak and Tibetan camps with their black and white circular tents and barking dogs. They rolled past the wide Yellow River, greedily gathering pale golden silt and pushing it sluggishly to the distant coast of Shandong Province before spilling into the Bohai Sea.

They rolled through fields of rapeseed and barley and, in the early morning, while the first rays of sun washed an eerie pink mist over Beishan Temple, perched high on North Mountain, they crossed a modern iron bridge leading into the city of Xining. Traffic increased as other stake trucks, carts drawn by donkeys, coal carts pulled by men, bicycles loaded with baskets of fowl, and cadres in their fancy automobiles, joined the morning rush. The long journey was coming to an end.

As the truck idled slowly into a compound, Chen Yu Hua woke up to the commotion and the sudden shaking of the tarp beneath her. The men, grabbing their meager belongings, scrambled down from the truck. Thick dust covered everything. She was so tired.

"Come, let me help you," came the voice belonging to the fine hands. This time she allowed herself to be lifted down. The hands were gentle.

"Thank you."

Chen Yu Hua waited by the truck. She pulled at her wrinkled clothes and rubbed her eyes, itching from dust and lack of sleep. She tried to smooth her hair and drew the sleeve of the coat her mother had made across her nose. Standing there, she looked every bit like a small unfortunate homeless waif.

"Chen Yu Hua," called a stern voice. A pregnant woman in a plain black jacket and trousers came striding out of the morning shadows. She had short straight black hair pulled back with tortoise shell combs. Her piercing eyes squinted and the corners of her mouth turned down sharply when she spoke. "I'm your Aunty Chen Fugui, your father's sister. Pick up your bag and come with me please."

The little girl from Hualong County looked up at the frowning face, so unlike her mother's face. Apprehension filled her heart. She felt like an animal, a poor timid rabbit captured in the snare in preparation for the evening meal.

"Yes, Aunty Chen Fugui," she answered obediently. She turned to the young man who had just helped her down from the truck. He smiled and nodded, pressing the palms of his hands together piously in Buddhist style.

"Goodbye," she said again in Salar dialect.

The excitement and bright lights of Beijing did not prepare us for the cluttered old frontier city of Xining.

A delegation was waiting to greet us at the airport. Foreign Affairs Deputy Director Madam Chen Jingjun smiled warmly and handed us a huge bouquet of spring flowers. Liu Li Xun welcomed us saying, "You will be a great asset to my department," and Deputy Mayor Li hoped our life in Xining would be happy. Deputy Mayor Yang Qi Lian told us we had the spirit of Norman Bethune, the Canadian doctor who served with Mao during the 1930s. Like all Canadians working in China, we would often hear this analogy.

We were bundled into the back of a big black Audi. The driver wound slowly along the bumpy crowded streets, dodging tractors and donkeys, trucks, cadre cars, people walking and people on bikes, until we reached Nan Guan Road.

Miss Chen was right; we had arrived in the real China.

Guards checked our three-car convoy through the gates of the municipal compound in which City Hall was located, and came to a stop in front of a narrow lane bordered by a high wall of concrete blocks plastered over with off-white stucco. In places the wall was crumbling away, leaving patterns of dark brown blotches, like someone had thrown mud at it. Our ten new friends hurried us along, eager to show off the newly-renovated house we would call home for the next year.

A rusty padlock clicked and a big yellowish wooden gate swung open to reveal a generous courtyard with lilac bushes, several large poplar trees and red Lobelia flowers blooming in the sandy soil. There was no grass, just newly turned earth. An uneven stone path led up to the red double doors of a single-story gray brick house. A tall leafy apple tree leaned over the slate roof.

"This house has been the home to four leaders," said Miss Chen proudly, pushing open the front door. We hesitated and peered into the gloom to see a dark hallway and wet concrete floor, looking musty and uninviting.

"Come. Come," she insisted and the smiling group pressed forward. We stepped over the puddles while Miss Chen explained that in China a floor is always freshly washed before the honored guests arrive ... "and you are the honored guests," she said, giving us one last nudge.

Looking around we were pleasantly surprised to find a solid brick and concrete seven room house built by Russian engineers in the early 1950s. It was small and well designed but extremely neglected. Only six of these homes had escaped demolition over the years, and in the future they would all be gone. The Chinese government could ill-afford to keep old private dwellings on such valuable land.

The living room, two bedrooms and an office were laid with wooden floors painted barn-red. Dust traced long straight lines as it squeezed up through every crack between the well-worn planks.

The floors in the kitchen, the washroom, toilet area, and hallway were the original unsightly, bare concrete.

Bright yellow polyester curtains framed three huge casement windows in the living room. Over the years careless workers simply forgot to clean up splashes of various paint colors on the panes, creating a sort of stained glass modern art effect when the sun filtered in. At one end of the room there were two black leather sofas trussed up in a film of plastic, and two new glass and chrome side-tables, a matching coffee table and a Peony television set. At the other end stood an old square table and four chairs. The genuine leather padding was barely intact on the seats while the carved design, although worn, was still distinct on the wooden backs. The only color in the room came from the decals on three thermos bottles: orange poppies, yellow sunflowers, and blue and white butterflies. A standard four-tube fluorescent light fixture dangled on chains from the twelve-foot ceiling.

Our new friends could hardly wait to show us the kitchen. It was certainly larger than the kitchens any one of them had in their tiny apartments. They waved their hands towards a state-of-the-art Hyer refrigerator, presenting it as though it was about to perform. The fridge was their pride and joy; it looked so white and so out-of-place against the faded yellowish casement paint of the windows and the damp floor. They opened the door and showed us the dials for setting the temperature, the ice trays, the egg trays and where to keep the vegetables, and we all had to smell the freshness of the freezer.

"Are you happy?" asked Miss Chen, "they want to know if you're happy."

"Of course," I said truthfully. We never expected to have such a large new refrigerator.

The rest of the kitchen was not so Western. There was a low metal purple cabinet containing a set of Blue Willow dishes and various cooking utensils including a giant cleaver for chopping, which I never learned to use. A white ceramic counter had been installed along one wall and held a two-burner gas stove with a shiny aluminum kettle sitting on top. "You will like this," said Miss Chen, "it whistles when it boils." The propane tank was securely tucked under one end of the counter, which was a little scary for us knowing it was so close to the stove, but every kitchen in China was equipped the same way and seemed to work.

Above the counter top ran a galvanized pipe leading to a single cold-water tap suspended over a square cast iron sink. When the water was turned on it ran through the sink and gushed out below, dropping onto a recessed floor and ever-so-slowly seeping away. Greasy residue had built up in gritty layers from fifty years of flushing dirty water without a proper drainpipe. Later, when I scraped and cleaned under that sink, I found myself in tears of frustration. "What am I doing here?" I wailed, "I left perfectly good plumbing at home."

The large toilet room next to the front entrance had sunny windows along the upper half of the wall and, thank goodness, a Western toilet had replaced the Asian squat type. In one corner a tap dripped water into a concrete box built around a squalid greenish drain on the floor. "They want you to know this is where you wash your mop," explained Miss Chen and she pointed to a faded gray dingy string floor mop slouched against the wall. A few days later we insisted the drain be cemented over, eliminating the sour smell, and bought a new white mop and red plastic pail. The wooden cover made for the top of the box provided a good place to set a plant, prompting the concerned workman to ask Miss Chen "now where will the foreigner wash her mop?"

A cast iron, high-backed English tub with ball and claw feet sat in an equally large washroom separated from the toilet area. The bottom was brown and gouged as though the former occupants had used it for storing rusting tools. With limited hot water, we couldn't use it if we wanted too, and we thought we would welcome the extra space if it were gone. In contrast to the ancient tub was a newly installed electric shower, a luxury we truly appreciated. As an added feature, the shower played the first notes of *Beethoven's Ninth* when the water was hot enough to use. A hand basin with a leaky tap hung precariously from two long nails driven half way into the cinder block wall. Water dripped little by little down the pipes, pooling in low spots on the wine-colored ceramic floor. Two more rusty nails pinned a lighted cabinet to the wall above the sink. Skimpy, unhealthy looking 220-volt wiring wound its way up to the high ceiling.

Next to the hand basin was a new automatic washing machine. It was a little more complicated to run than the one we had at home, but then we didn't expect to have a washing machine at all.

We were fortunate. We had everything we needed; new friends and a private home, which was rare for foreigners working in China. Usually they were housed together on college or university campuses, designated hotels or special areas. In fact, the Canadian Embassy in Beijing had never heard of foreign experts living in a single-family dwelling.

"Do you like the house?" Serious Chinese faces were all around us. "We hope you like it. You see … it's all equipped for Western foreign experts," and they produced a set of cutlery for eight.

"Yes," I said, and meant it, although my mind was busy with possible renovations. I knew we were in a very poor part of the country and the last thing I wanted to do was sound insulting about cleanliness, but my Western mind could not learn to live in anything other than an hygienic house. We would clean it; buy things to make it beautiful and make sure anyone who wanted to visit our home would be welcome.

"It's a very fine house," Bill said. Everyone smiled and shook our hands, relieved that the foreigners were happy with their new home.

Our six big suitcases, two smaller ones, numerous carry-ons, shopping bags and the box full of books were packed into the office. What must they have thought about all the stuff we brought? Little did they know we had important things like a queen-sized duvet (at the suggestion of friends who lived in Korea) and lots of clothes. We knew instinctively that our sizes, although not huge in North America, were huge by Chinese standards. We had aspirin, Tylenol and ten big bottles of Head & Shoulders shampoo. We had guessed correctly on most things, but we did find all the Head & Shoulders shampoo and Vaseline Protective hand cream we would ever need in the state-owned stores just down the street.

Miss Chen looked at her small watch. She shook her arm and

held her wrist to her ear just to make sure it was still running. "We'll be back to pick you up at five-thirty for a reception and dinner with our leaders at the Xining Dasha."

Bill and I tore open our suitcases. We had exactly thirty minutes to get ready for our first formal banquet in Xining.

Surrounded by six beautiful girls, the friendly manager was waiting at the front entrance of the Xining Dasha Hotel. The girls wore red, sequined, form-fitting gowns in the style of the traditional Chinese *qipao*, long skirts split to the thigh on one side and bodices with high Mandarin collars and short cap sleeves.

The lovely ladies smiled graciously and escorted us into the foyer of the old hotel where we walked up a wide elegant staircase curving to an open balcony. Although the stairs were chipped and scratched from lack of maintenance, and the rich French silk wall covering was peeling and blistering around us, there was an ambience of former elegance. A smooth mahogany banister glowed like brown satin. Balusters of brass and wrought iron were combined in Oriental and European designs and, above our heads, chandeliers dropped like clusters of dusty diamonds, catching the dim light from wall lamps. It was a pity, but the hotel could not afford the electricity to bring the lamps back to life; there were too many of them.

The Russians played an important part in the re-building of China after the 1949 Revolution and throughout the 1950s, leaving impressive architecture and quality buildings that could be seen in every city. The Xining Dasha was an excellent example.

"The hotel is presently under renovation," said Miss Chen, reading my mind. It would be under renovation until we left Xining, and we were sorry we never had the chance to see the staircase brought back to its original beauty.

The banquet was held in a small room. Wooden frescos decorated the walls, flowers and white linen cloths adorned every table. The restaurant dining tables were round with seating for eight to ten people; large glass circles rotated in the center to provide the diners with easy access to the various platters of food.

Time protocol at official banquets was very strict. Each

occasion began at 6:00pm and ended abruptly at 8pm. Even casual meals in restaurants or private homes started early and stopped early. There was no pre-dinner chitchat over cocktails. Tea, beer and alcoholic drinks were served with the food, but to make the evening last longer, the party usually moved on for Karaoke fun.

The Foreign Trade Commission hosted dinner and we were introduced to senior staff leaders, most of whom had never met a Western foreigner before. If they were shy at first, a few toasts with Qinghai Barley, a clear white liquor of local fame, soon relaxed the group.

The sequined red-clad ladies served dish after dish of appealing food, announcing each one by name. Every now and then curious chefs in their tall white hats would peek around corners trying to glimpse the foreigners who were asking for rice and soy sauce. Rice was never served with meals. It was only served at the end of the meal as filler for those who may still be hungry after eight or more courses. But we wanted rice, not realizing we were offending the chefs.

We were introduced to new and unfamiliar foods that night. Along with platters of raw vegetables artistically sculpted into flowers and peacocks, came Camel Palms, looking and tasting every bit like strips of tough gelatin; Qinghai Snake, cooked whole or sliced; Snow Mountain, a huge pile of sugarless frothy whipped egg whites; deep-fried sparrows; tripe and two heaps of chicken feet ... some steamed and some crispy. They also served our favorites: sesame chicken, snow peas, broccoli and white pearl onions, wok-fried prawns and crabmeat, and Tsingtao beer. And for dessert; wonderful sweet oranges, watermelons, and something I had never tried before ... the tart taste of star fruit. In the middle of one course, chopsticks from across the table plunked a piece of jellyroll on top of my mutton stew. A smiling face suggested he knew we Westerners liked desserts.

Then appeared *the* special dish. A large, whole Qinghai lake trout with the unusual name, Naked Carp. It was perched on its belly on a plate of rice and vegetables and was slowly being turned clockwise on the revolving glass. With mouth and eyes wide open, it came to rest staring straight at Bill.

"You're the honored guest, and must drink when the head of the fish is pointing at you," blurted Miss Chen. Bill did not hesitate and promptly downed ... one ... two ... three small glasses of Qinghai Barley to the applause of the Chinese.

"Be careful," whispered Miss Chen behind her hand, like she was telling us a bit of top-secret gossip, "too much alcohol will make you drunk."

The trout was toasted several times before the onslaught of chopsticks. Eyes and cheeks, considered the most delicious, vanished along with the plump body, leaving what looked like a cartoon mock-up of tail, spine, ribs and a faceless fish head revolving slowly in the center of the table.

The first juicy morsel of fish had been generously laid in the bowl of the honored foreign guest and there it remained uneaten. Not good manners.

"I think you should eat your Naked Carp," I said, "it's delicious. Besides everyone's watching you."

"Okay," said Bill under his breath, reaching for the chopsticks, "but I really don't like fish, especially trout with no scales."

The piece disappeared.

There were more toasts. A tiny glass of liquor was held in salute, then tapped twice on the table, "*Gambei*," they all shouted, and we laughed, "Cheers." We made promises to work together and further the promotion of Xining and Qinghai not realizing how complicated and, at times, frustrating it would be. We unfolded a large Canadian flag and presented it to the deputy mayors. More toasts. More speeches. More photos.

Driver Zhang drove us back to 83 Nanguan Road.

It had been a long day and we were now alone in our Chinese home. Everything was so strange. We missed our family. Did we really know what we were doing?

six

中国

The dream was beautiful.

She was back in Xunhua lying on fragrant dry hay piled high in the courtyard of her home. The night sky was the color of the new deep blue overcoat her mother had given her for the trip to Xining. She was with her siblings, happily counting stars, which curiously and magically dissolved into showers of golden coins falling around their feet. They ran and danced and sang, picking the bright coins from the dust until their pockets were heavy and they became exhausted, falling laughing to the ground. Round and round Chen Yu Hua glided, arms outstretched, eyes closed, black hair floating. Peace and contentment and a little sadness overwhelmed her as she watched herself fade silently into the cloudy vapors of her dream.

She was suddenly wide awake.

They were arguing again and this time Aunty Chen Fugui was screaming and crying. Uncle Xiao Zhan would be leaving in the morning to go back to Golmud, 500 miles away. He had been given time to come home for the birth of their baby girl and now he must return to his teaching position. Families were split; husbands and wives rarely saw one another. They were allowed to meet at home during Spring Festival once a year or a man could apply for leave to attend his wife for *zuo yue zi*, confinement after birth. Aunty Chen Fugui had given birth to her beautiful baby and now for the next month she would follow strict traditional rules. She must stay in her house with the windows closed tight, dark curtains pulled to shut out fresh air and sunlight. She washed only her face and hands, never took a bath or shampooed her hair. She was not allowed to exercise in any way and spent most of her time in bed resting, receiving no visitors except very close family members.

The poor baby also suffered. On the premise of keeping the spine straight it was bound tightly in blankets. Unable to move, hot and uncomfortable, it cried most of the time while fighting against its confinement; again, no fresh air, no sun for the newborn. Life was stressful and restricting for mother and child and no wonder Aunty Chen Fugui was distraught; her husband was leaving her again and she would not see him for several months. She was twenty-two years old with a job at the factory, a mother and new baby to care for and only her ten-year-old niece to help her out.

Chen Yu Hua sat up in bed when she heard the baby crying. She was worried about the argument; it was going on too long and was unusually violent. She could hear things being thrown in their bedroom, like glass breaking and crashing noises that frightened her. Aunty was screaming again, spitting out a tumble of words so incoherent that Chen Yu Hua could not understand what she was saying. In contrast her uncle's voice was low and steady, rather soothing she thought, and she wondered why her aunt was so agitated and could not be comforted.

Ever since she arrived at her new home several weeks before, Chen Yu Hua found her aunt cold and stern, treating her more like hired help than a family member.

She was grateful to be enrolled in Liberation Public School where she heard, for the first time, *Putonghua*, (Mandarin), the official language of China. Timid and scared, and far from her father's home, she was ignored by her classmates for being a country girl in looks, dress and certainly in her behavior, and they frowned at her inability to speak *Putonghua*.

There was endless work to do after school. As well as homework, there were vegetables to be washed for the evening meal and brick floors to be swept. She tended the stove, cleaning out the ashes and making sure there was always kindling and coal handy. No matter how unkind or inconsiderate Aunty Chen Fugui was to her, Uncle Xiao Zhan was the opposite. He took her shopping and taught her about the history of Qinghai and the old city of Xining. And he was genuinely interested in her stories of the family back in Xunhua County.

Chen Yu Hua had determination and moral strength, and a fervent desire to be educated. She especially wanted to learn Mandarin and remembered her father's words "listen and learn all you can this year, it will serve you well later". She knew she must be grateful for this opportunity but in her heart she was lonely. She remembered her siblings, so excited when they heard she would be going to the big city, and her mother, who made her a pair of underpants … her very first underwear. She cherished the smooth feel of the fine cotton and ran her fingers along the French seams, even touched them to her cheeks before folding them carefully into the old wooden chest in her room.

Another loud crash. Something smashed hard against the wall.

"You don't look after us as well as you should," Aunty Chen Fugui scolded her husband hysterically, "I can't do everything." She was sputtering and talking so fast she began to cough. A choking, belching cough … "It isn't fair that I should be alone with an old lady and a useless child … I can't look after everything here while the government sends you off teaching far away."

Chen Yu Hua's tiny feet felt the cold brick floor as she padded to her aunt's room and warily opened the door … just a crack. It creaked softly, enough to startle her but they didn't hear.

"Hush!" Her uncle's voice had turned harsh. "This is the plan of the Communist Party … you must not speak against the Party."

She could see them clearly. Uncle Xiao Zhan was sitting on the bed while his young wife paced at one end of the room. The baby was crying in the basket, straining against the tight blanket and frightened by the loud racket. A chair was overturned. Pieces of porcelain that once had been a blue and white basin lay smashed on the floor, as well as a filigree gold frame holding a photograph of two young faces staring out from behind fractured glass. A fragile fan had snapped in half. And clothes: dark rough Mao jackets, black silk trousers and black cloth shoes, had been pulled from a chest and flung everywhere.

Chen Yu Hua had never seen her aunt in such a state. Her short hair, always neatly pinned, was disheveled and tears of angry frustration ran down her swollen face. Her feet were bare and the long white cotton nightgown clung to her legs as she turned and stomped straight towards the door where the little girl was hiding. Chen Yu Hua froze. For a moment their eyes met, at least Chen Yu Hua thought they met, but the blank frenzied eyes she was staring into, saw nothing.

In a flash the young mother whipped around, arms flailing.

"I don't care about the Party ... I don't care about you ... or this." She screamed and in one quick heart-stopping movement plucked the tiny bundle from its basket and flung it at her husband.

Chen Yu Hua saw it all in semi-frozen slow motion. The baby flying through the air ... her uncle's horrified face ... his big hands thrust forward.

She closed the door.

Too sick, confused and shocked to watch anymore, she ran back to her small bed and pulled the blanket over her head. All she could think about was her mother.

"Mother," she whispered to the darkness. "I want to go home."

There was dead silence in the house all that night and the next morning uncle Xiao Zhan waved good-bye to Aunty Chen Fugui, patted the blanket-bound baby and smiled at Chen Yu Hua as if the night before was just a bad dream, not important and easily forgotten.

"See you at Spring Festival." And he was gone.

🍁

Bill and I woke the next morning to the sound of a sharp whistle. Six a.m. A rooster crowed. Guards coughed, cleared their throats and spat. Roll call was barked; at least we assumed it was roll call as there were eighteen to twenty young men housed in the barracks across from our bedroom window in the municipal compound. Like every government compound there were soldier guards stationed at the entrance to check traffic in and out. At least 3000 people lived in the seven-story gray apartment blocks stretching behind, and dwarfing our little home.

"I guess we'll be hearing this every morning," said Bill, as we dragged ourselves out of bed and tried to untangle a mess of half-opened suitcases. Clothes, make-up, shampoo, packages of soup mixes, cans of Canadian salmon and a toaster bought in Beijing cluttered the bedroom and office.

"And where are we going to put all this stuff? "

"We'll find a place."

It was a bright new morning, our first morning in Xining, and Miss Chen was coming to take us to buy food at the Shui Jing Xiang market at West Gate.

The chords of Beethoven's Ninth played from the shower, the big boiling kettle whistled, and the sun poured through our open windows along with the foot-stomping martial music from loud speakers. It was Tai Chi time at city hall and employees were exercising out in the square.

Xining sidewalks were more than a little perilous by our standards, and took some time getting used to. Open holes appeared when manhole covers vanished in the night, stolen by thieves who sold the iron. None of these pits had movable guard railings or anything to identify their existence. We dodged steel cables and kept an eye on flowerpots balancing on window ledges above us. There were loose bricks, loose rocks and ankle-breaking depressions in the concrete. Crowds of people moved in unison along these sidewalks, never increasing or decreasing their stride. What we called life-threatening hazards, were quite normal to them.

The entrance to the West Gate market was a five-minute walk from our house. It was then we discovered we lived in the heart of the old city. We bought vegetables familiar to us, including lettuce and plump red tomatoes and every type of fresh fruit, even small oranges we called Mandarin oranges. Miss Chen thought this was a very odd name. "I have never heard these oranges called by the name Mandarin," she frowned.

Fresh fruits ranging from grapes to pineapples, as well as the most delicious persimmons and litchi nuts, were imported from Southern China.

West Gate Market was huge, at least two city blocks in length with lanes running off the main walkway. Pots of boiling pepper soups and mutton kabob stands filled the air with spicy aromatic scents, and hungry customers downed "local flavor" noodles and steamed buns at long crowded tables.

The least favorite place for me in all the market was the fresh meat and fish section. Lake trout gasping for a breath of oxygen tried their best to swim in over-crowded tanks while live snakes and turtles moved sluggishly around in their container jails. Yak meat chunks, and blobs of pork and mutton lay on the counters in splatters of blood. Squatting behind these unappetizing piles of flesh were vendors, cigarettes dangling from their lips, patting and fluffing and rearranging each piece of stock. It always amazed us that this meat market, with its dubious health practices, had very little odor, even in summer. And since Xining was over 7000 feet above sea level we saw few flies and no mosquitoes.

Rows of counters loaded with cooked meats and hard-boiled Tea Eggs, and shops selling beer and liquor stood toward the far end of the market near the busy exit to West Street. Cakes, perched in glass display cases in a bakery, looked very much like any bakery in Canada. Happy Birthday Best Wish to You lay swirled in colored icing on the top of a birthday cake and a Western-style bride in white and a groom in black stood side by side on a three-tiered wedding cake. Along with Western cakes came Western bread, which we thought was perfect for our Beijing toaster. But the bread never really tasted like our bread at home no matter how many different shops we tried ... it always had a sweet flavor and crumbled in our hands.

Leading away from the main part of the market, reams of cloth fluttered in the breeze down the lanes. Treadle and electric sewing machines hummed as seamstresses and tailors designed the latest fashions for local clientele. There were stalls of shoes and underwear. Book stalls sold popular Western posters of smiling, blonde, pink-cheeked young children hugging puppy dogs and kittens. There were tools, knives and aluminum pots, and silversmiths tap-tapping out delicate jewelry with simple work tools.

Outside the gates and close to the post office, sitting at small desks on one-half of the sidewalk was a row of Letter Writers; reading, writing and filling out forms for their customers seated next to them. We watched one old Chinese grandfather. He was lean and wrinkled, with sparse white whiskers waving down from his chin. The long fingers of his right hand gestured in unison with his words as he dictated a letter.

When the letter was done he carefully folded it, stroking it slowly and tenderly, and then unfolded it, appearing to read the words over and over. I could only imagine what words were written on that single page or if the old gentleman could really read them. He did this several times. Again and again he ran his fingers over the letter sighing and, as though he hated to let it go, slipped it into his pocket and walked toward the post office.

But for us the sight on the street that was most disturbing was a man who was horribly burned and disfigured. He leaned against a building, one knee bent, his foot flat against the wall for balance; his arms dangled by his sides. A cap holding a few dull coins lay at his feet. It was as though a red rubber mask had been stretched over his face and neck, leaving a few wispy strands of sparse black hair sprouting from the back of his head. There were two holes where his nose had once been and two holes for lost ears, his mouth was a slit cut in the thick rubber mask. One eye had been completely burned shut, but the other eye shone like a child's marble from out of a little puckered opening, as if someone was standing behind a grotesque fabricated figure peeking through a slot in the mask.

We stopped while Bill dug in his pocket for extra yuan to drop in the hat. There was expression in that one, glinting, very much alive, eye. I may have imagined it, but I thought the eye said thank you. The man in the red mask never moved, never turned his head, but I know his bright eye followed us down the street.

"How did the poor man get so burned? Did a propane tank explode near him?" asked Bill, when we finally caught up with Miss Chen.

"I don't like him," she said sullenly, "He cheated on his wife. She threw acid over him and now she's in prison for life."

This was the first time we heard about the cruel, although rare, practice in China and parts of Asia of harsh revenge for infidelity. A man or woman would be scarred for life when families or friends of the betrayed spouse threw acid into the face of the guilty party.

Miss Chen said the man's sister brought him everyday to beg at the same spot, and this is where we saw him for the year we stayed in the city. He was paying a terrible price for his indiscretions, displaying his shame before the people of Xining, in hopes some would have compassion and toss a few coins into his hat.

Everything we ever needed or wanted was for sale in the market except, of course, cheese, butter and whipping cream. And only once did we see a lemon.

seven

中国

Qin Yan was only in her mid-sixties but had the demeanor of an older woman.

She hobbled and teetered and shuffled about the small kitchen on her golden lilies ... *san cun jin lian* ... stumps of feet that had been bound by her mother when she was five years old. Although they were less painful now, the old lady kept them tightly wrapped for support and concealed them inside her black-laced leather shoes. They had grown ugly and malformed over the years and were no longer desirable to the eyes of men.

As young as she was, Chen Yu Hua knew to be thankful she was not born in the years that promoted foot-binding. She could only imagine the excruciating pain when the four small toes on each foot were crushed and bound tightly back under the balls of the feet of a young girl. In time the arches bent slightly forward with the pressure until only the edge of her heel would support her weight, making it impossible to walk properly or stand very long.

The purpose of this trauma was to produce the legendary three-inch foot to fit a tiny silk Lotus shoe.

Qin Yan knew all about pain.

"When I was a little girl," she lectured, "my screams were soothed by my mother's whispers. She told me to just dream about my future husband and the comfortable life I would have someday. I was told over and over again the story of a loving Han mother who refused to have her daughter go through the ordeal of foot binding. When the child grew up to be a beautiful young woman she was unsuitable for a good marriage ... her feet were too big.

They looked too horrible to men of means and they did not want her ... she could only work in the kitchens of peasant farmers. The girl cursed her mother, saying she had doomed her to a hard life. She screamed at her, saying she could have borne the pain if only her mother had bound her feet. And you know what? The mother felt so guilty she ended her own life ... that was how important it was in those days to make sure your daughter had small feet."

"I don't think I would like to have my feet hurt," said Chen Yu Hua softly.

The old grandmother smoothed the little girl's hair and ran her fingers down the side of her face.

"You will never have to go through such pain ... you can thank the Father of Our Revolution, Doctor Sun Yat-sen ... he forbade the wrapping of little girls' feet a long time ago."

Chen Yu Hua liked Grandmother Qin Yan. She was full of stories of life before Liberation. She talked about her family, her husband, and her children. "I had nine babies," she would say, "life was hard ... but I had a good husband. He did not beat me and we always found enough to eat."

Chen Yu Hua cut the Chinese cabbage as she watched the old lady knead the dough on the board for the evening meal of noodles and vegetables. Beads of sweat glistened on her forehead, pasting drifts of gray hair to the weathered skin. Her bony hands clapped oil on the dough and cut and rolled it into long stretches of gleaming white cylinders two inches in diameter. She patted them carefully and laid them side-by-side like pieces of perfectly matched porcelain. A pot of water was warming on the coal stove. Aunty Chen Fugui would be home soon and Chen Yu Hua could hardly wait to taste the delicious meal they would have: noodles and vegetables, steamed buns and maybe a piece of fruit.

Today was not a good day for her. She was nervous. Under her bedroll was an exam paper from school she must show to her aunt. Lately she was having problems with the subject called General Knowledge, taught by a teacher from Sichuan Province who spoke in thick dialect. Chen Yu Hua found the teacher's speech difficult to understand and, try as she may, she could not grasp the meaning of any of the lessons. When exam time came she scored a zero.

She was trying her very best but she was tired all the time. The never-ending chores around the house were wearing her down and she had to rise too early each morning. Before she went to school the courtyard had to be swept, the diapers washed, the baby fed and dressed and grandma had to be helped with the cooking. It was late at night before she could study her homework and, longing for family and home kept her from getting a sound sleep.

Fear of her aunt was very real. Aunty Chen Fugui had been desperately unhappy since her husband left and she took it out on her ten-year-old ward. Chen Yu Hua endured her aunt's bad temper, but the beatings, endless scolding and the ridiculing added more misery to her already unhappy life.

The water started to boil in the aluminum pot and Chen Yu Hua dropped in the chopped greens. Qin Yan kneeled her swollen legs on one of the little stools that were strategically placed around the kitchen to eliminate unnecessary standing on her bound feet. She picked up a white cylinder of dough, stretched it out and wound it around her left arm. She began to tear off small pieces of the dough with her right hand, quickly, like plucking a goose. Fingers flying, she shaped the dough and pulled it across her left palm, propelling a white blizzard of flat identical little noodles into the steam. Chen Yu Hua watched with admiration. She had forgotten about school and her aunty. She was warm and safe, listening to the old grandmother prattle on with tales of her youth.

Suddenly the door rattled and flew open and Aunty Chen Fugui was standing before Chen Yu Hua.

"I happened to see your teacher just now," she lashed out angrily, "and she told me how poorly you did in one of your exams. Very poorly!"

Grandma Qin Yan stopped talking; stopped making noodles. The dough, hanging limp, gradually drooped from her left arm and, like a white snake, appeared to crawl down her traditional black pajamas.

"Is this true?"

The ten-year-old cringed. She could not move her eyes from her aunt's face, so severe and fierce it was.

"Yes," she said as a sharp slap burned her cheek. She winced but never shifted her eyes, now brimming with hot tears, from her aunt's dark face.

"What mark did you get?"

Chen Yu Hua could hear the water bubbling in the pot. She could smell the aroma of cooking greens, hear the old woman's hoarse breathing and the stirring of the baby girl in her bed.

"Zero," she said in a barely audible whisper.

"Zero? Zero?" Aunty shrieked. "You ungrateful girl. How could you get a zero? You are a lazy child ... you will never get a zero again. Do you hear me? Do you hear me? Do you hear me?" Each *do you hear me* was preceded by a sharp slap on the cheek until grandma Qin Yan threw up her hands and the remaining dough now swung in a long loop almost to the floor.

"Stop it!" She wailed.

Chen Yu Hua went to bed without her supper that night and made herself a promise. She would study General Knowledge in detail, memorizing the pages one by one. And so she did. In the final term exam she got 100%. Her aunt was thrilled, praising her to friends and colleagues, and told Chen Yu Hua's parents what a wonderful student she was and how proud they should be of her.

But the damage was done and Chen Yu Hua hated her aunt.

The twelve-story building on Huanghe Road looked very impressive. It didn't matter to anyone that we scattered a few pedestrians as Driver Zhang drove the old white Russian station wagon over the sidewalk to the front door. Director Liu Li Xun and Mr. Cheng were waiting to take us to meet the twenty-two staff members of the Trade Commission and to see our new office.

High rises in Qinghai were not always what they seemed. This was our first introduction to what lay within many of the smart-looking modern buildings we would be visiting in the following months ... damp, dreary concrete structures, dimly lit to conserve power. It was a shock to leave the sunshine and find yourself stumbling along freshly washed cold floors and climbing dark staircases.

"We'll take the elevator," said Miss Chen optimistically, trying to determine which one was working that day, "the meeting room is on the tenth floor."

The slow-moving crammed elevator, lit with one small light bulb, bumped its way up. We smiled to ourselves when each floor brought new riders startled to see foreigners on their elevator.

The staff clapped their hands as we entered the meeting room. They were a cheerful, friendly bunch and politely curious about us, stealing glances as though they had been briefed that it wasn't respectful to stare at the foreigners too much.

In this part of China, we soon realized, not only were conditions poor but also a great many employees had little or no important work to do except to scan new directives from head office or read local newspapers. There were too many people allocated to fill each position, leaving a listless work force and a frustrated administration trying to invent meaningful tasks for everyone. Endless reports were forwarded to senior government officials detailing the workload of each department, and employees justified their own existence with more reports. Whenever we commented to Miss Chen on the inordinate numbers of workers per job she would say, "China has too many people. The government must give them jobs."

"This is your second interpreter," said Lui Li Xun. "Her name is Wei Qin Hua. So now we have *Old Wei* ...that is you," he pointed to Bill, "and she is *Young Wei*." Everyone laughed.

Miss Wei, a fashionable, pretty twenty-three-year-old graduate from Qinghai Foreign Language School, was obviously nervous as Bill pinned a small maple leaf on her white collar. We would become very attached to this gentle young woman and follow her life through her love affair, marriage and birth of her baby boy.

"I'm sorry," she spoke softly, "my English is not so good."

Liu Li Xun, nicknamed Boss Liu, was forty years old; a short slender man with a wide smile. We found out later he possessed a velvety singing voice and never missed the opportunity to perform Karaoke at luncheons or banquets. We teased him about being a

Chinese version of Frank Sinatra. Boss Liu was well educated; an intelligent and able leader who had traveled to several countries including Canada. He had the challenging task of bringing economic development and the Opening to the West policy to remote Xining.

In the Foreign Trade Commission there were four Liu's, creating some humor as we struggled to sort out who was Liu. Liu is one of the five most common surnames. Director Liu became Boss Liu, and then there was a Second Boss Liu, and Miss Liu in finance. Office manager Liu Xiao Ning was Young Liu.

Mr. Cheng, our other boss, was a staunch loyal Communist and obeyed all rules to the letter. Mother China could do no wrong in Mr. Cheng's eyes. Although he had a good sense of humor and treated us with respect, we soon learned he was skeptical and not so receptive to new ideas regarding change of any kind. It would take a lot of hard work on our part to convince him that "foreign ways" were not all bad.

Senior Driver Zhang Yi Min and Driver Pei were two more important people in our Commission. In China, chauffeurs held high positions of trust; they protected the integrity and safety of the leaders and were privy to their confidential lives. Driver Zhang, in particular, became our good friend. For the next year his excellent driving skills would take us safely around Xining City and over the mountain roads of Qinghai.

After the staff meeting was over, and the one working elevator had retired for the day, our group shuffled its way down the dark stairwell with Young Liu racing ahead to turn on the lights on each landing.

Our office was located on the fifth floor and the staff had placed a large blackboard announcing in both English and Chinese, "We welcome Weigands to work in Xining."

Our big office was one-of-a-kind and extravagant. We were told it was designed especially for Foreign Experts. It was actually two offices separated by glass panels with a sliding door; one room was delegated for our use and the other for the two interpreters and Young Liu. Here they would develop our daily work schedules and arrange the industrial tours they called on-site investigations.

Everything was new and conspicuously out of place.

The floor was covered with a thick wall-to-wall Wedgwood blue rug, the only rug in the whole depressing building, and fine white lace doilies stretched on the backs of a pale blue sofa and two matching chairs. Two flags were displayed together in the same holder, the red and white maple leaf flag of Canada and the Chinese flag, with one large yellow star and four small ones on a crimson background. On the desk sat an English script manual typewriter and a current copy of the China Daily News. Pinned to the wall was a large map of the world. It was the first time we would see a map prominently displaying Asia in the center with North America allocated to the far right outer edge ... so unlike Mercator's Map we learned in our Western schools, making me realize we weren't the center of the world after all.

Boss Liu gave more speeches while we drank green tea from delicate English-style bone china cups and saucers. We applauded when he proudly announced the big news ... Miss Chen had been chosen as one of the ten women delegates from Xining to attend the United Nations Fourth Women's World Conference in Beijing in September.

Bill tried out his new desk. He would spend two days a week at this downtown office and the rest of the time working from the office in our home, promoting the Xining Foreign Economic Relations and Trade Commission.

We were now officially at work in China.

Something disquieting relating to that day stays in our memory. We had taken a roll of film of the office staff, sitting in groups of two or three. A few days later, one of the men, in his early twenties, died in a swimming accident. Miss Chen came to us as the family didn't own a picture of their son and hoped they could have the one taken at the office. "It's very sad for the family to lose their only son," she said, "we have this saying in China ... black hair has to send white hair first ... and some people consider an accidental death to be a very bad ending ... there will be no eternity for the soul."

I thought about how casually we reeled off pictures of our children all through the years. Hundreds of pictures; so many that we kept them in shoe boxes, and now we gave Miss Chen a small group snapshot, the only photo of a mother and father's dead son.

eight

中国

Chen Yu Hua heard soft knocking from the other room. At first she ignored it, thinking it was the wind. She bent lower over her math homework. It was the winter of 1971 and her school was beginning to teach selected subjects once again, along with the regular schedule of words of Chairman Mao and the Little Red Book.

The gentle knock grew louder.

She went to the kitchen, picked up an oil lamp and opened the back door that led to the small courtyard. It was the first part of November and the heavy padded blankets had not yet been hung over the outside doors to stop the cold air from entering the house.

"Yes?" she called out to the darkness.

The optical illusion of a giant moon racing out of control behind a stationary curtain of menacing clouds startled her and the feeble glow from the lamp was no help. She turned to go back inside just as a fierce wind caught the branches of an apple tree and scraped them like giant claws on the side of the old brick house. Aunty Chen Fugui was fortunate to have this house with a courtyard, where a vegetable garden, a lilac bush and two apple trees struggled to survive in the clay soil. It would be torn down one day to make room for a new apartment compound and the family would be moved into a warm flat with modern conveniences, but in doing so they would lose privacy and the freedom to grow their own garden.

"Hello," came a hesitant voice from the shadowy outline of a man huddled against the gray brick wall. Chen Yu Hua could barely hear the greeting. The relentless wind whipped the leaves from the frozen ground and whirled them into cone-shaped piles in the corners of the courtyard. It was a wild night, filled with noise. And apparitions.

"Who is it?" she called again. Her voice was edged with fear and she knew she should not have opened the door so hastily to this stranger. The lamp flickered.

"I don't know if you remember me," said the voice calmly. It was in Salar dialect. "I was on the truck a few months ago when we all came from Hualong County." He took a step forward holding up his hands with palms facing her, a sign of peaceful greeting. "Please ... don't be afraid of me. I saw your aunt meeting you that night and I found out where you lived."

She held the dim lamp higher until a glimmer of light caught his gaunt face. Instantly she recognized the young man who had helped her down from the truck.

"Please," he said again, "I wonder if you could give me a little food. I haven't eaten in a long time. There is no work here in Xining and I have go back to the farm before I starve to death."

She could see him plainly now as he moved towards her. His dirty, threadbare jacket, obviously too small, exposed his wrists, and he had no gloves on his rough red hands. Although the flaps on his cap were pulled down over his ears and his collar turned up, his face was chapped so badly that tiny fissures were bleeding on his cheeks. Nothing he did could ward off the icy winter wind.

"I really had nowhere to go," he shivered. "If you could just give me something to eat ... anything ... I will go away and you will never see me again."

Chen Yu Hua heard herself telling the young man to come in and get warm by the coal fire and to wait while she fixed some food. She poured hot tea in a glass and heard herself telling him to take her old gray gloves and scarf as her Aunty had given her new ones ... telling him she wished she were going home too, she didn't like the city, she didn't like her mean-spirited Aunty Chen Fugui or even her new school. She missed her mother and family, although she did admit to being fond of her aunt's baby girl and, of course, Grandma Qin Yan. It was the first time she had someone from

Xunhua to talk to, someone who knew who she was and where she came from. Tears of loneliness ran down her face as she wrapped some sunflower seeds, steamed buns and dried fruit in a square of cloth. She would like the young farm boy to stay longer but she knew if Aunty came home and found a stranger in the house she would be severely scolded or even beaten.

She pushed a bowl of noodles and some cold steamed buns towards him. He greedily downed the noodles, slurping them into his mouth and, with trembling hands, wiped up crumbs that had fallen on the table, licking them off his filthy fingers. He was so hungry.

Taking the food Chen Yu Hua had prepared, the Salar man stood up and started for the door. The storm shook the windows with renewed fury, battering the little house in Golden Plum Lane. This was the original name of the street but since the Revolution it had been changed to Victory Lane. To the older residents who still lived there it would always be Golden Plum Lane.

"I have to go and see about a ride back to the valley," he said, "I'm like you ... also missing my family. Life in the city is not as good as I thought it would be. I pulled coal carts for a month ... so hard ... all I did was dream about the apples and the nice weather and ..." He looked down sheepishly. "I have a girl, too. She is very beautiful and she didn't want me to come here ... she had bad feelings about Xining."

He hesitated and turned back, pulled Chen Yu Hua to him in a quick firm hug. "Thank you," he said. "I hope we meet again someday in Xunhua."

They did not hear the footsteps. The young Salar man had his hand on the door handle as Aunty Chen Fugui came into the room. She was stunned.

"What's this?" she yelled. "What's going on?"

Out the door he ran. The scarf wound around his neck and the old gray gloves hanging from one pocket. As he ran for the courtyard gates the little bundle of food caught on a branch from one of the raging trees, tearing the cloth from his hand, scattering the precious food; sunflower seeds and dried fruit. And out of the corner of his eye was the sad sight of the precious steamed bun rolling along the cold ground, pushed by the angry wind.

He had no time to stop.

Aunty Chen Fugui was hysterical.

"We've been robbed! There's a robber here! Get the police!"

She threw her arms above her head and bawled at the top of her lungs, alarming the neighbors. Then she sprinted down the lane to the Block Police Post before Chen Yu Hua could make her listen.

"He's my friend," she kept repeating. "He isn't a robber. He's my friend." But it did no good.

The little girl ran down the hall to Grandma Qin Yan's room and burst through the door.

"Grandma! Help me! Please!"

The old lady was swinging her legs out of the wooden bed while struggling to get her arms into a worn old housecoat.

Chen Yu Hua stopped and stared.

She saw, for the first time, the bare twisted stumps of feet, bluish-gray in color and ringed with rough calluses. How did this old lady walk?

She threw herself into Qin Yan's arms sobbing, and told her the story of the young Salar boy.

Several hours later, after the beating from Aunty Chen Fugui, and after much crying, she was lying in her bed. She could cry no more. She only hoped her new friend had escaped and would make it safely back to the valley where they both belonged.

The door to her room was pushed open and Aunty stood framed against the sparse light from the oil lamp behind her in the hall. Her fearful shadow loomed across the floor.

"They caught the robber," she said proudly. "Here are your stolen belongings. Unfortunately, the young thief wanted to run away so the police had to beat him to make him confess. The officer said he was in such poor physical condition that he died from the beating." She carelessly threw the gray crumpled wool gloves and scarf onto the bed.

Chen Yu Hua wanted to scream out the injustice of it all. She wanted to say the young man was no thief, that he came from her part of the world where people would have gladly given him food.

She wanted to say she hated this cruel place and longed for home. But she could only lie still, with dry eyes staring at the ceiling.

Mr. Wu was a handsome, stylish young man who was to become a most important person in our lives. He was every bit the well-dressed cadre, nodding and smiling as he adjusted the turned-up collar on his long coat, fashionably draped over his shoulders. He had a small leather pouch tucked under his arm. All the cadres carried these square zippered bags and at first I thought they were shaving kits. The bags contained note pads, pens, wallets and any important papers. Some had shoulder straps, but most were kept securely under the arm.

Mr. Wu was in charge of our house project and asked mistakenly if there was anything we needed.

"Mr. Wu wants you to know that his job is to assist you," translated Miss Chen.

He was taken aback when I said we would like to have the floors tiled, as well as the windows and doorframes and most of the walls painted. Could he help us find workers?

"And none of the doors close properly," said Bill. "We actually need a carpenter."

A deep discussion went on for several minutes between Mr. Wu and Miss Chen, mostly about the house having been completely renovated to *Western standards for Foreign Experts*. When we said we would pay for the expenses, it put a different light on the subject and Mr. Wu agreed to help. But he was still puzzled why we would spend money on a house that was to be demolished; couldn't we bear it for one year? I looked at the concrete floors and the scruffy yellow window casings with globs of old paint smeared on the panes, and in the washroom I could hear the steady dripping of water from poor-fitting rusty pipes.

"It's such a nice old house ... we'd like to make some changes ... to brighten it up." I wanted to tell him politely that we did not want to live this way for a full year without trying to improve the place. "But first, I'd like to have the old tub removed from the washroom. We can't use it … we have no hot water to fill it … someone else should have it."

This was too much for Mr. Wu. Anyone would love to have a big bathtub. Didn't we know that four leaders had used it?

"Please tell Mr. Wu we're flattered to have this lovely antique, but we really don't need it."

More talking. On and on. Mr. Wu wasn't buying any of this and he seemed to be resisting the fact we didn't want the old tub. Just when I was beginning to adjust to the idea of having the well-worn relic hanging around for the year, Miss Chen suddenly turned and said, "Mr. Wu says he will send some men here this afternoon to take it away."

The last we saw of the old cast iron tub, with the claw feet and high back, was the struggle of four young men as they dragged it down the lane. We always wondered where it finally ended up. We were told very few apartments had bathtubs. If they did, I presumed they must have been used for storage or knew the secret of getting enough hot water to have a bath. The flats had only cold running water. The people used communal shower rooms, with one day a week allotted for men and one day for women.

The tub had never been connected to the sewer pipe and, since the floor was unfinished under it, the water drained directly onto the ground. We had to find some matching ceramic red tiles and a man to do the job.

We hired four small ladies with well-worn brushes and homemade pole ladders to slap "whitewash" on the walls, which flaked like a snowstorm when the cold weather arrived. I tackled the doors and the mustard-colored window casements with bright white enamel. My eyes puffed from what I suspected was lead in the paint.

Miss Chen called from the courtyard gate. She was laughing hard, "Come and see Mr. Weigand."

They had been shopping all morning. Boxes of black and white linoleum tiles for the concrete floors and red ceramic tiles to finish the washroom, were piled high on a bicycle cart along with rolls of red carpet to cover the planks. I was amused to see Bill teetering on top of our supplies. Never having bought anything in China before, I thought the goods would be delivered by a small truck, but we later realized that everything was moved on these carts: bookcases, beds, three-piece sofa sets, and even large mirrors.

Two men arrived with one dull knife to share between them, and we settled on the sum of two hundred yuan ($32.00) to tile our hallway, toilet room and kitchen with the black and white lino tiles.

"You are paying too much," said Miss Chen. "It's a lucky day for them to have met the foreigners."

"Doesn't matter," we assured her.

The men had little idea how to match patterns or measure properly and obviously were not tile layers. We laid out the tiles for them and gave them our "Exacto" knife for cutting. But we just couldn't take Mr. Wu's good advice. He thought it would be wise to glue the tiles down on brown paper so we could pick them up and take them with us when we left. The house would be gone next year, he kept reminding us, and these were brand new tiles.

"Mr. Weigand, the ceramic man is here to do the floor in the washroom but he has no tools to cut the tiles," said Miss Chen.

"We have a ceramic man already?"

"He says he needs seventy five-yuan to buy a special tool."

Bill was staring at the skinny young man grinning in the doorway; the third man to be hired this day.

"No tools?" said Bill, digging in his pocket to hand Miss Chen the seventy five-yuan, "so do I get to keep the tools if I pay for them?"

In no time the house was filled with the high-pitched scream of a circular saw, and powdery red dust drifting out of the washroom, settling on everything.

"Does he have a facemask?" Bill yelled over the noise, "how about ear plugs?"

"We're worried about his lungs," I said.

Miss Chen's answer was to close the door to the washroom, leaving the ceramic man to work alone. "You can't do that," I argued, but I noticed the door remained shut all afternoon.

The carpenter hammered and chiseled at the doors with what

resembled a hunting knife, trying to make them fit. Before long he put his tools away and said he was finished.

"But the doors don't close," said Bill, staring at the gouges. "Tell him he has to make the doors close!"

Mr. Carpenter and Miss Chen went into another huddle with a lot of negative head-shaking on both sides.

"He says he's very tired," said Miss Chen … "and he can't finish today."

"Is he coming back tomorrow?"

More conversation. "No!"

"Then tell him he has to finish the doors today."

I felt sorry for Bill but I was glad it wasn't me trying to get a couple of hours of work out of Mr. Wu's unwilling man. Bill agreed to pay the "carpenter" a little more and finally the chips started flying again. Within half an hour the doors closed easily when they were slammed.

We had better luck with the washroom floor. It was neatly finished where the tub had been and we paid the tile man his wages, thanking him for the professional job. He was covered all over in fine dust; his hair, hands, clothes, every bit of him. His two brown eyes peered through a reddish-purple haze. He grinned and bought up his hand in some kind of salute then disappeared out the door with his new tool.

"Don't workmen ever have any of their own tools?" asked Bill. Miss Chen just shrugged. After all, what did she know about renovating a house? She was learning along with us.

The little ladies gossiped in shrill voices from their ladders. Thin white water dripped everywhere and discarded pieces of tile lay along the hall floor. At one time there were fifteen people milling around in the house and the noise was awful.

I heard Miss Chen call from the front door. "Mrs. Weigand, two doctors are here to take your blood pressure."

An attractive older woman came into the room followed by a lovely younger girl. Both were dressed in white medical coats and carried blood pressure gauges.

"What?" I couldn't believe my ears. I got down from the kitchen chair I had been using as a stepladder.

"Deputy Mayor Yang sent Dr. Ma to take Mr. Weigand's and your blood pressure."

Stepping over tile cuttings and curly bits of wood, we made our way to the living room, trying hard to ignore the noise while Miss Chen served tea.

"You must always offer tea to your guests as soon as they arrive," reminded Miss Chen. "This is why we keep several Thermos flasks of boiling water handy at all times."

We had our blood pressures taken. Quite normal, which was a surprise considering the commotion around us, and the giddy seven thousand foot altitude of Xining.

"Dr. Ma says she must listen to your heart," said Miss Chen, "she wants you to lift your blouse so she can use her stethoscope."

The room suddenly became quiet. Twelve workers stopped what they were doing and watched me as if something very interesting was about to happen.

"In front of all these men?" I said.

"*Mei Guan Xi.* It doesn't matter!"

The term *Mei Guan Xi* (May Guan Shee) is used every five minutes in China. It literally means no problem, don't worry, or, it doesn't really matter. I suddenly had visions of me sitting with my blouse held high, exposing my Western bosom for all the workers to see. I'm sure it would have given them a great topic of conversation for the dinner tables that night.

"I think it matters," I said and, with her pretty assistant in tow, I took Dr. Ma to our little kitchen where I could close the door and let her gently rest her stethoscope on my chest. Her blank expression didn't change but I knew she was impressed, having never viewed the ample chest of a foreign lady before.

Between our busy work and social schedules, it took about two weeks to clean and paint our new home. The wealth of cheap goods in department stores supplied us with some finishing touches: new cooking pots, crystal glasses, towels, a china teapot with six mugs, and we couldn't resist a silver-plated candelabrum and three red candles. We bought a colorful Oriental rug, table lamps and yards of white lace to dress the windows, and filled large glass vases with realistic silk flowers: red roses, sunflowers, branches of cherry blossoms and soft mauve irises. We bought extra pillows and linens for the beds, and searched out a thick piece of foam pad. Chinese beds and pillows were incredibly hard.

Miss Chen enjoyed shopping with us but every now and then she would ask why we needed so many *things*. "You are only in China for one year," she reminded us, "you are not in joint venture with the stores in Xining."

We found that the Chinese were great consumers. They loved to shop and were hampered only by lack of funds. They saved to buy all kinds of gadgets and 90% of families owned the biggest TV they could afford.

Later, we visited poor farm homes with dirt floors and very little furniture and there would always be a television, large or small. Chairman Mao had envisioned a TV in every home. It was his way to reach the masses and he succeeded, with over 500 million sets in China.

Our house changed to a cozy small piece of Canada. We tacked a huge Canadian flag on the wall of the office, along with a picture of our Prime Minister, and filled the window casing with framed photos of our family and friends. Maps, calendars, posters and pictures of Canada were everywhere.

I illustrated two famous Chinese scenes, the *Great Wall* and *Yellow Mountain*, with kid's poster paints on the white walls of the living room. Another mural, *Headwaters of the Yellow River*, ran along a 22-foot hallway to the office. This puzzled our visitors. They had never before seen anyone paint murals on the walls of their homes.

The plumbing in the washroom remained a problem. Although pipes were taken apart and put back together twice, there was always the same annoying drip and puddle just in front of the sink. We fixed it with a funnel and a long flexible plastic tube. The floor was dry but the sink was still loose and we had to remember to warn our guests to not lean on the sink.

The kitchen windows were hung with green and white curtains matching the wallpaper and I hand-sewed a chintz skirt to dress the big rusty propane tank we named "the pig." It was all very designer-looking but there was one distraction. In the high ceiling, a two-foot square black hole about sixteen inches deep extended to the roof, covered with a grimy window pane. Years ago it had been a chimney where smoke from a coal stove funneled out. To us it was unsightly, and I complained every day what an eyesore it was.

"Just don't look up," said Miss Chen, with her usual Chinese wisdom.

We couldn't help but look up. Bill bought large sheets of heavy white cardboard and thumbtacks and Miss Chen phoned Liu Xiao Ning. He must have wondered when she asked him to come and help put paper on a hole in the kitchen. Handsome Young Liu, with the infectious laugh, arrived for work detail in no time.

"He needs two chairs," said Miss Chen.

This was our first introduction to a Chinese-style stepladder. One chair placed on the other and, with Bill and Miss Chen holding the top chair, nimble Young Liu hopped up and secured the cardboard over the offending hole. This worked very well, except ever after, during a Xining wind the quick fix would moan, inhaling and exhaling, like the kitchen was breathing.

One day Miss Wei brought her charming mother, Song De Gui, and one of her aunts for a visit to meet the Foreign Experts in their Western-style home. The two ladies brought gift baskets bulging with eggs, oranges, grapes, bananas and six green jade liquor cups.

Song De Gui was a very successful entrepreneur, owning a brick-making factory and a lucrative liquor wholesale. She was the only businesswoman we actually met in Qinghai. Her business acumen and benevolence for the poor of Datong County, where she lived, won her "Citizen of the Year" and other awards.

Proudly, Miss Wei began the tour through the foreigners' house.

"Don't miss the bathroom, it's my pride and joy," I said, pointing down the hall.

The ladies smiled and frowned at the same time, then turned into the kitchen. Obviously they didn't know that we had the brightest, freshest-smelling, dirt-free, *Better Homes and Gardens*-looking bathroom in all of Northwest China. We painted the rusty lead pipes and the large window casements glossy white, bought a new toilet seat, hung frilly lace curtains. I filled a wire rack with colorful towels printed "hand towel" and "bath towel" in bold red

Chinese characters, and stood a healthy green philodendron in the corner. All kinds of interesting knick-knacks, an empty perfume bottle, paperweights and small teapots sat on a chrome and glass étagère we found in a second hand store. But the pièce de résistance was something else. I bought a square of fuzzy black synthetic material, cut a template for the base of the toilet and added a small luxurious rug on the black and white tiled floor.

Just as the three of them were about to leave I asked, "Are you not going to have a look at my bathroom?"

"No, no thank you," said Miss Wei. The other ladies shook their heads, giving me a weak smile.

"I would really like them to see the bathroom," I pressed, "we spent a lot of time fixing it up."

The "oh well" look of resignation was on their faces as Miss Wei warily pushed open the door to the huge bathroom and they went in, closing the door behind them. I could hear them giggling, imagining them examining everything including the black fuzzy rug. They reminded me of Mr. Cheng's saying ... "in China three women make a street."

"Where did the ladies go?" asked Bill.

"They've been in the bathroom for ten minutes," I said, "I think they really like it."

Miss Wei told us later she had never seen such a lovely bathroom, it was like a picture in a magazine, she said, and her aunt and mother were favorably impressed. "We never show our bathrooms to anyone," she sighed, all whispery, like it was a deep dark secret, "they are not very nice you know ... yeah?"

Early the next morning Miss Chen was on the phone, "I have good news for you."

We learned to be suspicious of this statement. It could mean really good news like a trip to the country but often as not it was a twenty-minute warning that we were about to have company. We didn't mind the company but sometimes the shortness of the warning was nerve wracking.

Everyone wanted to see what the foreigners did to the old house and today it was the leaders' turn to inspect the renovations.

"They wish to welcome you properly to your new home," said

Miss Chen.

The municipal government of Xining consisted of seven mayors appointed by the Central Government in Beijing. Out of these seven, one was chosen by the other six to be number one mayor. Unlike the elected mayors and councilors of a Canadian city, the Chinese mayors had much more power and, as we learned, a definite pecking order.

"Remember, Miss Chen, there's no smoking in the house." I knew this made her uneasy. She twitched her shoulders and hummed to herself when she didn't like what I said. We had numerous discussions about smoking and Bill and I agreed we should stick by our rule. This was really breaking new territory and most Chinese women would never challenge the men on smoking.

"I don't think the leaders will obey that rule."

"You have to *just tell them*," I said.

The morning visit went well. Our two sofas placed directly across from each other allowed us to chat face to face with our guests. In China the seating arrangements are rarely so intimate, as chairs and sofas are generally placed flat against the walls.

We had tea and small cakes and everyone inspected the renovated house. Comments were made about the murals, the kitchen with the painted white enamel cupboard that once was a drab bookcase and now held the Blue Willow dishes. The propane tank 'pig' with the skirt. The flowers. They studied the maps and pictures in Bill's office and asked him how we were doing for food and were we happy with the office downtown? Were we lonely? They worried about us being lonely.

Before they left I handed Mayor Li a thick black felt pen. Would they all please sign their names on the white wall behind the TV? It was the start of 260 Chinese and English names and humorous drawings to appear on our signature wall over the next year.

We laughed easily together, and with Miss Chen's superb translating, two cultures were comfortable with one another. She was a voice between friends. We depended on her to build trust and good communications and she never once failed us. But she was wrong about one thing. No one smoked!

As we said good-bye at the door, Mayor Yang swept his hand graciously around the room and spoke directly to Bill.
"What did he say?"
"Mayor Yang says … This is really living!"

nine

中国

Chen Yu Hua could not believe her eyes.

Was the tall man standing by the school gate really her father? She stopped abruptly and stared in amazement before realizing the figure was not an unkind trick played by her lonely mind. It was her father. He looked thinner now, his clothes more worn than when she last saw him. The familiar steel gray suit bore the stitches of repeated mending and re-mending by Jia Ying and his once white shirt was creased and soiled.

For a moment she was too shocked to move. Her feet stuck tight to the ground as if unseen iron shackles were holding her down by the ankles, and students jostled her, almost knocking the books from her grasp in their haste to leave the classrooms.

Six months had passed since the day her father secured a place on top of the old blue stake truck and sent her riding into a new life in Xining City. Spring Festival had come and gone. It had been so different when Uncle Xiao Zhan came home; his cheerful disposition lifted everyone's spirits during the holiday season. He had decked out the house perfectly, hanging large red and gold lanterns and pasting narrow red *cuplets* on each side of the front door. *Happiness, Prosperity, Long Life* leapt out in grand gold characters. He bought candies, and all the ingredients to make the traditional dessert, Eight Treasure Pudding: rice, honey, raisins and fruit pressed hard in a bowl, steamed and turned onto a platter, splashed with liquor and flamed. He also splurged on two red and gold candles. When Aunty saw these she scolded him for spending too much money, but he smiled and said simply, "it's the New

Year." At night they lit long strips of firecrackers in the courtyard and watched them crackle and dance, sending clouds of smoke billowing into the black sky. And during Lantern Festival, Chen Yu Hua's school made exquisite lighted lanterns designed in every conceivable image. When darkness fell they carried them like dancing stars along the streets to People's Park.

Chen Yu Hua ran to her father, clinging to him, tears streaming down her cheeks.

"Father! Father! I'm so happy to see you! Have you come to take me home? Please take me home."

Avoiding her questions and pleading eyes he explained that he was on his way to a job in another county, building houses he said, and he would be back in the city in a few weeks. They could talk about these things when he returned.

"How are you doing in school? This is a great opportunity for you to learn." He looked earnestly at her, "How about your lessons? Are your marks excellent?"

She did not answer. Why couldn't he just say he was here to take her home? Why did she have to beg?

"Father, take me home," she wept. "I can't stay with Aunty any longer. She hates me! Please!"

Chen Jian Pin spent one night in the house of his sister, Chen Fugui. That evening as they sat around the dinner table he talked about the hard life in Xunhua. The family was well, of course, there was a shortage of food but he was going to make extra money when he finished the job in the north. Chen Yu Hua never had any time alone with him; she wanted to tell him how miserable life had been for her at Aunty Chen Fugui's home but she never got the chance. He took no notice of her and simply ignored anything she tried to say to him. She went to bed frustrated and depressed, thinking her father didn't realize how unhappy she had become. He didn't care. Those thoughts were still with her the next morning as she said good-bye to him at the school gate. Much to her surprise, her father *had* been aware of her circumstances. He squeezed her small hand and whispered, "I know how unhappy you are. As soon as I come back in a few weeks, you'll be able to go home. I promise." And he left her alone and melted into the early morning crowds.

But it wasn't a few weeks, it was five long months before she heard he had returned to his home in Xunhua. She felt dejected and sick to her stomach all the time. She had headaches every day and she lost weight. She could not concentrate on her work. It was as though her mind was separate and in control of itself, wandering and languid. Aunty tried scolding and threatening her and when this didn't work she realized it was time to send her eleven-year-old niece back to Xunhua as soon as possible.

"All right," she said, "I know how much you miss your family." Her voice softened for the first time. "Your father told me if you really wanted to go home I must send you. You can go as soon as your father arranges a ride."

That night Chen Yu Hua made a wish. "I want to be home for Mid-Autumn Festival," she whispered to the darkness in her tiny bedroom.

But it was not to be; the festival was already here.

The only thing that made the waiting tolerable was having Uncle Xiao Zhan home for the celebration. Also Auntie's disposition had improved slightly.

"This is the time of year when the moon is at its very fullest and brightest," said Uncle Xiao Zhan. "What are you going to say to the big moon, Qing Ling?" He used the pet name her father always called her to make her feel less lonely.

"I'll think of my family far away in Xunhua and know they're seeing the very same moon as I do … I'll tell the moon to tell them I miss them." Chen Yu Hua suddenly slumped down in her chair and began to cry.

"Don't cry," soothed Grandma Qin Yan, wrapping her bony arms around the unhappy little shoulders.

"I know how to cheer you up, Qing Ling." Uncle Xiao Zhan clapped his big hands. "Everyone, sit down," he bellowed, "I'm going to tell you the story of my favorite goddess, the divinely beautiful … *but*," he stopped in mid-sentence and, with eyes shut tight, he wagged a finger in the air, "*ill-fated* Chang Oh."

The family huddled around the small table while Uncle Xiao Zhan inflated his barrel chest and stood poised like a performing storyteller from long ago.

"Chang Oh was married to a famous archer," he began, "Hou Yin, was his name. He was an officer in the Emperor's Imperial guards. One day ten blazing suns suddenly appeared without warning in the summer sky. The emperor was alarmed, afraid of the fearful sight and terrible damage that could be inflicted on his people. He called for his most skilled archer and ordered him to shoot the dreadful apparitions out of the sky."

The uncle, filled with exaggerated zeal, at once assumed the romantic stance of the archer.

"When the Goddess of Western Heaven heard about the great feat she rewarded Hou Yin with the promise of everlasting life. This came in the form of an elixir to be swallowed, but only after Hou Yin spent one full year fasting and meditating ... he had to obtain spiritual enlightenment, you know. Carefully he hid the potion in his home, but his wife Chang Oh discovered it and drank it down greedily. This angered the Goddess of Western Heaven and she punished Chang Oh."

Xiao Zhan swung both his long arms heavenward and lowered his voice to a raspy whisper. "And this is what she did ... she sent Chang Oh on a moonbeam to dwell alone on the moon ... forever and ever. Hou Yin loved his wife so much that he forgave her foolish act and tried desperately to follow her, but the goddess in her wrath sent a powerful typhoon and swept him back to earth."

Uncle Xiao Zhan made a wide, deep bow.

"Now you know the story," he said eloquently, "how the brilliant radiance of Chang Oh's beauty greatly enhanced the silver moon and for centuries we Chinese have admired it each year during Mid Autumn Festival ... but poor Chang Oh, as a poet once wrote ... she must regret stealing the elixir as she broods in loneliness night after night."

The baby girl laughed and squealed. Chen Yu Hua, Grandma Qin Yan, and Aunty Chen Fugui clapped loudly. Delicious Moon cakes, filled with nuts, dates, sesame seed and bean mash, were brought out to be eaten with fragrant hot tea, while uncle held a small cup of rice wine.

"Let us make a toast to beautiful Chang Oh!" he chimed.

Yak hides were piled so high on the floor they looked every bit like a giant mammoth; a longhaired indistinct mound minus head, tusks and feet.

It was another on-site investigation at a local factory listed on our daily work schedule. Today was the Qinghai Gelatin factory. We met the genial manager who took us step by step through the manufacture of gelatin capsules. It seemed to revolve around the rendering down of yak bones in large pressure vats until a sticky substance is somehow molded into small capsules, to be filled with everything medicinal from antibiotics to Chinese herbal medicine.

These visits always began in the executive office where we would be briefed about the operation of the business over a cup of tea and fresh fruit. Our minds were numbed with facts, figures, percentages, statistics, and well-rehearsed rhetoric delivered faithfully to the last word by every manager of a state-owned business. We suspected that the production figures and lucrative profit ratios were exaggerated, and there was always the request for a much-needed injection of foreign investment.

I looked at Bill and Miss Chen, both caught up in the exciting operation. Bill was busy taking notes. It was his job to send letters of introduction to Canadian companies seeking Chinese products. I found it hot and stuffy, my stomach churning at the thought of the bubbling yak.

The assistant manager, a serious young lady, decked us out in facemasks, white coats, plastic bags to pull over our shoes, and little white hospital caps. We looked every bit like a team of doctors. She led the way into the germ free zone where capsules of various sizes and colors floated along conveyor belts past quality control ladies dressed in space suit garb.

It seemed terribly sanitary, until we arrived at the shipping department. Rows of ladies sat, minus gloves, each with huge containers in front of them, scooping capsules by the handful, into plastic bags.

We made visits to a leather factory, gear factory, tractor factory, steel mill, chemical plant, and a gold jewelry manufacturing company. We sent detailed investment opportunity letters to Canada, re-wrote brochures, tried to simplify books of regulations and even polished business cards.

One successful operation in Xining was the production of yak hair and cashmere sweaters at Number One Knitting Mill. Soft blankets and clothing were produced skillfully on dangerous and antiquated machines. We watched one young girl who had the risky job of flipping a lever as she crawled beneath the fast shifting loom. Each time she let the arm go it immediately swung back with incredible force. The girl would duck with precision as the giant steel bar pitched over her head missing her by a few inches. Obviously it was her job for several hours at a time and we wondered how many serious accidents occurred. The noise was deafening; a thunderous *clank-clanking* delivered by archaic monsters.

"Do the workers have earplugs?" asked Bill pointing to his ears.

"What?" said Miss Chen leaning closer.

Before the answer came, a bobbin launched itself from a spool with lightning speed, striking the leather bound note pad that Bill was holding in front of his chest. He stumbled back from the wallop. The group had shocked looks on their faces as Miss Chen said, "oh, my," and Bill examined the dent in his new leather book. There must have been a sigh of relief from the Chinese to know that a flying missile in Number One Knitting Mill hadn't killed the foreigner that day.

A nervous Bill inquired, "Does this happen often?" No one answered. The group was already moving on, conveniently forgetting the query about earplugs and protective screens and any other non-existent safety rules.

Another memorable visit was to the Qinghai Carpet Factory, famous for its exquisite wool carpets and tucked inconspicuously behind imposing iron gates. We were surprised to find ourselves strolling under willow trees scuffing the ground with their long branches, past rows of boarded up warehouses and shops, and uninhabited workers' homes, each with a neat little courtyard.

Birds nested in these trees high above an old bone-dry fountain showing signs of cracks. Wild flowers blossomed in abundance. Long ago this community would have bustled with life, families gossiping at the water pumps and calling for their children. But now the vegetable gardens were over-grown and the courtyards silent and empty.

"This place looks abandoned," I said to Miss Chen, "are you sure we know where we're going?"

We stopped in front of an imposing four-story warehouse, the only one with huge *unboarded* windows, and met the managers of the Qinghai Carpet Factory. The factory must have been built sometime in the 20s or 30s, no one knew exactly when.

It was always like that, as though China never really existed before Chairman Mao came on the scene. When we talked about history, Miss Chen would say "You know more about China than I do," and this was often true.

Like many state-owned businesses the carpet factory was suffering from lack of cash flow. Years of declining markets after China cut off trade with the outside world and mounting expenses were taking a toll on the company.

"How many employees do you have in this company?" asked Bill.

"Seven thousand five hundred," came the surprising reply.

Taking a quick look around the building we said we would have guessed at maybe two thousand workers. The manager shook his head then enlightened us on the theory of the *Iron Rice Bowl*, the Chinese Communist way of looking after its people from cradle to grave. He explained that every person who ever worked for the carpet factory was entitled to the same ongoing paycheck, apartment and benefits when he or she retired. Literally the company had one third working employees and two-thirds retirees.

With this financial drain on companies there was never enough money to buy modern machinery or develop new markets. In fact, as the employees retired and payrolls increased with new workers, there was the sad fate the company would slip into an impossible debt, devastating for everyone. Beijing was propping up these companies as much as possible, but eventually tremendous pressure was put on the managers to become more productive, an impossible task without more investment. From the carpet rooms we heard the steady rhythmic swishing sounds of an ancient art: knotting, pulling, combing and clipping, with the shuttle slipping smoothly forward and backward adding one more thread to the pattern.

Thick wool carpets in various sizes and shapes, from traditional Chinese designs to modern works of art, lay in piles on the floor: Tibetan motif carpets in royal blue and flame red, with the famous Phoenix and Dragon tossing a magic ball above the clouds; willow patterns in blue and creamy tans, and small square prayer rugs of deep burgundy with images of yak woven in the center.

One of the young managers noticed we were looking at the windows. "These were boarded over during the Cultural Revolution," he said, and explained how the carpet company had fallen out of favor with the Red Guards because of the foreign investment involved. It was ordered to shut down. The managers at the time made the buildings appear as desolate and empty as they could by covering the windows and letting the weeds grow. He hesitated for a moment and I wondered if he was thinking perhaps he shouldn't be telling secrets to foreigners, but he soon continued. "No one got suspicious ... and the weavers came to work every day and produced carpets by dim lights. They did this for ten years before they could take the boards off the windows and replace the glass broken by the Red Guards."

ten

中国

Chen Yu Hua forgot about the unhappy times in her aunt's house and, as long as Uncle Xiao Zhan was around, life was bearable.

One day in the warm sun of spring, the two of them walked to the busiest part of the city to a place called "The Cross" where a high overpass spanned the intersection of two main streets named East and West. The Xining Post Office and three large department stores stood at this junction. Overhead a giant circular walkway not only served as a safe passage for the people but also a social gathering place and viewing stand. From here the old city looked impressive with its tree-lined avenues, and later, after dusk, the streets below would be transformed, as if by magic, into the Night Market, where sidewalk vendors set up shop in the midst of teeming crowds flowing around them.

The Post Office was busy. Long line-ups met them inside the front door. People sat at desks addressing envelopes or stood around a table in the middle of the room where the essential glue pot rested. It was a huge bowl of brown, honey-textured paste punctured with gummed-up sticks, ready to seal envelopes or dab postage stamps. Others waited for the Postal Clerk to inspect their open parcels before they wrapped them in durable white cotton sacking and sewed them taut by needle and thread.

As they left the post office on West Street Uncle Xiao Zhan pointed to the long line of people, mostly poor farmers waiting patiently outside the local pharmacy. "They are waiting to see a doctor," he said, "For a small payment they can discuss their health problems." He explained that very few words would be exchanged, just the nature of the ailment and a limp attempt to take the patient's pulse. Headache pills, plasters for sore joints or powders for stomach aches would be hastily jotted on a prescription pad to be purchased, of course, in the pharmacy positioned behind the doctor.

They walked together through the market at *Ximenkuo* (West Gate) where wooden stands groaned with fresh fruits and vegetables. Her uncle pointed out persimmons and bananas from the southern provinces, potatoes and corn from neighboring Ganzu and the delicious red apples from her hometown.

He stopped in front of a display of litchi nuts and asked Chen Yu Hua if she wanted to hear a story about an emperor and a beautiful lady. Chen Yu Hua loved stories. China was filled with stories, and her uncle seemed to know them all.

"This story is about Emperor Tang Xuanzon and his favorite concubine, Yang Yu Huan ... who loved litchi nuts. When the Emperor became aware of her fondness for the fruit he ordered the leaders of the southern provinces of Fujian and Guangdong to pay tribute to his court in the form of fresh litchi nuts. He even started a pony express to bring the fruit as fast as possible to the lovely lady. Can you imagine Chen Yu Hua, how powerful the Emperor was ... there in his magnificent palace in Chang'an?"

They strolled past wire cages piled high with chickens and geese. Some were ready for the axe while the customer waited, and some to be taken home live, dangling upside down, wings flapping and gasping for air, from bicycle handlebars.

There were sacks of finely ground Oriental spices, chili and jalapeno peppers, and barrels of peanuts, cashews and sunflower seeds. Tables displayed stacks of Mao posters, large and small, and little red books of Mao's sayings.

It all seemed so lavish to Chen Yu Hua compared with the meager markets in Xunhua.

"So did she get lots of litchi nuts to eat, Uncle?"

"Every day the lovely Yang Yu Huan watched from her casement window for the flying hooves of the horses, knowing that fresh juicy litchi fruit was nestled in the cargo baskets," said the uncle, theatrically waving his hand in a great arc. "She had lots and lots of fresh fruit to eat."

"That was a good story. I wish I was a concubine."

The uncle stopped, looked down at the little girl and drew in a deep satisfying lungful of cigarette smoke. "No, you don't," he said.

When Uncle went back to Golmud, the mood in the house resumed its meanness. Grandma spent most of her time attending to the needs of the baby, who was now a year old, and Aunty became unusually quiet. It was another two weeks before a long-distance truck driver came to the house to tell Chen Yu Hua he would take her back to Xunhua. He was a good friend of her father and said he would make sure she got home safely.

The next morning she was up very early, packed her belongings, ate a steamed bun and drank some hot water. Dutifully she thanked Aunty Chen Fugui, hugged old Grandma Qin Yan, kissed the baby girl, and climbed into the truck beside the driver. She was so happy as they pulled out and headed for home, she thought her heart would burst in her chest.

She never once looked back down Victory Lane.

That night she walked into her father's house. When she saw her mother she cried and wiped her tears with her sleeves. She greeted her father and threw her arms about her siblings, and gave them colored pencils to share her happiness. They were all together again.

A few days later she put on a new pair of nylon socks her aunt had given her, slung her fashionable Peoples Liberation Army type bag, so popular in the city, over her shoulder and went to school. The teachers commented on her excellent Mandarin and mature behavior and were intrigued by Chen Yu Hua's new ballpoint pens and schoolbooks. They had never seen these things before. The students loved her big-city clothes and marveled at her white face; apparently it had paled from her year indoors and away from the fields. She was envied and sought after by classmates who were eager to hear stories about Liberation Primary School.

Gradually she turned away the bad thoughts of the year with Aunty Chen Fugui and in due course recognized the many good things she had learned. She had broadened her views on life, learned more about China, learned to cook, and learned how to save and spend money wisely. It was Grandma Qin Yan who taught her to sew and do exquisite embroidery. Aunty bought many new clothes for her and taught her how to dress properly, attend to her hair and have good manners. But for Chen Yu Hua the most important trait learned that year, and the one most admired by the Chinese, was how to muster the strength to bear anything harsh and unfair. This *how to bear* would shape her personality and help her cope with difficult situations all her life.

Not once did she tell her family about the awful things that happened in the year away. The beatings, the fights between husband and wife, the poor Salar boy who only wanted a little food, and all those empty nights when she cried herself to sleep.

And for years after, Chen Yu Hua reflected on her relationship with Aunty Chen Fugui. She never saw her again, but heard she had died at age forty-six. She felt nothing at the news one way or another, no real sadness at her aunt's early demise, but little by little a grudging respect and forgiveness began to grow in her heart and she tried to remember only the good things that came from her year in Xining.

"We are going to Qinghai Lake tomorrow ... yeah?"

Miss Wei chose her English words carefully and thoughtfully, not wanting to make any glaring mistakes, but she had this habit of saying "yeah" after most of her statements. Not a harsh *yeah* but a long breathless, whispery drawn out *yeahh*. "We will stay the night at the Birds Island Hotel and come home the following day ... yeah?"

Miss Wei, beautiful Miss Wei, came to the door the next morning looking every bit like a model ready to march down a Paris catwalk. She wore a long slim black skirt, laced up high-heeled leather boots and a crisp white blouse. Her black hair hung straight and shiny to her waist and a curved comb of pearls pulled it back from her face, sitting like a small royal tiara on the top of her head.

She was exceptionally glamorous.

"You're all dressed up?" I spouted, meaning she didn't look casual enough for a trip to the country, like me, in jeans and T-shirt and running shoes. She didn't quite understand my English and seemed puzzled.

"Yes, of course I dressed," she breathed in a voice soft and youthful, "We're going to Qinghai Lake … remember? Yeah?"

I felt stupid. "You look great." I said.

Five of us packed our station wagon with snacks, bottled water and juices and, with Driver Zhang at the wheel, headed out of the busy city.

The road to Qinghai Lake, the largest lake in China, was also the road to Tibet. Trucks bound for Golmud and Lhasa were piled high with supplies and belching black smoke. Long distance buses choked the road, as did donkeys, wagons, and farm tractors with dangerous open flywheels on the side. It was the first time we had a good look at this popular tough three-wheeled workhorse nicknamed the *mechanical buffalo*.

We rolled past yellow rapeseed fields squared off against the green fields of early barley and caught glimpses of the Riyui Mountains in the distance. Here stood two wooden Chinese pavilions built to honor the twin mountains called the Sun and Moon.

"Have you heard the story of Princess Wen Chen?" asked Miss Wei, "It is a fascinating story about a lady who lived long ago."

By the time we got to the mountains she had finished telling us the part myth and part historical legend.

During the glory days of the peaceful and affluent Tang Dynasty, Emperor Tai Zong was on the throne of China. Foreign trading was at an all time high, Buddhism flourished and the Silk Road was a prosperous route from the capital city of Chang'an to the rich cities of Europe. This is when Songtsen Gampo, the powerful Dharma king of neighboring Tibet, decided to promote his country's position with China by requesting a daughter of the Emperor Tai Zong for his bride.

Historians disagree as to whether the practice of marrying Chinese Princesses to kings of other countries even existed. Although it was thought that these young daughters were sent to various states outside China to appease warlords of barbaric tribes or to bond powerful countries peacefully with China, this may not have happened. According to the annals of the Tang court, Emperor Tai Zong had twenty-two legitimate daughters, but he never once sent any of them away from the royal city to be married in a foreign land. He always feigned that he had no daughters to send and proceeded to find a suitable high borne lady of his court to go in place of a princess.

This was the fate of eighteen-year-old Wen Chen, given the title of Princess so she could marry the king of Tibet. Little is known of her background but she is surmised to be the daughter of the famous General Li, who accompanied her on the two-year journey across the mountains to Lhasa.

The story tells us that Emperor Tai Zong at first ignored the request of Songtsen Gampo, considering the king to be a barbarian and less than important. But when one hundred thousand Tibetan soldiers marched towards Chang'an he was alarmed. The Emperor sent a larger army to terrify the Tibetans and engage them in a scuffle, but they refused to retreat. Another emissary was dispatched from the Tibetan camp to inform the Emperor that the king and his troops would stay on the plains not far from Xining until a princess was delivered.

One can imagine the discussions at court.

"Find me a suitable young woman," the Emperor might have said, "she must be clever, talented, beautiful and learned. Although the king is a barbarian we must keep peace with Tibet. Prepare a large dowry of scholars and intellectuals, and send with them Buddhist scriptures to be translated into the Tibetan language. Send Chinese writings, medicines and seeds to grow crops: maize, wheat, soybean and grape. Send horses, yak, camels, and families to settle in Tibet near Wen Chen, and soldiers to guard her on her long trip."

What a sight it must have been to watch the cortege leaving Chang'an with a tearful young girl, a future queen, bidding farewell to her family, knowing she would never see them again.

"Take this magic mirror, Wen Chen," said her mother, "and every time you feel lonely, look into it and you will see me and all your family and friends. We will be with you forever."

The long journey brought the young princess to the Sun and Moon Mountains. There on the very top where the land is divided, one side in China and the other side sweeping down towards Tibet, she looked into the mirror and saw her mother and her past life. She was so sad that she threw the mirror back towards her home and cried a flood of tears. So many tears that a small river formed and began to wind its way to Chang'an.

The princess realized what she had done and fell to her knees, kowtowing to the gods.

"Please turn the river around and make it flow towards Tibet," she pleaded, "I never want my family to know how unhappy I am. I promise never to look back ... I will go forward to my future and be a good queen." And she dried her tears and kept her word.

The meeting between King Songtsen Gampo and Princess Wen Chen took place on a vast, desolate plain. The thirty five-year-old king was overwhelmed with joy when he saw the princess. He took her to Lhasa and she became his queen in the year 641 AD in the Tubo era. He built a great palace called the Potala and brought the enlightenment of Buddhism to Tibet. His reign was considered the zenith of the Tsanpo Period (127 BC – 842 AD). Unfortunately he died nine years later but, during his short life, he established his country as a major power in Asia. After the king's death, the respected and much loved Wen Chen Kongjo lived for another thirty years, teaching and advising the Tibetan people.

"So you see ... yeah," said Miss Wei, "there is a strange river called the *Dao Tang He* that runs opposite to all the other rivers."

We stood on the same spot where the young princess once stood, and stared back down the ancient road twisting up Sun and Moon mountains. It was a golden brown world; no trees, just rock outcroppings and prairie grasses. The cool wind pulled at our clothes as we walked to the pavilions, one on each side of the highway. They stood like gates to an exotic place where a sad princess might, just *might*, have thrown a hand mirror long ago.

Beyond the mountains lay the great legendary grasslands of Qinghai. An immense space opened before us, overwhelming our senses. Carpets of tiny red and white flowers rolled away forever and we knew the highest peaks in the world were at the edge of this vast plateau. These were the high plains, the home of the Tibetan tribesman with their legions of *maoniu* (yak) and sheep. It was the time of year to drive the yak to new pastures and whole families were on the move with tents, cooking stoves and clothing, and everything needed for a summer camp was strapped to the backs of these mountain beasts. The families rode fine horses, their bridles and saddle blankets decorated skillfully in traditional artistry. A small boy balancing behind his father turned and waved to us as we passed.

"We need to take some pictures. Please stop for a moment."

Driver Zhang couldn't believe we were getting excited over seeing Tibetans and *maoniu*, especially the *maoniu*.

"Driver Zhang is asking me why you want to take pictures of yak," said Miss Wei, "he wants to know if Chinese yak are different from Canadian yak."

He was quite amazed when we told him there were no animals like these in Canada.

We stopped to spend an hour at the viewing room at Birds Island Sanctuary. This is the breeding ground for thousands of migrating birds and in the spring the skies are filled with sandpipers, gulls, rare black-neck cranes and a particular type of geese that cross the lofty Himalayas. Unfortunately for us, it was the wrong season and we found ourselves viewing thousands of common seagulls through the slots in the concrete bunker. Later, as we walked along the cliffs, we spied a rookery of cormorants perched on a massive jagged rock poking out of dreamlike turquoise water that once was known as the Western Sea.

It was late afternoon when we reached our hotel. The Birds Island Hotel should have been the loveliest hotel in the world. It was beautifully framed against the blue sky and rolling mountains. It had perfect *feng shui*. A rambling place, its open marble walks meandered under empty planters intended for hanging flowers. The arbors, trellises and archways testified to the designer's vision for a splendid garden that never was. It remained bare and unattended. There were no flowers, no vines and no color.

At first our room looked impressive enough with twin beds and a garish red and yellow neon ceiling light fixture in the shape of an oversized rose. Then we opened the bathroom door. There was a two-inch layer of cold water on the floor and a stale odor stung our nostrils and lingered at the back of our throats. It was a large Western bathroom with water dripping from every pipe. The white porcelain on the tub, toilet and sink had seeped by osmosis into brown rust, and the only light in the room was from a tiny bulb dangling from the ceiling.

"Miss Wei," I said, "could we get a room ... maybe, with a dry bathroom floor?"

"You don't like your room?"

"It's not that," I muttered humbly, trying to justify my Western point of view. "We'd like to be able to walk around in the bathroom without soaking our feet."

I'm sure Miss Wei thought this sounded self-righteous and we felt the usual guilt about complaining, but then it annoyed us to realize it would only take elbow grease and some repairs to keep the place in good shape. Unfortunately the management missed this point. They took a beautifully constructed tourist hotel and let it slip into disorder. We found out later the staff resented being sent to remote Birds Island, considering it a punishment, like prison. When we discussed this with Miss Chen, she admitted a group of Germans on tour the previous year had complained bitterly to the government tourist bureau, but to no avail. Japanese thought better than to patronize the place and built their own hotel, strictly for the Japanese trade.

Nervously, Miss Wei took us to the front desk and explained carefully to a clerk why the foreigners were not happy with the water on the bathroom floor. The lady lacked any sympathy.

"Tell the foreigner she can have any room she wants," Miss Wei translated, "the floors in all the bathrooms are wet. They have been freshly washed for the guests."

We had been to homes where the floors were damp, and understood it meant good etiquette to wash them for visitors, but this was ridiculous, we actually sloshed through the water. Every bathroom floor was the same, including Miss Wei's, who felt helpless that she was unable to do anything for us. We gave up and went back to our original room.

The dining room was equally unappealing, although the beer was cold and tasted good. Young Liu and Driver Zhang played a hand game, pointing fingers and shouting numbers over their Qinghai Barley drinks, while Miss Wei worried about us not having enough to eat.

We walked out into the lovely cool evening. The sky was brilliant cobalt blue, layering down to a pale white iridescence shimmering on the horizon. Nothing mattered now; we could feel the closeness of the boundless universe and the slow revolution of the earth. It was the top of the world at ten thousand feet.

eleven

中国

"You must be able to cook well," said Chen Jian Pin, teaching his daughter how to make dough for steamed buns and noodles, the staple foods of northern China.

He sat cross-legged on the kang near the small kitchen, with his elbows supported by his knees, and his arms crossed palms up in front of him. A thin hand-rolled cigarette drooped from the corner of his mouth, flapping when he spoke. "What do you think your new husband and his family will say if you can't cook properly? They will laugh at you." He took the cigarette from his lips, pinched the fire from the end and tucked the butt into his shirt pocket for later. "They would even laugh at *me* and call me inadequate … not a good teacher if I couldn't make you understand the art of cooking."

As usual it was her father who did the vocal teaching. Her mother was far too busy to converse with her daughter about anything. But Chen Jian Pin, a true educator, loved to instruct and teach. He longed for his past life in Gandu Normal School when he had knowledge to share and students willing, yes, even wanting to listen and absorb. He told himself he was not meant to work in the fields like a peasant; he was a teacher. Life would improve and he would teach again, but in the meantime he had his children to guide and instruct, especially Chen Yu Hua.

His one big obsession in life was to arrange a good marriage for his oldest daughter.

Chen Yu Hua was small for her age and had to stand on a stool to reach the top of the counter. She could hardly wind her fingers around the large pile of dough to start the essential kneading. When she had lived in Xining, she helped Grandma with evening meals and, with only three mouths and one baby to feed, the cooking had been easier. She admitted to herself the meals at Aunty Chen Fugui's home were more delicious. Often they had bits of chicken or fresh fish from *KoKo Nor*, Qinghai Lake, the largest lake in China and very close to the capital city. There always seemed to be a variety of fish, vegetables and fruits. Here at home there were no such luxuries. Meals consisted of buns and hot water for breakfast, buns and hot water for lunch and buns or noodles and green vegetables for dinner. Eight members of the family had to be fed, not three.

Although meals were simple, the cooking of the meals was slow and frustrating. The most difficult part was to keep the stove burning evenly with enough hay and wood to boil the water. If the fuel was not burned properly, smoke permeated the kitchen making everyone's eyes burn and tears run down their faces.

Just as she was about to roll the dough on the table and prepare the small buns for the bamboo steamer, her father jumped from the kang and snatched the long thin rolling stick from her hands. More demonstrations followed.

"You must do it this way," he ordered impatiently, "and remember, the more you practice, the easier it will become." Next, he preached the virtues of his mother.

"My mother was a remarkable woman," he said with enormous pride. "She was a wonderful cook. Everyone admired her capabilities: her skills in managing a family, teaching her children, her sewing and beautiful embroidery. She was a typical capable Chinese woman." He handed the rolling stick to the little girl … "and *you* must be just like your grandmother."

He bounced back on the kang, repeating the story of the laughing husband and the ridiculing parents-in-law. She would hear these words over and over again until the day she married.

It was almost time for the evening meal and Chen Yu Hua checked her steamed buns rising in the bamboo containers. The streets outside the courtyard were especially noisy today. The family was used to noise; students marched, shouted slogans, beat drums and gongs and hoisted banners into the air proclaiming Chairman

Mao's latest words.

At the age of seven, Chen Yu Hua started to memorize Chairman Mao's quotations. She loved learning them. She was good at it. Teachers would often ask her to demonstrate her ability to recite and she would be told to stand out of rank, face her classmates and, in a clear voice, recount Mao's latest sayings. This year, her favorite teacher was Mi Lan, an enthusiastic supporter of Chairman Mao, who insisted all her students memorize every new slogan and revolutionary statement that came from the mouth of the great leader. She was also a supporter of Chen Jian Pin's young daughter. "Notice how eloquently Chen Yu Hua recites," she would say to the students and the little girl would smile and stand proudly, relishing the admiration.

The hungry family gathered at the table for their evening meal, just as a loudspeaker bellowed from the streets heralding Chairman Mao's latest proclamations. This was a regular event in their lives and meant the adults would be ordered to gather outside their homes, perhaps at midnight or even later, to learn the new words verbatim.

"I must go and see," said eldest brother Chen Yan, who now called himself *Yong Hong*, Forever Red. Red was the most popular color in those years, it signified revolution, the dawn of a new China and Mao Zedong Thoughts. It was also the color adopted by the Red Guards. When Chen Jian Pin found out his son had changed his name he was furious. He scolded him again and again but the young man refused to change his name back to Chen Yan.

The loudspeaker stopped abruptly. Everyone listened. There was one quiet choking moment then came the chilling scream of a terrified woman. This was followed by the punchy voice of a man, provoking and menacing, stirring the crowd into boisterous cheers that came after each political diatribe.

The family was alarmed. It showed on their faces as they turned their heads towards the uproar coming from the street. Jian Pin frowned, put his finger to his lips and spoke softly, "We can't go out there." He closed the door at the front of the house, muffling the sounds of drums and shouting voices. "We can't get involved … it's far too dangerous."

"But I have to see what's happening," said Chen Yan, "it's my duty father," and before he could be stopped he rushed from the house.

The family sat looking at one another, too frightened to speak. No one, not even the youngest child, ate the steamed buns.

It wasn't long before the door opened, flooding the room with street noises. Chen Yan glanced at Chen Yu Hua with a puzzled look mixed with fear. She felt cold. She didn't know why she felt that way or why a sinister message was coming from her brother.

"What's the matter?" she asked anxiously.

For a moment Chen Yan did not speak.

"Tell us ... what's happening?" said Jian Pin.

"There's a struggle going on father," he hesitated ... "a very bad one ... I fear for the teacher."

What teacher?

Chen Yu Hua *knew* 'what teacher'. She kicked her little stool, sending it spinning as she jumped from the table. Two chopsticks dropped, bouncing one by one on the dirt floor. She ran as fast as she could in the direction of the shouting. She knew! It must be Teacher Mi. *Please don't let it be teacher Mi.*

She could hear her father's voice ordering her to stop. She never hesitated or looked back. She had to go. She had to disobey him this one time.

An excited crowd had gathered, chanting slogans. She remembered seeing students circle unlucky adults before, criticizing and calling them demeaning names. She knew it was cruel, but the situation never turned truly threatening and the crowds would usually disperse without incident. But this one was different. She could smell the ugliness in the air; feel the tension; hear the belligerent voices. Looking around, Chen Yu Hua was astounded to see such a large number of Red Guards in the street, each one wearing a red armband with markings identifying their particular factions. She pushed her way to the front of the jeering circle to look upon a young woman with her head bowed down and her hands tied behind her back with a red scarf. Tangles of black hair spilled over her face as one of the Red Guards shouted, "get down on your knees, you daughter of a Capitalist Roader." And she dropped to the dirty street on her knees, gravel digging through her pant legs.

It was Teacher Mi.

Chen Yu Hua gasped. "What has Teacher Mi done?" she asked a girl who was in her class, looking equally shocked. "What could our teacher have done?"

"Is it true you are the daughter of a Capitalist? We found out your father was a landowner. Is this true?"

The young Red Guard slapped her head making her black hair bounce absurdly.

"No," she sobbed. "I'm only a grade school teacher."

The Red Guard struck her again, this time hard enough to knock her over into the dust and, as she lay there, he kicked her with his heavy boot until she screamed. The crowd continued chanting, laughing, jeering.

"She's my teacher," Chen Yu Hua cried and sprinted to the side of beleaguered Mi Yan.

"Get this child out of here," yelled the Red Guard above the clamor. He tried to drag her away from the screaming teacher. Chen Yu Hua kicked viciously at the young man, jabbing his ankle, making him flinch and curse and, when he bent over to touch it, she hit his face with as much strength as she could muster in her small arms. She grabbed his hair and hung on, pulling out tufts and sending them flying. She scratched and punched and stuck to the furious man like a small dog attacking a bear. The astonished crowd grew quiet for a moment then began to laugh uproariously at the ridiculous sight of the Red Guard with the small girl clinging to his back, her thin arms choking his neck and her heels digging into his ribs. It was all too funny. Someone picked up the confused teacher and untied her hands, brushing the dust from her clothes, and sent her scampering through the crowds to safety.

A terrified Chen Yan ran up to the frantic Red Guard who was now drenched in sweat and howling with rage. He plucked his squirming, screaming sister from the back of the young man and ran for home.

"Yong Hong," called a laughing bystander, "your little sister is a real tiger."

Real tiger or not, Chen Yan recognized the danger into which his sister had put the family, and he only hoped nothing would come of it.

Later in the streets, the crowd lost interest and the Red Guards marched off, possibly to find another victim for their denunciation crusade.

A quiet uneasiness settled around the dinner table that night. Someone said that Chen Yu Hua was a good cook. Chen Jian Pin did not chastise his daughter but neither did he condone her wild and naive actions.

Much to the family's relief, nothing ever came of the frightening incident, and Teacher Mi somehow managed to be transferred to another work unit. But not before she sent a message of thanks to her young student.

My advice to anyone wanting to work in China ... it helps to have a very good sense of humor.

I was sitting at our desk in the downtown office going through some letters. Bill had gone to experience yet another factory tour with Miss Wei.

"Boss Liu asked me to ask you something," Miss Chen said casually as she stepped into the room with two cups of green tea. "Do you think Mr. Weigand would throw the opening *hand grenade* at the annual Sports Day next week?"

I was stunned. "Grenade! You mean ... throw a hand grenade?"

Miss Chen was oblivious to the surprised look on my face. She sat down and blew the tea leaves around in the cup. "Yes, of course." She was quite serious. "We always start the sports day with a grenade throwing competition for the men."

"Are you talking about ... like, a hand grenade?" I pretended to throw an invisible something, imitating John Wayne in a war movie.

She suddenly started to laugh crazily. Miss Chen always held her stomach when she laughed, tears glistening at the corners of her eyes. She could hardly talk.

"They aren't *real*," she choked, wiping her eyes, "they're made of wood."

The minute she left the room I could hear her voice burbling in the hall to Boss Liu and anyone else who would listen. Later, every time she related our conversation, there would be howls of laughter as she demonstrated me throwing a grenade and vocalizing ... *boom*.

Actually I laughed at myself for being caught again. Miss Chen and the others were always teasing us and telling humorous stories about our naiveté towards Chinese customs. The way we mispronounced the Chinese language was also a common joke, as well as our fear of bacteria; we insisted on having clean chopsticks and wiped our hands with *Wet Ones* before we ate.

Arrangements were made for us to meet with Mrs. Ding Qin Lin, Director of the Xining Women's Federation, and her colleague Mrs. Yang, president of Datong Women's Federation, regarding a poverty alleviation program. Although I had always been interested in women's issues, I never gave this meeting too much thought; it would be the same rhetoric, note-taking and letter-writing. In 1995, the internet was just a fledgling power and we had to rely on mail and fax machines to communicate with the world.

But this meeting was different. It affected me deeply, making me think about women and poverty and examine my own life. How fortunate I was to live in a developed country, where the hospitals were clean and medicine was available.

Mrs. Ding was tall and thin. She had a round face and pale complexion. Every time she smiled her cheeks puffed up like little rose-colored apples. But what made Mrs. Ding different were her uniquely expressive eyes, revealing her true emotions. At times I wondered about the ancestry of the people we met. I was sure some of them had European blood in their ancestry, and Mrs. Ding was one of these people; I expected her to bring forth English every time she spoke.

It didn't take long to realize Mrs. Ding was a passionate feminist; this was made clear in the translations. She was angry about injustices to women and her big goal was to build a shelter for abused and destitute women and children. She chose an old building in the middle of Xining and had elaborate plans designed for its renovation. She was, sadly, going nowhere with this dream as there were too many priorities the government deemed more important than women's issues. No doubt she would be waiting a long time for a shelter in Qinghai Province. Western countries, with all their wealth, had only in recent years begun to build these crucial facilities.

"Mrs. Ding wants to train four hundred midwives in Datong County, about twenty miles from here," said Miss Chen, "She says they have never had proper training and the infant mortality rate is unacceptable ... but the Federation has no money to do this."

The wide brown eyes of Mrs. Ding glanced from me to Bill and back to me.

"What can we do?" I asked.

"She says, would you please come with her to Datong County and see for yourself. Perhaps the Canadian Government has funds to help with this project."

We were both surprised that Mrs. Ding mentioned Canadian funding until we realized that all cadres were well aware of sourcing foreign monies for poverty alleviation, health and education. China was a developing country and Canada was no stranger in Qinghai. CIDA (Canadian International Development Agency) had already implemented many projects in this province.

How could we refuse Mrs. Ding? We would go to Datong, but no promises. Mrs. Ding's smile lit up the room. She shook our hands vigorously, as though the deal was done and the money was on the way.

"What is this, the road to hell?" Bill whispered to me as Mr. Cheng, Miss Chen, Bill and I, with Driver Zhang at the wheel, bumped along the unfinished road to Datong in our white station wagon. The road was built up with boulders, shale and gravel. Vehicles snail-crawled for twenty miles dodging huge rocks, damaging tires, breaking springs and shock absorbers. Cars and buses shook so violently that tail pipes and mufflers fell off. We closed the windows tight to keep out the choking dust, only to be confined in suffocating heat.

"When are they going to finish the road?" we asked.

"Driver Zhang says paving is coming soon ... when the traffic has packed the surface down hard enough," said Miss Chen indifferently. We knew the last thing she wanted to do was listen to our complaining. She crossed her arms, stared out the window and hummed to herself every time a wheel dropped into a deep pothole as though it was just one more character-building moment.

"It's going to be great when you get pavement." I jerked the words out of my throat.

Wrong words. Our patriotic boss Mr. Cheng, thoroughly fed up with the foreigner's grumbling, rested his head on the back of the seat and closed his eyes, reminding us not to insult Mother China. "The road will be done when it's done," he said and spoke with such reverence that I peeked to see if he had placed his right hand over his heart.

We made at least ten trips to Datong County over the next year and there was still no pavement. The road wore down into twisting ruts and, with each trip, even though we had long given up worrying about it, Driver Zhang always commented, "paving is coming soon." What he really should have said was "there's simply no money in the coffers to pave this very important road to the second largest city in Qinghai."

Today we were to visit Mrs. Ding and her assistants.

Western foreigners were a rarity in Datong County. The word got out fast that there were 'big noses' in town ... 'white skinned, yellow haired, round-eyed aliens'. By now we were used to being stared at by onlookers but these crowds were huge, trailing us everywhere. Mrs. Ding had orchestrated this tour very well to get the most publicity possible; there was a TV camera team from Xining filming every move of our group's visit.

The first stop was a visit to a foreign-funded project in the poorest part of the city. A young lady had received a small grant, bought a treadle sewing machine and went into business. Her home was overflowing with clothes. Finished and half-finished jackets, pants and shirts hung from the ceiling. Bundles of cloth, spools of thread and colored scraps of material were piled high on the dirt floor in the one room where she and her husband lived with their little baby. The lady was obviously successful at what she did. She was so overwhelmed with work that she had to buy another sewing machine, squeezing it and a new employee into a corner between the bed and the stove. Beside it stood a wobbly table holding a steam iron with a frayed cord stretching dangerously across the floor to an uncovered wall plug. "She says she will move to a larger place someday soon," said Miss Chen, nodding towards the lady. "She has developed a new idea … all by herself … making car seat covers, and has many orders already."

We were handed a pair of zebra-striped covers to examine and someone remarked, "What a good designer." Mrs. Ding praised the smiling young woman for her hard work, entrepreneurial spirit and creative imagination. We also praised and admired her, to think she could carry on this thriving sewing business from such cramped quarters, with a husband to cook for and a baby lying sleeping on half-sewn winter coats strewn on the bed.

Outside, the crowds were curious. Young men pressed their faces against the windows trying to get a glimpse of the important cadres and the two foreigners all the way from Xining, and the pretty seamstress who was now an instant celebrity.

Our second visit was to the spotless farmhouse of Midwife Ma Xiuying. Modern Scandinavian blonde furniture and a new TV stood prominently against a wall in the front room. A matching glass cabinet, an armoire and several smaller pieces lined the other wall.

We were asked to sit at a long rectangular table, unusual in a Chinese home as *Feng Shui* dictates that tables should be round for the *Chi* to circulate; no sharp edges to block the flow. While the three women talked seriously, Bill and I sipped chrysanthemum tea and waited.

The dirt floor had been swept and polished into something comparable to smooth dark concrete. Only in the corners and along the walls was the floor slightly broken and dusty, betraying the fact that it was just plain ground. Around the bottom of each piece of furniture there appeared signs of dampness seeping up into the blonde wood. I wondered if I would ever set my priorities on buying fancy cabinets and a color TV before I built a floor. Perhaps I would. I didn't think so, but then I never had to choose.

We could smell the air; a mixture of hay and wild flowers, farm animals and the odd wisp of car exhaust drifted in through the open windows.

"Midwife Ma Xiuying wants to talk to you now," said Miss Chen. We listened carefully to an emotional translation about the suffering of people in the small villages, and especially the dangers of childbirth that all pregnant women faced.

"Poor women cannot afford to go to the hospital; they must rely on midwives. But very few midwives in Datong County have had the chance to take any formal training and not one person owns a proper birthing kit." We watched the midwife unwrap a towel and show us a basin, scissors, a piece of cord and some antibiotic pills, tools of the trade she had learned from her mother.

"This is what all the women have ever owned, and some women don't have this much," explained Miss Chen, "Midwife Ma says they need modern tools and hospital training to save babies' lives ... they just can't afford to buy new medical things on their own. They need help. You must understand ... they are all very poor."

Miss Chen's voice cracked and I could see the beginning of tears as she listened to the midwife.

"She wants to tell you that midwives are honorable and dedicated ... they will help the village women even if they don't get paid." The midwife smiled, her face flushed. She shrugged, spreading her hands towards us, as if to say, "What else can I tell you?"

In this remote part of the country, ethnic farmers made up most of the population: Muslims, Mongolians, Tibetans and Tu People. It was almost impossible for the state to collect true official figures on the mortality rate of infants, but the "black" figures indicated as many as fifty deaths per thousand. Compared with five deaths per thousand in Canada these numbers were extreme.

The somber mood suddenly changed. "Come," said Miss Chen, "Midwife Ma Xiuying has a surprise for you." And we followed her out to the courtyard. "She wants you to meet eight of her many *babies*." They stood in a row, healthy laughing boys and girls of all ages and the midwife hugged them one at a time. She had brought them all safely into this world.

Before we left Datong we made a commitment to get in touch with the Canadian Embassy in Beijing for advice about submitting a project proposal for a Midwives Training Program for the women of Datong.

The contacts we had made in Beijing with Acting Ambassador Ken Sunquist proved to be most helpful. After discussing our ideas on the phone with him, we promptly received a call from Scot Slessor, Canada Fund Coordinator for CIDA. He would send us the necessary forms and guidelines to be completed and returned for approval. He was even coming to Xining on business in a few weeks and was curious about our private home.

"I'll bring butter, cheese, chocolates and some good red wine," he promised.

The Sports Day had arrived. Bill and I felt honored to be special guests. I was ushered to the bleachers to sit front and center with the visiting dignitaries while Bill and the Commission staff prepared for the parade. The band struck up and the march was on. Out came Bill, directly behind the standard bearers, followed by Miss Chen and a thousand marchers. There were banners and flags and Bill said he felt like General MacArthur leading the troops. It certainly was a first! No other foreigner had ever been seen walking in a parade in Xining City that anyone could remember.

Bill found the grenade throwing to be tougher than he expected. He grasped the long wooden handle and, with his arm stretched out behind like an Olympian javelin thrower, raced towards the line, and let fly the grenade with all his might. It fell a short distance away in an eruption of dust. "Ooooh Kaaay," someone said, and he was applauded for being a good sport and got the thumbs up sign from the old army vets.

With small white sun hats squatting on our heads and tied under our chins, we watched ping pong, broad-jumping, sack races for kids, horseshoes, relay races with fresh eggs used as batons, and we cheered on Miss Wei as she finished *first* in the hundred yard dash.

Food was plentiful but no delicious fried onion smells drifted on the air; no hot dogs or hamburgers. There was lots of *shuanghui*, a type of cooked meat like wieners, wrapped in red plastic, as well as fruit and dried snacks of every kind.

Later we sat with the Commission staff in the cool shade of some old trees, eating bananas and drinking bottled water.

"It's better to peel it this way," said one of the men as he took the banana from my hand, turned it upside down, peeled it almost all the way to the bottom and, holding the stem in his fingers, gave it back to me.

"Now you have a handle to hold your banana," said Miss Chen.

"They even peel bananas differently in this part of the world," I laughed.

Knowing Miss Chen

Chen Yu Hua and Jerrine.
First meeting – Whitehorse, Yukon.

Mayor Yang, Bill, Miss Chen, Jerrine, Mayor Li, Boss Liu.
Front steps of 83 Nan Guan Road.

Main room with its *Great Wall* mural.
83 Nan Guan Road.

Interpreters Miss Wei, Miss Chen and Young Liu, with Bill, preparing notes for a Foreign Trade meeting.

Tibetan family herding Yak on the plateau.

Audrey McLaughlin in Tibetan dress.

Miss Wei and children washing up for dinner.

No. 14 Middle School English teachers in our courtyard.

Tibetan girls at Ta'er Monastery.

Dr. Ma signing 'The Wall'.

Looking over Longyang Gorge from top of dam.

Bill receiving hot Yak milk in Tibetan Yurt (tent).

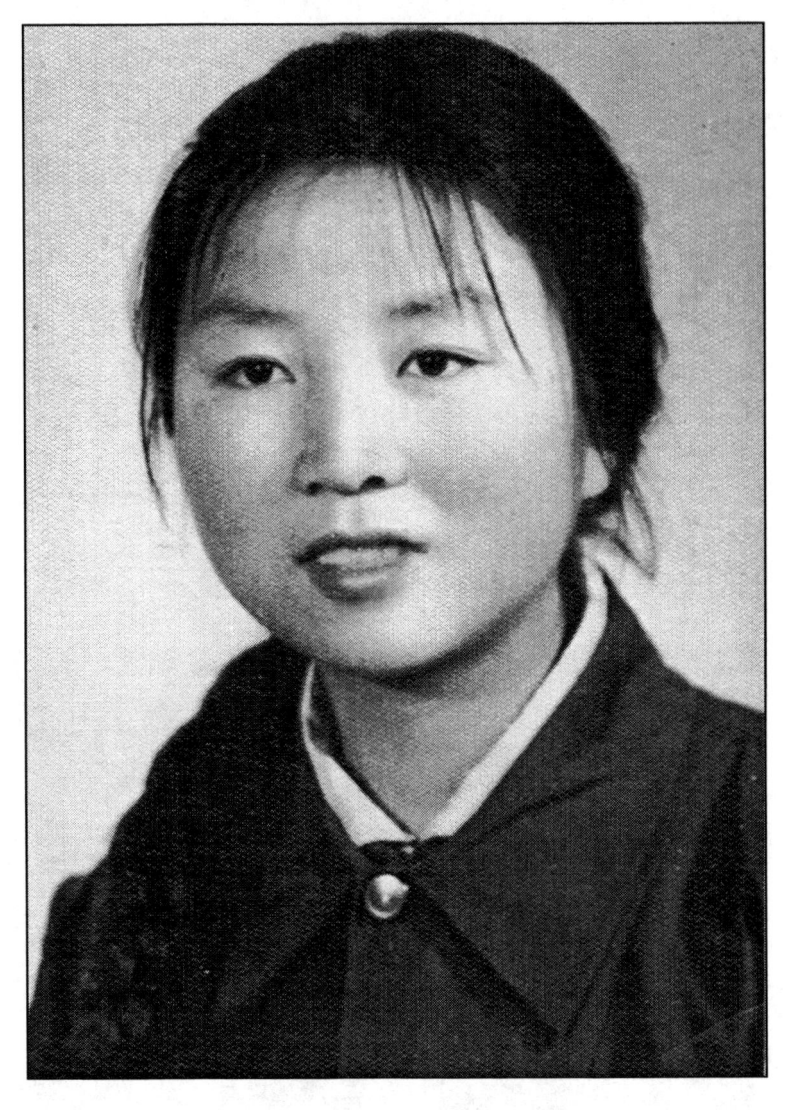

Teacher Chen – 1978. 18 years of age.
Qinghai Normal School, Xining.

Beijing Opera theatre cast, Xining.

Santa Claus and helpers, Qinghai Hotel.

Keith Dede and Erin Schulz, Christmas dinner, 1995.

Si Xian receives her first Barbie Doll for Christmas.

Bill and Shirley Read, New Year's Eve, Lanzhou.

The Chen Family, New Year's Eve, Lanzhou.

twelve

中国

With the beginning of the Great Proletarian Cultural Revolution on August 8, 1966, a system of education, closely tied to Mao's teachings, was instituted. Campuses were controlled by the propaganda teams of Red Guards and soldiers from the People's Liberation Army; conflict between these two factions, as well as with workers and peasants, resulted in total disruption of classes.

When Chen Yu Hua began school in 1967, the old traditional way of teaching was almost non-existent, though students were still required to attend classes.

Primary education, although least affected, was notably shortened, sometimes by as much as two years. The curriculum was reduced to practical subjects, including simple math and Chinese language, whereas history, geography and literature were excluded. Little importance was placed on any other learning.

In fact, when students took exams they were allowed to copy the answers from textbooks. This was conveniently called "open book learning." There was no homework, no accusations of cheating and no burden of achieving any serious knowledge in the schools during the Cultural Revolution. These ten years deprived a whole generation of proper education in primary and middle schools, universities and other higher learning institutions. As loudspeakers blasted out Chairman Mao's slogans, students chanted passages from the Little Red Book, over and over, and were told, "Cherish these like your eyes." Huge portraits of the Great Chairman dominated every classroom and *People's Daily*, the official newspaper of China, proclaimed him "in absolute authority."

Chen Yu Hua carried a small picture of Chairman Mao, everyone did, and each morning at her school desk she would place the picture in front of her and silently, reverently ask, "what shall I do today?" Before leaving for home in the afternoon she would address the picture again, this time reporting her deeds of the day, good or bad. She wrote diligently about her good deeds. And, like a Christian child asking Jesus for forgiveness with head bowed, hands clasped, eyes closed in prayer, she would sit on her bed at night staring at the picture, promising never to do bad deeds. There was no need for a higher being in Chen Yu Hua's young life. Chairman Mao replaced God, Buddha, Allah ... he was supreme leader and she would follow him forever. In fact, she was told to love Mao above the love she felt for her mother and father. This was not easy for her. She loved and obeyed her parents, and she was burdened with the secret that her father taught classical Chinese to his family out of books that were forbidden in the schools; a very good reason for constant self-criticism.

If only she could be more like Lei Feng.

Chairman Mao immortalized this soldier, who died in 1962 when still a young man. He was the perfect example of one who selflessly served the people by helping his neighbors, the elderly and the sick, donating his meager pay to the poor. He was deeply admired and revered by everyone for his devotion to Chairman Mao. There was a rumor suggesting Lei Feng was simply created as the flawless model for Chinese socialist youth, but to Chen Yu Hua, his exemplary life portrayed an ideal paragon for her young mind.

Chen Yu Hua idolized Lei Feng. All through her primary school years she scrubbed toilets, swept the compound area, cleaned blackboards and made fires in the stoves. She helped small children carry baskets and helped women push heavy carts. She and her classmates were often over-zealous when performing their splendid deeds; unwary old people would be startled when umbrellas suddenly unfurled in the rain above their heads and a couple of smiling twelve-year-olds hustled them across a busy street. It may not have been the street they wanted to cross, but the good deed had been done.

Above all else, these virtuous acts were to be carried out as unobtrusively as possible; no bragging or performing singular good deeds in full view of classmates, as this could be considered "showing off" in hopes of receiving the award given at the end of each school term. This coveted award was presented to three outstanding students for excellent morals, healthy mind and body, devotion to school studies and, of course, for performing many good deeds.

The dilemma felt by Chen Yu Hua about all this good-Samaritanism was the fact that no matter how hard she worked or how much time she spent helping others it was to no avail if it was done in secret.

"I should win the award," she grumbled to her father one day, "I work all the time. I'm the one who cleans the toilets the most … no one knows how hard I work."

If she was expecting any praise or sympathy from her father she was wrong. He listened to her briefly and shrugged off her complaints.

But she did win the award. In fact she won it three times, and now she felt more like Lei Feng. She memorized his poem "The Four Seasons" word for word.

> *Like spring, I treat my comrades warmly.*
> *Like summer, I am full of ardor for my revolutionary work.*
> *I eliminate my individualism as an autumn gale sweeps away fallen leaves,*
> *And to the class enemy, I am cruel and ruthless like harsh winter.*

Primary school days passed easily and life was exciting for Chen Yu Hua. The turmoil and frenzy in other parts of the country had little effect on her and her classmates. Their young lives were caught up belonging to the Mao Zedong Thought Propaganda Team, giving performances of Tibetan, Mongolian and Salar folk music, or taking part in the latest Revolutionary play written by local playwrights. Sometimes they had the opportunity to watch a Beijing Opera; it was always an opera, of course, that had been approved by Mao's wife Jiang Qing.

In 1938 in Yanan province, Jiang Qing, a young actress from Shanghai, became Mao Zedong's fourth wife. She remained discreetly out of the public eye until the early 1960s when she unexpectedly appeared on the political stage beside her husband. By 1963 she commanded enormous power in her new portfolio as the overseer of culture, observing and reporting to Mao on the state of theater, literature, dance troupes and especially Beijing Opera. She was ever alert to spot old influences that could be lurking in the new world of Chinese culture; these would not be tolerated and must be dealt with harshly. It was time to wipe out The Four Olds: Old Ideas, Old Culture, Old Customs and Old Habits, and the First Lady was good at her job.

As her power grew so did her vindictiveness toward her real and imagined enemies. Writers, actors, musicians and even renowned physicians, fell into suffering and despair under the heavy hand of Madam Mao, and many died in prison during the Cultural Revolution. Beijing Opera was a particular thorn in her side. The old programs were still enjoyed by the general population and members of the Party alike. The ancient stories, Farewell To My Concubine and Li Huiniang were soon banned and relegated to obscurity. Only eight model Revolutionary operas were sanctioned for public performance.

"Hurry, Chen Yu Hua," called Wang Yan. "We don't want to be late."

Wang Yan was young Chen's best friend. She was much too tall and not terribly pretty, but she had a good mind and was totally trustworthy and loyal. Chen Yu Hua could tell her anything; confess family secrets, her worries for the future, discuss the teachers at school, anything. Her thoughts would be safe with Wang Yan and their friendship would last for years.

Tonight they were hurrying to see one of the most popular operas, The Red Lamp; a real tearjerker being performed by a group of visiting actors from Shanghai. Many such troupes were obliged to travel throughout China giving performances in remote country villages and small cities. This evening Chen Yu Hua's hometown was privileged to watch the handsome, talented actor, known simply by the name Ji, whose fame was growing as a Beijing Opera star. This young man was especially good in the role of Li Yuhe, the main character in The Red Lamp, and everyone agreed that he had a great future in Beijing Opera.

The old meeting hall next to the school was filled with smoke and noise and excitement. There were farmers in mud-spattered boots, local cadres smoking Hong Ta Shan cigarettes, and fellow students, spitting sunflower seed husks on the dirt floor or dropping pits and skins from their fruit. On the front row bench sat militant Red Guards, arrogant in their prominent red armbands, eyes warily searching the crowd for any flicker of suspicious behavior.

Chen Yu Hua and Wang Yan found a crowded bench, pushing themselves between other students. Soon they were laughing and gossiping, waiting for the curtain to open on their favorite opera and the handsome Ji.

The Red Lamp was a complicated story of three revolutionaries whose lives were interwoven by the troubled times in which they lived; the Japanese invasion, the struggle between the Kuomintang forces and the Communist Movement.

The plot of the story centered on a bachelor named Zhang Yuhe who lived with an elderly woman called Grandmother Li. Her husband had been killed during the Railway Workers' Strike in the 1920s. There was also a child, a young orphan girl called Chen Tie Mei who helped Grandmother Li with the housework and shopping. These three; a grandmother, a bachelor and a child, decided to become one family, adopting one another and giving themselves the surname Li.

It was a story of the Communist underground movement, full of intrigue and suspense, centering around a red gas lamp once used by Grandmother Li's husband for giving covert signals on the railway. The lamp was passed down to Li Yuhe to carry on the Communist fight to free China. Later he was caught and killed by Japanese invaders and the lamp again passed to other hands. Li Tie Mei, now a young woman, was the new keeper of the flame and at the end of the opera she sang a beautiful aria holding the red lamp high, signifying her determination and belief in the revolution and the Communist cause. These old days, as the years before 1949 were called, were compared to a long, cold, dark night in Chinese history. The red lamp symbolized the lighting of the way to Communism and freedom for the people, who suffered from the oppression of the Three Big Mountains: Imperialism, Feudalism and Bureaucratic Capitalism.

The opera ended and the curtain closed on a tearful, emotional audience.

It took a minute before Actor Ji reappeared. He bowed low. The crowd went crazy, stomping and whistling and calling his name.

"He is so beautiful," sighed Chen Yu Hua, her eyes pinned on Actor Ji.

"Yes, I love him," whispered Wang Yan, wiping away her tears. The two girls giggled to think they had said such sensuous words out loud for one another to hear. The opera was so patriotic. So moving. Actor Ji had stolen their young girlish hearts. Small wonder there were tears.

It was almost a month later when the real tears came to Chen Yu Hua and her friend. It was when they were told the story of what happened to Actor Ji in a country village in another province.

During a performance of The Red Lamp there was a part of the show where Li Yuhe was supposed to hide a small secret codebook from Japanese soldiers. He was to place the book into a peddler's lunch box, so the story goes, where it would be safely hidden from enemy eyes. Actor Ji had forgotten to bring the prop book and in one fateful moment of haste decided to carry on with the opera using his copy of Mao's Little Red Book, kept in his pocket at all times. It happened to be the same size as the book called for in the opera. A sharp-eyed Brigade Leader sitting in the front row observed all this. Straight away the Leader jumped up on the stage, pulled the Little Red Book from the lunch box and waved it at Actor Ji, calling him a traitor for using the precious Red Book as a mere stage prop. Ji was frightened. He tried to explain he meant no harm but the curtain was closed and the show stopped. The confused actor had his hands tied together behind his back. A wooden board was quickly scribbled with the words "down with actor Ji" and placed around his neck. He was forced to stand, shivering with fear, in front of the very people he had just been entertaining minutes before. He was devastated.

"I did not do such a thing on purpose," he pleaded. "I would never do such a thing. I would never insult our Great Helmsman."

The leader shouted "traitor, traitor" and smashed the ill-fated actor's face with his fist. He did this so many times and with such ferocity that he complained about being tired and how much his hand was aching. He then called upon the audience to punch Actor Ji on the head and criticize him for his guilty wrongdoing.

One by one the audience, enraged by the screaming Brigade Leader, lined up and took turns beating the young man until he fell, bleeding from both ears, to the floor.

"Look at my hands," one man shouted and they all looked at the red theatrical paint that had come off the actor's face and stuck to their hands and fists.

They laughed and jeered and found it quite humorous.

Actor Ji survived the terrible beating. He became completely deaf and would never sing Beijing Opera again. Sadly, this patriotic, high spirited and once loved young actor was given the menial task of collecting rubbish for the rest of his life.

It was a tragic end to a promising career.

"What are you laughing at?" Miss Chen asked me.

She and Driver Zhang had arrived at our house early in the morning to take us to a local clinic for blood tests. We had been arguing with the Commission about our International Health Certificates. These were recognized around the world and our blood tests confirmed we were free of HIV or any other infectious disease, but the Chinese health service refused to accept our Canadian documents and more tests were scheduled.

"I shouldn't tell you," I said sheepishly, "but I was reading the English on this jar of face cream I bought at Dasha Zu."

She burst out laughing as she read aloud, "Guaranteed to remove skin from face and neck."

"I sure hope not," I said, "You know, Miss Chen ... you could make a fortune doing translations for these companies."

The English language is often mangled in China. We were intrigued by the way a mixed bag of English words or letters were often looped together in the off chance they might make sense. Like hailing a red van with the letters IXAT written boldly across one side and TAXI on the other, or when we received a gift wrapped in pretty blue paper with EVOL stamped in gold all over it. Some misnomers were wonderfully amusing and I always felt a bit guilty when I enjoyed reading directions on make-up, medicines or foodstuffs just to get a chuckle from the creative use of English. Mascara named MY STIFFY or throat lozenges that "prevent loss of voice in people whose voice is their livelihood." Never mind the rest of us who can't sing. One of the best examples was told to us by a friend, "I just bought a bag of cookies at the store," he said, "and I'm not sure if I should eat them. It says on the package ... 100% Cotton."

Who would not enjoy the following witches brew, reminiscent of Shakespeare's Macbeth, written on a brochure about Jun Porcelain? Here is an apt description of the beautiful markings on this famous porcelain first produced in the Song Dynasty:

> *It looks like a fragment but is smooth to the touch. In glazing, spectacular patterns occur; pearl-like spot, roe vein, crab scratch, thread of rabbit hair, spider net, earthworm zigzagging in the mud, and etc.*

And further charming descriptions:

> *The following scenery can be formed with kiln variations; the glow of a sunset, jackdaw returning to woods, stars adorning the skies, jeweled palace on fairy mountain, apricot flower falling down like rain south of the Yangtze River.*

I relished the poetic verse, never before having read such lyrical writing about porcelain, in Canada or anywhere else.

Driver Zhang called from the gate.

"We shouldn't be late," said Miss Chen, "because after your tests we have a surprise for you. It's such a nice day we're going to Ta'er Monastery."

We followed Miss Chen and Driver Zhang through a maze of alleys and back streets to a miserable little room belonging to the Public Health Commission, and presented our papers to two nurses in white uniforms seated at a table. They were the only clean spots in the dark surroundings.

"Tell them we had our AIDS tests before we left Canada two months ago," Bill insisted, "tell them these are the papers to prove it."

The older nurse did all the talking. "It doesn't matter about Canadian papers," said Miss Chen, "the nurse says you could have contracted AIDS in your travels from Canada ... and besides, you must have Chinese papers." It was the first time Miss Chen actually uttered the word AIDS. She usually referred to it as, "you know, that disease."

"We have our own needles," I said hopefully, producing two small packages from my pocket and holding them out to Head Nurse. "And we're sure we didn't get infected on our trip."

"Doesn't matter. She says those won't be necessary, we have better needles here," and Miss Chen pointed to large flimsily wrapped needles lying on the table, "This is the type used by all our leaders."

For a second Bill studied the messy table in need of a good scrubbing and the jar of menacing black antiseptic mud, which looked like thick molasses and was bloated with swabs.

"Please use ours," he said flatly.

Head Nurse was not very happy when she heard these words but reluctantly opened my needle package. My arm gave up blood easily but when she tried to draw a few drops of blood from Bill's arm she couldn't find a proper vein.

By now we had attracted a crowd of curious Chinese, watching the spectacle of Head Nurse and foreigner in a battle for blood. The stubborn vein refused to produce, which made her rather aggressive, and she randomly pushed the needle up and down his forearm, plunging it anywhere she assumed there might be a vein.

I thought Bill looked pale ... pale enough to faint. I imagined he was hyperventilating in the confining stale air of the little room. Miss Chen was also getting pale and seemed to be arguing with the nurses.

"She wants to use the bigger needle ... she says your needle is too small and not good."

Bill gritted his teeth, "Please ... just tell her to keep trying."

It took a few weeks for the greenish-yellowish-bluish bruises on Bill's arm to completely fade ... just around the time when two official Chinese certificates with large red seals arrived from the Ministry of Health stating for all the world to see that the foreigners did not have AIDS or any other dreadful virus.

Ta'er Monastery, (Kumbum in Tibetan), is nestled in the hills 16 miles south of Xining. A rambling nucleus of towers and halls built in 1577, it was home to the Yellow Hat sect, one of the great monasteries of Tibetan Buddhism. The famous Butter Sculptures were housed here. Intricate scenes of animals, flowers, birds and human figures unfolding historical sagas and myths were carved from vividly colored solid, and rancid, yak butter. This religious art developed and flourished in Tibet for thirteen hundred years before being brought to Ta'er in the late 1600s.

We walked the flagstone lane, past rows of prayer wheels, and through each cold dark temple crowded with Buddha statues: fierce bug-eyed angry Buddhas, and laughing Buddhas, hands flung high above their heads, covered with dust, their fat tummies plastered with yuan.

"I don't think I want to go into another temple today," I said, deciding I'd rather wait outside and give my lungs a rest from the rancid smoke of hundreds of yak tallow candles.

The gleaming gold tiles on the roof of the Grand Scripture Hall blinded me in the bright sun as I stood on a small concrete bridge watching the road below. There were very few people around; some monks in flowing red gowns hurried to a temple and small groups of peasant farmers moved along the hard-packed road.

One desperately poor Tibetan family caught my eye. Their

clothes were rags, barely hanging together enough to cover them as they walked slowly, bracing up an old woman bent with years of hardship, her gray hair tangled from the wind of the high plateau. The patient little group had to stop repeatedly to let the old mother sit on a curb and rest. They were on their way to the temple to give offerings of money and prostrate their thin bodies; pressing palms together in prayer, raising them above their heads, bringing them down to their breasts, falling on knees on battered prayer rugs, and stretching out on the polished floor. Standing, praying, falling, stretching ... over and over again. They would burn incense and spin the prayer wheels, called *Mani*, to spread spiritual blessings and bring peace and harmony into their own lives. They were devout Tibetan Buddhists.

I turned to find five young Tibetan girls, perhaps 18 or 19 years of age, standing behind me. They must have been walking on air, as I never heard them approach. They were slightly shorter than I, large boned and strong looking with heavy black pigtails falling to the smalls of their backs. Their intense dark eyes, fringed with thick eyelashes, blazed at me out of their round faces; cheeks ruddy and wind chapped. In contrast to the pathetic little family they were robust and healthy. They circled me and stood about a foot away, chatting and looking me up and down, eyeing my jacket, my gold wedding ring, my running shoes and my nose. I never felt threatened, but neither did I stop smiling.

Finally they became quite bold and patted my sweater and touched my ears. They pointed to my eyes, then to their own eyes, my nose, and then their nose. They softly pulled at my hair like they might straighten out the curly parts. They talked amongst themselves as if I didn't exist, as though I was nothing more than a store mannequin to touch and observe and probably criticize.

They were startled when I put out my hand and jangled their large silver earrings, ran my fingers down their fat pigtails and pulled wide their long black cotton skirts so I could admire the colorful red, white and green striped apron design. I kept smiling and making sounds of approval, saying *"piaoliang* ... beautiful." They broke into instant wide smiles, showing strong perfect white teeth, their round black eyes squeezed together in sudden amusement.

"Can I take your picture?" I asked, waving my camera.

They indicated "no" and seemed quite excited. I thought they were insulted because I had asked for pictures or perhaps they wanted money. I put the camera back in my purse.

Fortunately Bill and Driver Zhang returned with Miss Chen to do the translating.

"They say they have walked many days from their high mountain village to come here to prostrate themselves," said Miss Chen, "They are Buddhist, you know … they must keep their faith and visit this holy place."

"Did I insult them?" I worried, "they didn't seem to want their pictures taken."

"Yes, yes, they want their pictures taken," she said, "but they want to prepare themselves first." And we watched as they took off their outer rain jackets and wound long red silk scarves around their waists. One of the five girls pulled a compact from her gown pocket and began to straighten her hair and powder her face. She shared the compact with the others and soon they were camera ready. Eagerly they grouped together in a chorus line to pose for the curious foreign lady with the big nose and flimsy blonde hair. It was the first time I regretted not having a Polaroid camera, as I knew these smiling young women would not likely have much chance to see themselves in photos.

As for me, those few precious minutes looking deep into the black eyes of the Tibetan girls was unforgettable. To one another we were strange alien creatures but somehow we crossed the line of fear and mistrust and became friends for a brief moment in time. We gave them a few yuan and waved *zai jian*, wishing them a safe journey home.

Contrary to the argument that money given to the poor was demeaning, I always felt the opposite. Money, whether we like it or not, will buy food and people need food.

Walking back to the monastery gates we passed the small ragged family I had seen from the bridge. Bill handed Miss Chen yuan for them, asking her to go back and wish them well. No sooner had he done this than a man approached Miss Chen and spoke to her.

"I hope he doesn't tell us not to give to the poor," I said, "maybe there's a sign around here saying no panhandling."

But it wasn't that at all.

"The man says to thank you for helping the Tibetan family," said Miss Chen. "He wants to tell you he has never before seen a foreigner give money to poor Chinese people."

"That's very hard to believe," said Bill.

"It's true," said Miss Chen, "it's not their fault but foreigners rarely have the opportunity to give to the poor. Tour guides discourage them and they probably don't want to offend anyone either. You must have noticed too, Chinese people don't like to beg. To beg is to lose face ... and they believe families must look after one another. If the extended family has 200 members, lets say, and a few of them have money, it's their obligation to help the people who have none."

Never a day went by that we did not learn something new about the Chinese culture.

The next morning Driver Zhang called from our courtyard. He always yelled my name at the top of his husky voice as soon as he approached our gate.

"Jeree! Jereeee!"

He never called "Bill." I suppose he thought that would be disrespectful. He also never knocked, just bellowed my name until I opened the door.

Somewhere I read that back in history Chinese never knocked on doors but would gently make a scratching sound to draw attention to their visit. Even in 1995 our friends usually called to us as they neared our house or made some kind of noise to let us know they were there.

"Jeree! Fax! Fax!" And with his face turned up in his usual broad grin he handed the flimsy paper to Bill. Driver Zhang brought all our mail and messages and every delivery was as exciting for him as it was for us.

Bill read the fax out loud "I am going to the Women's conference in Beijing and will be coming to visit you first. I will be arriving in Xining by train on August 26." Signed, The Honorable

Audrey McLaughlin, our very own Member of Parliament for Yukon and a good friend.

We were thrilled. We could hardly wait to share our life in China with someone from home. It would also be the first time in two months to speak to another Western person in our own language.

thirteen

中国

Chen Yu Hua finished buttoning her black cloth shoes when her friend, Wang Yan, came to the back door of the house. It was 1973 and the two childhood friends were in Junior Middle School.

"I have a great idea for you and me to make lots of money," she beamed, "it will be easy, and I have this plan."

Life had improved for Chen Yu Hua and her family in the two years since Jia Ying had been assigned a teaching job in a country school twenty miles away. Her pay of fifteen yuan a month, plus a little grain, made a significant difference in the living standards of the family. Jia Ying hated leaving her family; she was allowed only one day every two weeks to go home. She took the old county bus and rattled into Xunhua on Saturday evening. On Sunday afternoon she had to make the journey back to her school, back to her dreary cell of a room with a dirt floor, where mildew lurked in every corner and a small window faced into shadows. The coal stove filled the air with a sulfurous odor and stood far too close to the scorched wall. Perched on its shoulders like a tin hat, sat a large blackened aluminum kettle. There was a desk, a chair, a rickety table and a kerosene oil lamp with a cracked glass globe in need of a good scrubbing. Two folded gray wool blankets, threads hanging from frayed edges, lay on a straw mattress tucked into a simple wooden bed frame. This was the furnished lodging supplied to the resident teacher.

With Jia Ying's absence from home the kitchen chores fell on Chen Yu Hua. Especially hard was the preparation of three meals a day and, by the time she finished feeding her siblings breakfast every morning, she did not have time to comb her hair or get herself properly dressed. She would go to school unkempt and tired with a dirty face and clothes. Her teachers criticized her and called her "wild looking."

But now her mother was back home to stay. It was summer holidays and her best friend was about to make them rich.

"So what do we do?"

Wang Yan explained that her father worked in a food factory that produced packaged dried rice, noodles and confectioneries. The factory people decided to make frozen food stuffs, ice cream and something new called "Ice-lollies." Chen Yu Hua was familiar with these sweets while living at her aunt's home in Xining but her friend had never seen such luxuries.

"The factory wants people to sell Ice-lollies on the street," Wang Yan gushed. Her eyes grew wide and her face glowed with excitement, thinking about the capitalistic opportunity close at hand. Money bounced around in her head. Wow. They might even afford the Ping-Pong bats featured in the store window for three yuan each, not like the ones they had tried to shape out of thin wood. She shuddered when she thought of the deep cut that Chen Yu Hua got when, accidentally, she sliced her thumb with the sharp knife. They had to burn a piece of filthy old cloth to make enough white ash to put on the wound to stop the bleeding. It was painful and took about three weeks to heal, but Chen Yu Hua had to bear it, she was too afraid to tell her parents what she had done.

"OK, let's go," Wang Yan nodded, looking down at Chen Yu Hua.

It was a happy bright day for the two girls. They pulled their cart to the factory and loaded it with one hundred Ice-lollies in an ice-packed cooler.

"You can sell them for five fen each," explained the lady manager, "and you can keep one fen each ... four fen each must come back to the factory."

It was noon and the streets were crowded with office workers, shoppers and cadres in from the countryside. Chen Yu Hua and Wang Yan cried their wares, calling out how delicious a cold Ice-lollie would taste on such a hot day. "Four flavors," they shouted, "only five fen each."

Several young Tibetan men from the high plateau stood on the sidelines watching people buying frozen delights. Although it was a hot day the men wore traditional working costumes, heavy ankle-length brown coats lined with sheepskin. The exaggerated right sleeve, usually brought over the shoulder to hang down freely on the front of the chest, was thrown back "toga style," exposing the shoulder. The other sleeve was long enough to cover the left hand. Rough gray wool pants and shirts were worn under this garment in winter but in the heat of summer, they had changed to light cottons. The wide deep pockets of the coat offered a safe place to keep the legendary silver daggers, money, food and other valuables. Their boots were leather, their hats fur-lined with high crowns.

They watched carefully, now and then chatting to one another about the strange looking food being sold to the people who crowded around the two young girls in the town square. Finally the young Tibetans, perhaps on their first visit to Xunhua, shyly approached the little salesgirls and, with broad smiles showing beautiful white teeth, they bought many of the colored translucent treats.

It was a successful day for Chen Yu Hua and her friend. They sold out the first one hundred Ice-lollies in no time and rushed back to the factory to get one hundred more. Capitalism wasn't so bad after all. They counted their money, packed up their cart and started for home.

Chen Yu Hua stopped. She pulled the sleeve of her friend's jacket.

"Oh, no," she said. "Look at the poor Tibetans."

The men were walking just ahead of them and each had a noticeable wet sticky mess around the pockets of their gowns. Apparently, not realizing the Ice-lollies would soon melt they had stored them in their pockets to take home to their families. The two girls put their heads down and rushed on by, pulling the cart as fast as they could, hoping the Tibetans wouldn't see them and want their money back. It was another side of capitalism ... stand behind your products.

In three days Chen Yu Hua and Wang Yan sold six hundred

Ice-lollies but on the fourth day people had tired of the new fun food and no one bought. Just another side to capitalism … the rule of supply and demand. They quit the food business and decided to look for another job.

Chen Yu Hua's parents were pleased when she turned over three yuan to them. Oh, how they praised her. How proud they were.

A few days later Wang Yan had more good news.

"Come on Chen Yu Hua," she urged, "we've been hired to carry bricks at the site of the new county post office."

Fired-up and eager to get more money, the two young friends showed up for brick-carrying early the next morning. The distance to move the bricks was about thirty yards. Chen Yu Hua carried five bricks at a time while Wang Yan, being stronger and taller, carried six or seven; adults carried eight or nine bricks. Unfortunately, no one was satisfied with her measly five bricks and they grumbled about Chen Yu Hua's inability to work as steadily as the rest of the team. She ran as fast as her thin legs would carry her, trying her best to keep up with her friend …to no avail. That night she went home too exhausted to listen to her parents' praise as she turned over another three yuan for her hard day's work. Her legs ached, her back felt like it was broken and her hands were rough and cut; even her little cloth shoes were scuffed and torn.

She swore she would never do such grueling physical work again.

"I will have to use my intelligence to get ahead in this world. I'm not big enough or strong enough to do such heavy labor."

And, as a young student in middle school, she decided then and there to study hard to be an "intellectual."

Life for us was becoming very interesting in Xining. What we expected to be dull routine office work, visits to industrial factories, and evenings spent watching Chinese TV before the late twelve-minute broadcast of *selected* English news came on, was turning into a parade of fascinating people and events.

We were invited to be on local TV with number one Mayor Liu Guang Zhong. We talked about Canada and our life in Xining, and presented a Canadian flag to the leaders. They mistakenly held it upside down for the photo shoot and were hurriedly corrected by Miss Chen. The next evening we were surprised to see most of our interview shown on CCTV, the national news broadcast out of Beijing.

"At least 800 million people saw you on national TV last night," beamed Miss Chen.

"And saw you too," I said.

Everyone was having fun but not Mr. Cheng. He was negative about the whole thing. "He thinks you're acting like movie stars," said Miss Chen, "he doesn't realize, like the mayor does, that this is good publicity for Qinghai."

"It's fine by us if they want to use our foreign faces," we said.

Letters came from all over China; some from people wanting to know Canadian immigration policies, some from students requesting names of Canadian colleges and universities, and some very warm letters praising us for living in the hinterland. But they all started with a line or two about how we had the spirit of Dr. Norman Bethune. Heady stuff.

There was also a spread in the China Daily, and the local paper called us "Peacocks" who flew north instead of south, referring to talented people leaving the cold of Qinghai to seek their fortunes in the warm southern provinces. One day a reporter from the Shanghai *Jie Feng* newspaper arrived on our doorstep. He had picked up our story from *Xinhua News Agency* and wanted an interview.

We had to laugh when Miss Chen later translated the article describing our sofas facing one another, the signature wall where the reporter had signed, the spirit of Bethune and, of course, the Peacock story.

It was Mid Autumn Festival, the night when the moon is the biggest and brightest, the fifteenth day of the eighth month of the Chinese Lunar Calendar, and the second most popular celebration in China, dating back hundreds of years to the Tang dynasty. Mayor Yang and some other leaders arrived early in the morning with a huge cake, gifts and the famous Moon cakes; delicious pastries filled with nuts, dates, sesame seeds and bean mash.

"Mayor Yang wants to tell you the story of the origin of the Moon cakes," said Miss Chen.

We settled into our black sofas, poured tea and listened while she translated the story of a fourteenth century Han uprising led by rebel leader Lui Fu Tong against the ruling Mongols. Han Chinese were under great hardship imposed by the Mongols, and revolution was in the air. Since small gatherings and meetings were forbidden, Lui Fu Tong had to find another way to reach the people and tell them when to rise up. He had an ingenious idea; secret notes were baked into small round cakes and delivered to every household in the province. When the Han Chinese cut into the cakes they were surprised to discover messages that instructed them to take up arms on the night of the Mid Autumn Festival.

"So when the moon was huge the people rose up and killed the Mongols," said Miss Chen. "It was the eventual demise of the Mongol Empire."

"We call the big moon this time of year the Harvest Moon," I said proudly. The mayor nodded politely with noticeable indifference, no doubt thinking what a colorless name it was. And it didn't help when I told them we had a "man in the moon" and not Chang Oh, the beautiful goddess that inhabits the Chinese moon.

As we drank our tea and enjoyed the delicious cakes, noisy hammering came from outside the office. Miss Chen went to the front door and called back, "the workmen are here to install the window bars."

The PSB (Public Security Bureau) had recently paid a visit to our home to discuss security. Did we have any concerns with our safety? Any fears? We said "no, we feel very secure," so you can imagine how surprised we were when the casements on the windows were being drilled for heavy cast-iron bars. Our little brick house was turning into a fortress with soldier guards across the lane, a locked gate in the courtyard and now bars on the windows. It turned out bars were put everywhere except in the bathroom where the window swung out instead of up and down.

"But they should put bars in the bathroom, too," said Bill, "that's where a burglar could get in."

Patiently, Miss Chen explained, "of course that could be true, but they say if they put bars on the bathroom window you would never be able to open it!"

I was always interested in calligraphy but knew little about it, so when we were invited to a well-known and respected calligrapher's home for the early evening of Mid Autumn Festival, I was thrilled. We would meet Mr. Mi, a man honored in Japan and Taiwan as well as in China.

His home and beautiful peaceful gardens were tucked away in the Muslim district of the city. He was in his 80s and had lived in this house most of his life. It was filled with priceless collections of teapots, porcelains, countless medals and awards, trophy cups and framed photos. The walls were covered with long narrow pieces of calligraphy.

Calligraphy is one of the highest forms of Chinese art; old as China itself.

To the Western eye, it is usually thought to be merely Chinese characters written with brushes on fine rice paper and, because we are unable to understand the language, we believe we can't relate to it. But if calligraphy is treated as a work of abstract art, we can appreciate it. One does not have to be able to decipher Chinese characters in order to feel the rhythm, line and structure of calligraphy, any more than one has to know the meaning of a Jackson Pollock painting to enjoy it.

We sat in a cool shady gazebo made from bamboo poles and drank green tea with Mr. Mi's family and the other guests. Later he showed us the techniques of calligraphy.

He spread a long sheet of white paper on his work table, ground the solid black ink stick with a little water on a slate stone engraved with flowers and birds, and then dipped one of his many writing brushes into this mixture. Holding his wrist high and the brush straight up, he made swift strokes, drawing within the three forms allowed in calligraphy ... circle, triangle and square, catching a living moment with his own distinctive pattern of writing.

"Mr. Mi says he uses only brushes that have a mixture of goat and weasel hair, which have just the right amount of flexibility," explained Miss Chen, and motioned to his plump writing brushes, pointed and smooth with shafts made from sandalwood and bamboo. "And sometimes, precious ivory, jade or porcelain are also used for the shafts," she added.

Mr. Mi invited all of us to try our hand under his guidance. I tried. Where the master's strokes were feathery light, mine were heavy and clumsy; where his free natural characters flowed along the paper, mine were rigid, divided and expressionless. Not very professional.

After our visit to Mr. Mi's studio I viewed as much calligraphy as possible at art shows and in private homes. One of the most popular, and my favorite, calligraphy pieces was "The Tiger." Round swirls of ink for the body, dropping down with hit-and-miss brush strokes on the long straight line of the tail. There are many such famous subjects painted over and over again. The single Chinese character for mountain has been brushed in many forms; bold, geometric, free-style and graceful, yet they are completely distinct from one another. It all depends on the concentration of the mind of the artist.

That night we stood in our courtyard and stared at the huge moon. It never meant so much to us as it did at that moment and, like the Chinese, we echoed a greeting.

"Hello family ... hello friends ... wherever you are."

We met with the Women's Federation and leaders from our Commission to lay out plans for the Midwives Project. The provincial and municipal governments would bear the costs of classroom expenses and wages for the doctors and nurses selected as instructors to go to county villages. Estimates for Canada's portion of the costs for student midwives, such as per diem food allowance, medical birthing kits, and the printing of bilingual instruction books in Tibetan and Chinese, were to be submitted to CIDA.

Getting estimates was interesting. Mrs. Ding and the committee shrugged off any suggestions that we must obtain three estimates for each order. Definitely not the Chinese way! Why would we bother with estimates when they all knew *someone* who could supply *everything* at a good price?

We insisted ... we got estimates.

Miss Wei was our interpreter this day and when Bill was explaining to everyone about the four hundred midwives involved in the project, Boss Liu's mouth fell open. Excited voices spun around us with Miss Wei in the middle of the heated discussion.

"What's the matter?" asked Bill.

The group suddenly laughed and Miss Wei, blushing a lovely pink, explained she had made a very bad error.

"I'm so sorry," she said self-consciously, "but I told them there were 250 thousand midwives ... I got mixed up in my translation of numbers."

"Good thing we weren't talking money, right?" said Bill.

Misinterpreting words could be amusing at times but always there was an important responsibility to make sure two languages used simultaneously were translated correctly.

Constantly, Bill reminded the leaders that skilled well-trained interpreters were a necessity; not only skilled in translating words into another language but also interpreting emotions. If the dialogue is happy, sad or comical in one language, it should be related in the same context to the other. Sometimes conversation turns into heated discussion over policy or management with the participants speaking too fast, making it confusing for interpreters to perform a good job. Often they forgot what was said, or were too embarrassed to admit they hadn't completely understood the exchanges. This could be disastrous when specific ideas, money or precise names were involved.

There is a story about Mao and Khrushchev having a falling-out over some regrettable translations by a Russian interpreter. The Chairman was so insulted he went back to China in a huff and it was several years before the split was mended. True story or not, there is a serious obligation for interpreters to be accurate.

Bill tried to promote our two interpreters but it was difficult.

"I find it hard to translate to my bosses all the kind things you say about me," said Miss Chen. "They would just think I'm bragging … or they might not believe that you even said them."

This was our dilemma. Respect and encouragement were at a premium and as one leader remarked to Bill after he had made reference to a skilled interpreter, "she's only doing her job."

The forms were filled out; estimates for the necessary items for the birthing kits were gathered from medical supply companies as far away as Shanghai. We met Naida Jean Willis, a nurse from Seattle who gave us immeasurable help in this field. The printing of the books and the royal blue kit bags with the Canadian and Chinese flags embossed on the sides would be done locally.

"I think we should ask the women what else they want in their kits," I said, holding a sheet of paper from the World Health Organization. "Perhaps there are different items they need that aren't shown on this list."

Sure enough, requests came back from the trainees to include a tape measure and a scale to weigh the babies.

The forms were sent. All we had to do was wait.

We had never planned to have a project when we came to Xining. Not until we met the persuasive Mrs. Ding and the needy midwives of Datong County did we imagine we would convince the Canadian government to help us.

fourteen

中国

After Chen Yu Hua's brush with hard labor, where she was unable to pull her weight carrying bricks, she was secretly dismayed to find out all middle school students were required to visit factories and learn from workers the *real* meaning of hard labor.

She knew this was a decree from Chairman Mao and she would gladly do her best, even if her small stature prevented her from carrying heavy objects or pulling such things as loaded carts. After the students had completed their training by shoveling sand in the cement factory, sorting nuts and bolts in the machine factory, and collecting garbage on the construction sites, they were trundled off to the countryside to live with Tibetan peasants for one month.

She enjoyed farm work much more than factory work. She cherished the camaraderie shared with other students, especially with her friend Wang Yan, and she loved the feeling of freedom from her father's endless scolding. She knew he was not in favor of sending students to work in the fields. He thought they should all be attending classes; but no one, not even Chen Jian Pin, dared to say such a thing.

Chen Yu Hua and her friends hauled water, cut the ripened golden wheat with a scythe, tied it with hemp twine and carried it to the threshing site. The weather was pleasant enough and warm, but after long days in the fields their hands became dry and cracked and their hair matted with wheat chaff. Wearily, at the end of the day, they made their way back to the compound for the evening meal of noodles, sometimes laced with bits of yak meat or mutton. Exhausted but happy with their day's labor, they fell onto hard bedrolls on the dirt floor.

Chen Yu Hua and Wang Yan convinced each other there was great satisfaction in helping poor peasant farmers, and the trials they suffered when serving Chairman Mao and Mother China made them spiritual. Or so they imagined. They were completely brainwashed and never once questioned Mao's theories. It never occurred to them at the time that being sent to work in the countryside may have been punishment, having school and family life denied to them, and in many cases becoming a burden on the very farmers they came to help.

Pity the poor farmers, obliged to accept these misguided dedicated teens, who had never in their lives walked in a field of wheat, and had soft hands and bodies that tired easily. It was also a burden for the farmers to share their paltry food supply with the *intellectual youths* from the city.

Between 1967 and 1976 millions of Chinese students were sent to rural China as part of Mao's Thought Reform Campaign to have them experience hard labor; something he believed to be more important than formal schooling.

"I'm glad you're in my class, Wang Yan."

Chen Yu Hua and her friend, now in their final year of middle school, were attending a basic medical class given by traditional Chinese doctors, explaining proper identification and use of herbs, and how to take blood pressure and recognize simple illnesses. The study of medicine was particularly interesting to Chen Yu Hua, who seriously considered becoming a doctor. In 1976 it was relatively easy for sons and daughters from 'virtuous families' (workers, peasants or soldiers) or even from 'bad families' like hers, (intellectuals who had been re-educated through Thought Reform) to enter university. Making it easier was the fact that entrance exams were not required in the universities since the Cultural Revolution began in 1966. Students suffered through watered-down or non-existent curricula due to the chaos caused by Revolutionary struggles. Moreover, through all these years students graduated en masse without ever having to write even one exam.

This unusual state of affairs ended for a brief period in 1973 when Chairman Mao reinstated Deng Xiaoping to his former post as vice-premier. Deng had been purged from the Politburo seven years before and sent to the countryside for re-education. When he returned to power, one of his first reforms, though protested by the indomitable Madam Mao and the Gang of Four, was to make entrance exams a prerequisite for universities.

Less than one month later an absurd story appeared in the *People's Daily* about a young man named Zhang Tie Sheng. He charged that the questions on the exam papers were too difficult and that he was too busy to have time for such "meaningless things." He handed in a blank paper with those defiant words scrawled across the top and to everyone's surprise Madam Mao agreed with him. She immediately overruled Deng Xiaoping and unquestionably decreed that exams were not necessary. It wasn't until early 1977, after the death of Mao, that university entrance exams once again became mandatory.

"Today we will be learning about acupuncture," said the doctor, and he held up an assortment of various lengths of steel needles. "We will learn how to place one needle into a specific point in our bodies. Acupuncture is the ancient medical art of inserting steel needles skillfully into acupoints in the body to connect with certain organs, joints and nerves. Although there are 708 classic acupoints and many Ashi points, only a couple of hundred are commonly used ... mostly for pain control."

The doctor ceased his talk when he heard a commotion from the back of the room. It was Chen Yu Hua. She was wailing, tears stinging her eyes. "I can't get the needle out!"

She had followed the doctor's instructions, and carefully placed a needle in an acupoint in her right leg. It stuck there. No matter how hard she tried to pull the thin metal out it would not budge. Her heart beat faster, her mouth went dry and she panicked and began to weep in front of the class. Yanking up her pant leg, she exposed the tiny quivering needle, feeling now like a steel pole.

"Don't worry, Chen Yu Hua," said Wang Yan, patting the arm of her distressed friend. This did not help.

"Get this thing out of my leg," howled Chen Yu Hua again until the doctor made his way through the crowd of astonished students and quickly embedded another needle beside the first one.

"The leg muscle has tensed up," he explained, "and when I put the second needle into the muscle at the right acupoint, it relaxes the leg muscle … so I can pull the two needles out … like this … " And he pulled.

"Everything is fine now."

He tugged down the pant leg and smiled at Chen Yu Hua, who was terribly embarrassed by the whole episode.

Because of the limited curriculum Chen Yu Hua was becoming frustrated with her school lessons. She planned to go to university someday but knew little about chemistry, physics, or math. It was almost impossible to learn from indifferent teachers who felt they were in a useless, even demeaning profession. Respect for teachers during the Cultural Revolution was at an all time low. They were ridiculed and abused by students or beaten by Red Guards, very often to death. It was no wonder their self-confidence had suffered. Reality for teachers was to make it through daily classes without drawing criticism or attention to themselves.

At least Chen Yu Hua's Classical Chinese language was excellent, her father had seen to that. She had good stage presence and a clear strong voice and, for five years in middle school, the good fortune of being sought after for public speaking. She was an announcer for school events, traveling around her county, reaching every corner of the nine communes and giving performances with the Mao Zedong Thought Team. Their programs were praised and enjoyed by the villagers, who elevated the troupe to celebrity status, rewarding them with delicious meals of tender mutton and chicken.

Chen Yu Hua loved all music. She sang and danced, and learned to play many instruments. Her favorite, and the one she excelled at, was the Chinese *erhu*, a two-stringed melancholy type of fiddle held and played as a cello.

All these thoughts were going through Chen Yu Hua's head as she walked along the crowded halls of the school. Abruptly, the loud speaker system screeched to life. "Stand by for an important announcement," it boomed.

Wang Yan caught up with her friend.

"What's the announcement going to be? Any idea?"

At once her question was answered by a disembodied voice

rising above the crackling static from the loud speaker. "Chairman Mao," it hesitated, "our great helmsman ... has died." A hush fell over the students. Wang Yan looked anxiously at Chen Yu Hua. "Did he say Chairman Mao *died*?"

It was too awful. It couldn't be. Then suddenly the tears began. Howling, crying, hair-pulling and fainting into one another's arms; each student isolated in his or her own inconsolable lamenting.

"Go to the meeting hall now," ordered the loud speaker.

Chen Yu Hua felt the hollow feeling that comes with loss. She thought the sky would fall on China. Although Chairman Mao had thrown the country into chaos and his policies caused death, destruction and turmoil during the last part of his twenty-seven-year reign, Chen Yu Hua never kept such thoughts. After all, he freed China in 1949 and he was the only leader she had ever known.

It was September 9, 1976.

Many important events had happened that year: a favorite leader of the people, Premier Zhou Enlai, died in January; Deng Xiaoping was purged yet again from the Politburo; and a devastating earthquake claimed over 200,000 lives in July.

And now Chairman Mao was dead.

"China is poised on a precipice," said the students with apprehension. "What could possibly happen next?"

They could never have envisioned the times that were yet to come. In October, the very next month, Madam Mao and the Gang of Four were arrested, ordered to stand trial and subsequently sent to jail. Known as the "Gang of Four," Jiang Qing and three of her allies had gained unpopular and destructive power during the Cultural Revolution. She opposed the more liberal views of Zhou Enlai and Deng Xiaoping, launching smear campaigns against both, and accusing them of selling out to foreigners. Chairman Mao tolerated her group and let her take much of the criticism for his own mistakes, leading the public to suspect that there was really a "Gang of Five." And although Jiang Qing assumed she would retain power after the death of Mao, it did not happen. She and her cohorts were completely ignored by the Politburo and her future would be suicide after spending many years in jail.

But reforms were coming and the long years of ignorance would soon be over. Deng Xioaping would be reinstated, for the third time, to all his former posts. He was committed to the new, forward way of thinking, that Communism and a free market system could survive side by side allowing China to prosper. Deng believed China would rise from the ruinous years of the Cultural Revolution and *open to the outside world.*

Chen Yu Hua was sixteen years and six months and twenty-two days old.

It was already the end of August.

We were standing on the Xining station platform waiting for Audrey McLaughlin to arrive. The summer weather was warm and dry with pleasant temperatures rarely above 75° Fahrenheit. The pink hollyhocks in the lane towered over our heads and the green apple tree at the front door had been plucked bare.

Two weeks earlier Mr. Cheng and Miss Chen made a visit to our house for a briefing. We were unaware of a serious problem brewing at the Commission over Mrs. McLaughlin's visit. "We are uncomfortable," they said "to tell you that Mrs. McLaughlin cannot stay with you in your home while she is in Xining. She must stay at the Qinghai Bingwan (hotel for foreign guests) as the regulations state clearly that foreigners cannot stay with other foreigners in private homes while visiting China."

"What would be the reason for this?" I asked, totally surprised.

Mr. Cheng kept fingering his small book of regulations. He understood how disappointed we were. "It's something to do with passports … it says that foreigners must surrender their passports to hotels for safekeeping," translated Miss Chen.

"But we want Mrs. McLaughlin to visit us in our home," said Bill. "She's our friend and we have a bedroom right here for her and besides, the hotel is very expensive for foreigners … perhaps the Commission can get special authorization for her to stay with us."

"Mr. Cheng doesn't think so, but he'll discuss it with our leaders," said Miss Chen, "you must understand this is complicated for us, we've never had this situation before. We are only following rules ... and he's very embarrassed by it."

As it turned out we received permission to have our first visitor stay in our home, something we had never imagined having to worry about. We filled out the necessary forms at the Public Security Bureau and later, when Mrs. McLaughlin was settled at the house, Mr. Cheng came over and uncomfortably went through the motions of examining her passport.

"Mrs. McLaughlin just got off the train," said Miss Wei. "Mr. Cheng says he saw her."

We started down the station platform when I asked foolishly "How does Mr. Cheng know it's Mrs. McLaughlin?" No one answered me as we spotted Audrey with a pack on her back, the only Western tourist, standing out like a sore thumb in the milling crowd of Chinese.

"I'm here," said Audrey throwing her arms wide for a hug, "and I've brought a care parcel ... coffee and soup mixes and something really important ... canned Sockeye salmon. I know it's the only fish that Bill will eat."

It was wonderful to see her. Anyone who has ever lived in a foreign country knows the thrill of having a visitor from home. During the next ten months, four more people would arrive from the "outside world", each with a humorous account of their trip and something special from home.

We laughed when Audrey related her one and a half day excursion in the "soft seat" compartment on the train from Xian, cooped up in a fog of cigarette smoke with three smiling good-natured male comrades.

"So, did they snore all night?" I asked.

"I don't know," she said, "I was too tired to even notice."

In the five days of Audrey's stay we squeezed in a picnic at Qinghai Lake, a Tibetan hospital visit, dim sums and official dinners with city and provincial leaders, including the Governor of Qinghai.

A ceremony at the Tibetan Tent Manufacturing Company was most interesting. When Audrey was presented with an authentic Tibetan dress, it proved to be six inches too small to fit around her waist. A seamstress was hurriedly called and lost no time remodeling it. Audrey looked impressive in blue and gold silk, with an orange *Hada*, an honorary Tibetan scarf, draped around her neck. "I knew I was putting on a little weight," she teased "but I never thought I'd be getting my clothes sewn by a tent company."

Driving to Qinghai Lake, we were once again awed by the Sun and Moon Mountains and the great Tibetan plains. We spread blankets on tufted clumps of prairie grass and Mr. Cheng and Young Liu brought food from the vehicles: tea eggs, cold Naked Carp, Tsingtao beer, potato chips, *shuanghui* and cakes. The Chinese love their food and they love to share it with their guests. After all, any culture that uses *Ni Chi Fan Le Ma* (have you eaten yet?) as a foremost greeting to one another *must* love food.

"Please help yourself," said Miss Wei, but we had our own potato salad made with real Miracle Whip, miraculously found in a new Muslim store and, of course, our sandwiches. We offered our food in return but knew they were not as adventuresome as we were expected to be. They would never enjoy the creamy potato salad and they didn't realize salmon was fish.

Mr. Cheng nodded towards Bill, "You know this ... Mr. Weigand never eats fish," translated Miss Wei. Audrey winked from under her coned Chinese straw hat, "yes I know," she said.

A whole new world opened up for us in September. We met four new friends: teachers Julie Cox, from England, and Australian Carol Ames. Also, Erin Schulz, an accomplished artist, and her husband Keith Dede, from Seattle. Keith was studying Tibetan language at the Minorities University. We now had seasoned expats to tell us where to find margarine (tasteless lardy stuff in big tin containers imported from Australia), the best chicken legs, Del Monte ketchup, and a semblance of Western-type bread for our toaster. Living without butter and other fats, such as ice cream, whipping cream and cheese, we had dropped over twenty pounds each since arriving in China.

Bill was getting so thin that Mayor Yang made a surprise visit to our house to see how he was feeling. He wiggled the skin under Bill's chin.

"Mayor Yang says he is concerned about your health, you are getting too thin," scolded Miss Chen, with the authority of the mayor. "We must find you something to eat. He says he will send you some fresh meat ... you must eat more meat!"

The next day a huge bloody roast of yak, the deep color of burgundy wine, was delivered. Bill bought a pressure cooker and Julie made stew. Although we appreciated the kind thoughts from Mayor Yang, we did not enjoy the strong-tasting meat, and one meal was enough for us. We gave the rest of the yak, along with the cooker, to the neighbors and went back to eating chicken legs.

A couple of days later Miss Wei came to the house to teach us how to make Tea Eggs, one of our favorite foods. We suspected she was sent by our concerned leaders to make certain we were eating enough protein. She started by hard-boiling a dozen eggs. When these were cool she cracked the shells by tapping them lightly all over on the ceramic counter. She did not remove the shells but put the eggs in a large pot of water and gently simmered them for an hour with a special strong tea, chunks of fresh ginger and a spoonful of Chinese Four Spices.

"My mother always told me if you boil eggs too long they become tough," I said, but Miss Wei assured me they would not be over-cooked.

The heat was turned off and the eggs were left to cool in the tea water, drawing in delicious flavors, leaving a marbled patina effect when the shells were removed.

"I think I'd like these wonderful eggs at the dinner party we're planning, Miss Wei. We've decided to invite Mr. Cheng and his wife and young Liu and his wife ... and you, of course," I said.

"A dinner party? You mean you will have them to your home for dinner?"

"Yes," I said, "they are always asking how to eat Western ... so we'll show them. We'll eat with our cutlery and have Western food. It will be fun. Do you think they'll come?"

Miss Wei frowned and pursed her lips as though she had been asked a very profound question, "I think so ... yeah?"

When Bill did the shopping at West Gate Market, he always patronized special stalls. His "chicken lady" ... "tomato lady" ... "egg lady" and "potato lady" smiled and gave him good service but charged him a little extra. Miss Chen forever reminded him, "You are paying too much."

That night the table looked very *Martha Stewartish* with the new lace cloth from Dasha Zu Department Store. Clerks at this store still used the abacus and made change from loose money kept in large basins. I polished the stainless steel knives and forks until they gleamed, popped blue and white napkins into the wineglasses and lit red candles around the room. Chicken legs with gravy bubbled in an electric frying pan in the kitchen. Bill whipped the potatoes into frothy mounds and chilled a bottle of Great Wall chardonnay. I tossed the salad, and we were ready.

The guests were right on time.

I thought the Western food looked deliciously appetizing on the Chinese Blue Willow plates until I heard Mr. Cheng say something that sounded like the equivalent of "oh god." He punctured a chicken leg with his fork and swung his knife in the air, not quite knowing what to do with it. The women were more adept at using the cutlery but they, too, had awkward moments. Beer was the drink of choice. This was a good thing since the cork on the Great Wall had dried up and refused to budge. No one seemed enthusiastic about the salad. The tiny baby carrots coated in Australian margarine were ignored, and each guest meticulously scraped every last drop of gravy from the chicken legs.

"What's the matter?" I asked, noticing Mr. Cheng making gestures and pointing to his mouth, all the while taking great gulps of beer.

"Mr. Cheng says the potatoes are sticking to the top of his mouth," said Miss Wei, embarrassed by having to repeat such rude news. She lowered her voice slightly, "he says they're not his favorite ... yeah."

"Mei guan xi. It doesn't matter," I exhaled.

Along with the beers, the Mao Tais and the Qinghai Barleys, we somehow got through the meal.

"I think the driver will be here very soon," said Miss Wei and they all studied their watches.

I'm a failure, I thought. No one enjoyed the food. They can't wait to go and find something good to eat.

"I have a very special drink from Canada," said Bill, his voice tinged with pride as he poured each of us a small glass of golden liquid from his treasured bottle of Crown Royal whiskey. "It's one of the most famous liquors in the world. Let's have a last toast before you leave."

The men acquired an instant fondness for the only bottle of Crown Royal in Qinghai Province and the toasts went on and on. Suddenly no one was in a hurry to leave. Driver Zhang came to pick up his charges and he too joined in the toasting while Mr. Cheng, in a loud voice, launched into a saga about life passing him by. We gathered from the dialogue that he wanted to become an engineer when he was young but the Cultural Revolution interrupted his education and he lost ten years of schooling. It was an all-too-familiar story. A drained Miss Wei tried to carry on with the translations but she was wearing down and just gave up.

"It was a great evening," were her last husky words as they noisily left. We were alone. The candles had burned away leaving red wax drippings on my new tablecloth and the single portable CD player bought in Beijing had infused our ears with "Butterfly Lovers" for the umpteenth time.

Bill waved his empty Crown Royal bottle. "I guess the party was a success after all," he smiled, "I don't know about the food but *this* was a hit."

October 1st was National Day. Chairman Mao Zedong had proclaimed the new Communist People's Republic of China on this date in 1949 and ever since, it has been marked with patriotic speeches, parades and cultural events. Magnificent stage productions, with literally thousands of entertainers, and lavish celebrations were held each year in Beijing and throughout the country.

In Mao's time the parade in Beijing was an overwhelming show of power, with rows and rows of goose-stepping soldiers, hundreds of tanks, rockets and firepower, reviewed in Tiananmen Square by

Politburo Leaders. The military might of China was displayed to the world annually from 1949 to 1959.

But we watched parades that were truly for the people, filled with children, ethnic minorities, singers, dancers and acrobats. Red flags waved everywhere, and the national anthem poured from every loudspeaker.

We celebrated in Xining by viewing an art show and watching local entertainers perform on an outdoor stage in a piercing cold wind in People's Park. At night we went to a "guns and gore" Chinese movie called *The Last Eight Days of General Yang* with Miss Chen whispering translations a little too loudly about this hero of the Liberation.

The cold weather had arrived. Drab gray mists settled on North Mountain and swirled around Beishan Temple. Our house was about the same temperature as the inside of the *Hyer* fridge in our kitchen.

One day Bill came home saying he had some good news and some bad news. "The good news is," he said, "in winter the homes north of the Yellow River will get heat."

"That's us," I interrupted.

"The bad news is, it won't be fired up until October 15, another two weeks."

"What will we do 'til then?" I said, "I'm freezing. It's warmer outside than inside." Here we were, sniveling again, and being soft *never-can-bear* Western foreigners. I knew the family next door was also cold. Twelve-year-old BeiBei and her old grandma had told us their house was not as warm as the apartments nearby and they said they wouldn't be sorry to leave it when the time came to move.

Apparently our dilemma was being discussed at city hall.

"Mayor Yang suggests you take a holiday for a week or so until the heat comes on," advised Miss Chen. "He says that perhaps you should go to Xian and see the Terra Cotta Warriors." Miss Chen cleared her throat. "At your expense, of course," she added.

We never planned to take a costly trip to get away from our freezing home, but on October 10 we boarded an antiquated Russian plane for Xian, along with six New Zealanders who had been on a trade mission to Qinghai.

"I don't have any buckle on my seat belt," I grumbled to Bill, who mentioned this to the busy flight attendant. She indicated for me to tie the belts around my waist in a knot. I complied and she nodded. Just as the plane was shuddering down the runway, the seat across from us snapped back, dropping the lady passenger mere inches from the lap of the surprised man behind her. She stayed that way during the flight and even ate her meal and read her magazines as though this was the proper way to fly. Further up the aisle, the side of another seat collapsed onto the floor.

"Excuse me sir, I believe this is yours," said one of the New Zealanders, and he handed the piece of metal to his friend across from him. The men laughed uproariously. The flight attendant (we saw only one) went about her business like a robot, dishing out drinks and lunch boxes without so much as a change in her expression. As far as she was concerned everything was okay. Maybe a few minor glitches here and there, but nothing she had not seen before.

The Hyatt Regency in Xian was paradise; luxurious and warm with very few guests. We spent six days in this splendid hotel, exotic music drifting through the lobby as lovely ladies plucked stringed instruments called *guzeng*. During the evenings in the dining room we were serenaded by classical piano music, Bach and Chopin, offered up by the nimble fingers of a smiling gentleman, sitting stiff and straight in his formal tails. We ordered German beer and grilled cheese sandwiches with fries, and sat in the spacious bar where, above us, songbirds flew in and out of tall trees under a great glass canopy.

East of Xian lies the Eighth Wonder of the World.

It's hard to describe the magnificent Terracotta Warriors except to say, once seen, they are never to be forgotten. Built to protect the tomb of Emperor Qin Shi Huang (221-207 BC), they stand in silent rows; a mute army of 7,000 soldiers meticulously detailed, representing ancient crossbowmen and cavalry. One hundred chariots and 660 horses, ready for battle, are locked in a time warp from a two thousand year old dynasty.

Emperor Qin thought nothing of sacrificing the lives of laborers to build his projects. Seven hundred thousand alone perished in the construction of his tomb, and millions more on his imaginative schemes. He was a cruel tyrant, yet greatly admired in history for his important policies and radical ideas.

After conquering six neighboring states and unifying China into one nation, he introduced a common script, established a uniform measurement and monetary system, and clarified laws. He replaced the hereditary rights of rulers with a centrally appointed administration and began a defense system to keep out the barbarians.

We read that more remarkable sites were waiting to be excavated. Apparently, a tomb lies hidden somewhere in an earthen mound, with more soldiers and treacherous booby-traps guarding the entrance to the Emperor's eternal afterlife. According to historical writings, a map of the Chinese Kingdom at the time of the Emperor's reign is portrayed on a stone floor, and rivers of mercury flow through mountains of precious gems and pearls.

We roamed the old walled city, and spent time in Bampo Village and the Shaanxi History Museum, learning about the legendary beginnings of the Chinese civilization. This was where we learned of the interesting *Double Six Magic Square*, buried in the foundations of new homes in the Yuan Dynasty (1271-1368) to exorcise evil spirits.

28	4	3	31	35	10
36	18	21	24	11	1
7	23	12	17	22	30
8	13	26	19	16	29
5	20	15	14	25	32
27	33	34	6	2	9

Vertical, horizontal and diagonal lines add up to 111.

It was time to leave Xian and our lovely hotel. We bought groceries from the American chef, who felt sorry for us when he heard we were living in, as he called it, the hinterland of China: butter, cheese, olive oil, loaves of Italian bread, and a big bottle of lemon juice to take back to our warm cozy house in Xining.

We were surprised and pleased to find eleven office staff waiting to greet us at the airport. "We're so glad you're back safely," said Miss Chen, mumbling something about the plane not looking so safe, and someone handed me a big bouquet of red roses.

Our house was toasty for two whole days then cooled down. Heat was rationed, causing the old gray radiators to sputter on and off at intervals. The Commission installed a heavier power line into our living room and we bought an electric heater, which raised the temperature slightly. At least we couldn't see our breath anymore, and there were days we would open the front door and let in, hopefully, a little heat from the winter sun.

fifteen

中国

Dong Feng was her destination.

She climbed into the mud-spattered faded green long distance bus filled with bedrolls and baggage and the odd trussed-up goat strapped to the roof. The bus was packed, as usual, and the air hung stale with cigarette smoke and sweaty unwashed clothes. Women with crying babies clinging to their breasts, carried cloth bags of onions and potatoes and jostled for seats. Chen Yu Hua was lucky to find a seat two rows behind the driver and tried to wipe a clear viewing spot on the window with her sleeve but the dust was clinging to the outside of the glass; still she could glimpse her father and older brother through the grime. She took a deep breath, waved and smiled to them briefly, then turned her face forward as the bus pulled away from the roadside.

She was on her way to independence.

Dong Feng was a tiny Salar village tucked at the foot of a mountain. Here Chen Yu Hua would begin her work as a primary school teacher, with no proper training or Normal school education, armed only with her intelligence and resourcefulness. At seventeen, she was small and beautiful; her short black hair had grown, almost to her shoulders. Mao was gone, the Cultural Revolution was gone, conformity was now less severe for the young, and she was young and spirited and eager, longing to start a new life away from her father's house.

It was her first real job and she smiled to herself as she thought how pleased her parents had been, especially her father, when she was chosen to be a teacher.

"Teacher Chen." Her father had said proudly. "I like it."

"It might not be forever," she teased them, as she handed her mother ten yuan out of the fifteen of her allotted monthly pay. "If I don't like teaching I may want to try something else."

With the remaining five yuan she bought herself three things. One was a shiny washbasin with large red poppies and deep green leaves glowing out of the smooth white enamel. Color was just beginning to explode into Chinese daily life after so many dreary years without it. A few months ago she would have purchased a plain white basin with a cobalt rim. But now, she traced the flowers with her fingers. It was the prettiest thing she had ever owned. Her second purchase was a large blue cotton bath towel and the third was a heavy package of folded, rough gray toilet paper. Her first possessions. Her very own *things*.

It was late in the evening when she reached her new home, a small room housed in a grey dormitory building. A fine mist, not quite rain, was shrouding the countryside in dampness. She looked around the sparsely furnished room: a bed, a desk, a chair and, standing in the corner, a long willow broom for the dirt floor. A single 15-watt electric bulb dangled from the middle of the ceiling casting a circle of pale light directly beneath it. At least the room was warm; someone thoughtfully had made a welcoming fire and now a kettle of water was boiling on the black coal stove.

Chen Yu Hua sat all alone on the edge of the bed and sighed, her hands cradling the white enamel cup as she sipped the precious hot water.

"This is only temporary," she said to herself, "soon I'll be going to college."

She unwrapped her few articles of clothing, her towel and toilet paper, the kerosene lamp and small stove she had brought from home. She placed a round mirror on the desk, along with a comb and hair clips. She had two old school books that Jian Pin had insisted she take with her, and a black and white picture of her mother and father when they were young.

She thought about Zhang Qi, the man who met her at the bus and helped carry her belongings to the room.

"I'm Teacher Zhang," he had smiled pleasantly as he shook her hand, "we're so glad you're here. I hope your bus trip wasn't too uncomfortable."

He was handsome. Maybe five years older, friendly and soft-spoken. Excellent Mandarin. A tingling feeling came over her as she remembered how strong he was as he picked up all her baggage, insisting he carry everything. Never had she been alone with a man before other than her father, and it felt good to walk along the dark unfamiliar path with this stranger in control.

The satin basin gleamed. It was the only color in the room. A residue of hot water left from washing herself caught the faint light as she twisted the basin around, watching diamond droplets run down the sides. It was so lovely. She stared at it for a very long time. Then she stared at her own young face in the mirror, turning this way and that way, studying her brown eyes and pretty mouth. She touched the soft skin on her cheeks and ran her fingers through her hair, pulling it back, pulling it forward, piling it on top of her head, and she was pleased with the glowing image smiling back. For the first time in her life she had the luxury of being alone, with only herself to think about.

"Good night." She waved at the mirror and turned out the fifteen-watt bulb. "Good night ... *Teacher Chen.*"

The typical poor country school was cold and cheerless with low ceilings and mildewed walls. The blackboards lacked any black paint and were so scarred and rough she could barely see the white chalk writing. Old wooden desks, two students to each desk, stood in rows on the dirt floor and in front of the class there was a wobbly lectern on a raised platform on which the teacher would stand.

Chen Yu Hua was one of nine teachers and in charge of teaching grade five level Classical Chinese Language to twenty-three Salar students, five of whom were girls. Salar people did not encourage education for women. It was thought to be a waste of time. Their mothers and grandmothers would teach them whatever education was reasonably important and, besides, they were needed on the farms to work. As for the boys, very limited education was tolerated; only the minimum required by Chinese law. Most Salar people living around Dong Feng were self-sufficient farmers with an ancient history. They followed Islam, did not eat pork, grew crops of wheat and barley and were shrewd business people.

Chen Yu Hua was happy with her small class and she became very good at learning on the job. She taught traditional songs of the Han people to the whole school and, in return, she learned the folk ballads and dances of the Salar people.

Like her mother before her, she became a very popular and respected teacher, for this was the primary school where Jia Ying had spent two years when she once went away, leaving her small daughter to manage the house.

One day as Chen Yu Hua passed the library room, she was curious to see Teacher Zhang and two students huddled over a small radio listening intently to a voice speaking in a strange language.

She stopped.

"What language is that, Teacher Zhang?"

"English," he answered curtly.

"What is he saying?"

Teacher Zhang looked up, openly irritated. He beckoned Chen Yu Hua to sit down as he pulled a nearby chair close to the table.

"Shhh, he is talking about American Imperialism and Soviet Revisionism," he translated, "and the broadcast is from Beijing."

Chen Yu Hua was in awe of the teacher and students who could understand this foreign language.

"What else is he saying?" She urged Teacher Zhang. "Please, can you tell me more?"

At that very moment in her life Chen Yu Hua decided to learn English.

English was not a required subject in schools and very few students were interested in the language, especially in this remote Salar village. She wondered about Teacher Zhang. He was obviously over-educated for such an out-of-the way school and she knew he must be longing to share his knowledge with other educated minds. She sensed his frustration as he tried in vain to teach English words every chance he got, speaking them to his students and writing them in the margins of their notebooks. And always the parents, who were ignorant about languages, chastised him and felt that studying Mandarin was burden enough for their children.

Teacher Zhang and Teacher Chen became good friends. Every spare moment they had together, he would speak to her in English. Walking under the trees he would point and say "trees" and she would repeat the word. He would say "grass" and she would repeat it. Sky. Clouds. Sun. Moon. Stars ... Me ... You.

They talked and laughed together and she told him the story of how she had spent hours preparing an extensive study on the "Basic Knowledge of Agriculture."

"Today I was telling the class how to grow potatoes, what the potato is composed of ... like root ... vein, leaf ... you know." She laughed so much she could hardly go on. "And right in the middle of my boring lecture this young boy stood up and said very seriously, Teacher Chen you don't have to tell us this ... we're farmers ... we know all about potatoes."

It was hilarious to both of them.

"I was so embarrassed ... I must have showed my red face."

She dried her laughing tears with the back of her hand and related more humorous stories about teaching. She failed to notice the way her new friend was looking at her.

Teacher Zhang Qi was falling in love.

Friday nights were spent with Julie.

We bought one of the two toaster ovens available at the department store and Julie made the most delicious bread rolls. I deep-fried a mountain of potato chips, like English chips minus the fish, and Bill went around the corner to his favorite beer-man for quarts of Tsingtao. We flopped on the black leather couches, dipped the hot chips in a bowl of packaged gravy mix and watched "Empress Wu" on TV.

We were addicted to this glossy historic tale of Wu Zetian, the only woman in Chinese history to be declared "Emperor" (625 to

705 AD) during the Tang Dynasty. It ran nightly in a series of thirty-six programs and every morning when Miss Chen arrived at work, she translated the events in our favorite soap opera. Why did the poor fellow get beheaded? What was said when the empress sent the minister from the throne room? Why did Empress Wu murder her baby? The story was confusing until Miss Chen enlightened us each morning. But on Friday nights Julie did the translating, speaking Chinese well enough to tell us the latest gossip and scandals of our endearing empress.

"You're a good teacher," I often told Julie. I admired her for all the years she served in foreign countries. These teachers asked for nothing, living in hardship postings with little pay, content to have students who just wanted to learn. Julie decided to go home to England after Christmas for a much-needed rest. We would miss her friendship.

While Bill was at the office one afternoon, reviewing project proposal applications and writing endless letters with Miss Wei, I was fortunate to accompany Miss Chen to meet the ten Chinese English teachers and the students of No.14 Middle School.

The supervisor was Miss Sun, a broad-smiling, quick-witted lady who told me she had never spoken to a native English speaker in her twenty-eight years of teaching. I was the first. The day we met she was studying about American festivals in her teacher's workbook.

"What is the meaning of *halloring* or *hallowing*?" she asked.

"Do you mean Halloween?" I said.

"We call it All Saints Day ... but you say *hallo* ... what?"

"Halloween is October 31 ... the *eve* of All Saints Day," I explained. "It's supposed to be named after Samhain, the pagan god of death for the Celtic people ... and it's celebrated mostly in North America. Children dress up in masks and costumes and go from house to house with a sack collecting gifts of candy, apples and other treats ... and adults have masquerade parties ... and contests for the scariest costumes." Miss Sun had never before heard stories of Halloween. I decided to get theatrical. "This is the day when witches, goblins and ghouls, black cats and bats haunt the world under a full moon ... and graves open wide ... and rotting corpses crawl out and frighten us." I put my hands up and gnarled my fingers. "Boo!"

Miss Sun was startled.

I also told her about the Halloween party we had for the neighbor kids on Nan Guan Road, about dressing the girls as Empresses and the boys as Tigers. Naturally they couldn't "trick or treat" but in the market we found a type of green squash, half the size of a pumpkin, and Julie and Carol showed the mothers and kids how to carve grimacing faces on them. We put candles in each one and when the lights were turned off, the parade of green pumpkins was superb.

When I finished, Miss Sun's astonished eyes had stretched into flat brown circles.

"Yes, and if you think about it," I said, "it doesn't even resemble the Festival of Samhaim, so don't ask me why a Christian nation like ours celebrates a fictitious pagan festival with witches and demons ... it's just fun I guess!"

Miss Sun looked very thoughtful, trying to digest my words. "Oh ... yes, fun," she mumbled.

I went to the high school with Miss Chen twice a week to speak with students in the English classes and there was always time to chat with the teachers before lessons. They constantly asked me complicated questions on grammar.

"I'm not a teacher," I protested, and got the usual stare. So I would rub my forehead and search back to my past education for an intelligent answer. I tried, but who knows how many times I was wrong.

The teachers and students were particularly interested in our festivals and holidays, and explaining one's own customs can be amusing at times. Christmas was always a favorite, but not being of Christian faith they found the story of the birth of Jesus confusing. They loved to hear about our festive foods and decorating a tree with lights *inside* our homes. They tried to picture Santa Claus flying through the night sky on a sleigh pulled by reindeer and delivering gifts to "good" children. When I talked about a fowl as large as the turkey, I wasn't sure they even believed me. Trying to describe such a creature never entered my mind before I went to China, and I had to sketch this ridiculous looking bird on the blackboard to prove it existed. The fact that it was roasted in a large oven made it even more unbelievable; there are no turkeys and few ovens in China.

There were also humorous misunderstandings and "lost in translations" that occurred at times in our conversations. One day I was explaining in detail the preparation of the Christmas turkey. I talked about cooking it for hours until it was golden brown, how we made the stuffing, spiced cranberry sauce and tasty wine gravy, and decorated a serving platter with fruit, presenting the delicious turkey whole to the dinner guests.

The group sat in a daze and I wondered if they had visions of this "thing" looming on a carousel in the center of the table while hungry diners attacked it with chopsticks. You can imagine how silly I felt when one young lady broke the silence, bent towards me and said in hushed tones something that sounded like ... "Do you wash it before you eat it?"

"Wash it!" I said, stunned that my long-winded descriptions went nowhere. "Yes, we wash it. We cook it for hours."

"No ... no," came the soft, reverent voice again. "I think you misunderstood me. I wondered ... do you *worship* before you eat it?"

After several visits to the crowded classrooms, the teachers decided to meet in smaller groups in the music room, where our talks with the students would be more informal. Here they asked many questions. They wanted to know if Canadians and Americans *liked* the Chinese people and were they interested in their lives. They asked about the students in Canada, about their sports, subjects they studied and were they allowed to have boyfriends and girlfriends. They grumbled about never being permitted such relationships, compelling the teacher to clap her hands sharply for attention. "You can do those things when you're older" she would say, "right now you must obey your parents and devote all your time to your studies."

The students were naive about life. They would hold their hands over their mouths and giggle whenever anyone mentioned love or marriage. They were especially curious about Western girls getting engaged and wearing a diamond ring, and they wanted to know how it felt to walk down the aisle in a long white gown in a big church. Honeymoons. Hearts and flowers. Anything to do with love and romance intrigued them, boys and girls alike.

One young lady raised her hand. "Miss Jeri," she said, "why do Western parents throw their children out of the home when they become eighteen?" I had been asked this puzzling question before. Even Miss Chen had made references to "throwing the children out, never to have them back again" but she didn't want to offend me so she added, "this is *only* in United States, I think." I assumed some old TV or movie show had the theme of an irate parent tossing an unruly teenager out into the night, "to never darken the door again." But now all I could do was explain to my skeptical listeners that the rumor was misleading.

"We do encourage our young people to be independent," I said defensively.

In a culture where daughters live at home until they marry and babies and grandparents live under one roof in a proper nuclear family, try explaining that we in the West actually encourage our young people to leave home. To them this was unthinkable. The first duty for parents was to look after their children's needs and, besides, why would any young man or woman want to live on their own, away from their loving family?

Not only were there questions and free talk in our get-togethers, but folk dancing, poetry and short story readings, superb piano recitals and lots of singing. I collected several drawings created for me by the students, as well as a cherished note in fine Chinese handwriting. Below it Miss Chen had translated:

"A foreign lady from Canada came to our school today. She was not too old or too young. She had blonde hair and her eyes were the color of the sky. Her clothes fit her very well and I did not understand a word she said."

So much for my English teaching ability!

I loved being with these children, watching them perform and converse in broken English, what we called *Chinglish*, in a room where the walls were flaking and the floor was bare concrete. And later, in the winter, we would sit in wool coats and overshoes and gloves. No one complained about the cold. They kept singing and dancing and asking questions, behaving towards me with the greatest respect, letting me into their private world.

The dreary music room was also the backdrop for the pretty Chinese English teachers. Wearing the latest stylish outfits and elegant colorful scarves, they were so fashionable we gave them names like Miss Paris and Miss New York.

One day the teachers invited Bill to the school.

"Would you like the class to sing a folk song for you Mr. Weigand?" asked Miss San Francisco.

"I would really like to hear them sing their national anthem," he said.

This pleased the teacher. She clapped her small hands together and the students jumped to attention. At her signal they burst into a stirring and patriotic rendition of "March of the Volunteers."

Hanging on the front wall of the room were three large portraits. One was Mozart and one was Beethoven and the third was a serious looking handsome young Chinese man, perhaps in his twenties.

"Miss Chen, who is that person?" I nodded towards the black and white photograph.

"That is Nie Er, the composer of our national anthem."

"He looks so young ... is he still alive?"

"No ... a long time ago he fell from a window."

"You mean he was pushed?" She ignored me. "You mean he was pushed out a window and fell to his death?" I insisted.

"I don't think he was pushed ... he just fell out a window."

Miss Chen started to hum. She was cautious and always sidestepped the bad facts, that there was a possibility Nie Er could have been murdered, that some people had AIDS in China, that some people had alternate lifestyles. We always tried to understand and never put her into a situation where she had to explain.

I really regretted having pressed her about the composer.

sixteen

中国

Spring had arrived in Dong Feng, the remote village where Chen Yu Hua had been teaching for almost nine months.

She took a deep breath. It was one of those amazing afternoons the whole world loves; warm enough to open the classroom door to the sun, and a lovely fresh breeze. Class was over for another day and she finished packing up her books and the twenty-three exam papers she would be correcting later at home.

"*Nihao*, Teacher Chen," a young woman called from the open door, "I'm looking for student LiLi. Have I missed her?"

Chen Yu Hua recognized her as a Salar lady, although she wore no distinguishing costume, jewelry or hairstyle. The Salar people, unlike Tibetans or Hui Muslims, had adapted comfortably to life with the Han people, accepting their dress and mannerisms, building similar houses and learning Mandarin, yet retaining their own culture and language.

"Come in. Come in. I'm sorry ... everyone has gone," said Chen Yu Hua. "Is LiLi your child?"

"No, my little sister, I was on my way home early today and thought I would come by and walk with her."

"She is a very clever young girl," said Chen Yu Hua, "I wish more girls came to my class ... more in the school."

"I know what you mean," said the lady, "LiLi is only the second girl in our family that my father has *reluctantly* allowed to go to school. I was the first. My father was persuaded by my mother to let me go and I persuaded my father to let my little sister go ... she wanted so much to learn to read and write. I think it's important for a woman to be educated no matter what our people believe."

Chen Yu Hua nodded in agreement. She noticed that the Salar lady could speak Mandarin very well. "Are you working in the village?" she asked.

"Yes, I work at the Commune Office in the education department and I'm very happy with my job."

"Is your husband a farmer?" More questions. Chen Yu Hua might be asking too many questions. After all, they had just met, and she knew that Salar people were timid, never revealing their emotions to strangers.

"No ... I never married," the lady said, "you can imagine how my family is reacting to this!"

They both smiled, knowing the tremendous pressure put on a woman of marriageable age to take a husband, preferably one that a matchmaker had recommended.

"But I did once have a young man," she offered bluntly, hesitating before going on, "we loved one another and planned to marry."

She told Chen Yu Hua about her farm boy and how they grew up together. "We were educated in this very school ... this very room. He was a good choice in my father's eyes, too," she said. "But year after year the harvest was too little and finally we were all starving. He *had* to do something so he went with a lot of other men to find work in the city."

"He went to Xining?" asked Chen Yu Hua, "I also went to Xining for a year of schooling."

"That must be why you speak such excellent Mandarin," said the lady. She smiled a wide, warm smile, but there was sadness about her, as though some long forgotten unhappy incident was pushing its way into her heart and she did not want to remember. "I really must go. My father expects his dinner on time. I'm so glad to have met you ... I hope we meet again."

The Salar lady was smaller than Chen Yu Hua, her fine oval face held high cheekbones that hinted at her European bloodlines. Seven hundred years ago the Salar people, spreading the word of Islam, migrated from somewhere in Turkey. They crossed the great Himalayas to Kashgar and followed the Silk Road through the

Taklimakan Desert to Dunuang, turning directly south to the old garrison at Xining. From there they drove their camels to settle in the fertile valleys of the southern reaches of the Yellow River in this region called *Hua Long*.

The Salar lady turned to leave.

Chen Yu Hua couldn't explain the eerie feeling that, in an instant, crept over her. She could not let this woman go … turn her back and simply walk away.

"Did he not come home to you?"

Chen Yu Hua felt guilty at once, asking such a private, personal question. Why did she say that? It was none of her business but then again something about the Salar lady seemed so open and sincere. Chen Yu Hua sensed that she wanted to talk about this part of her life.

"No," came the answer, "he died … in Xining."

The lady turned her head and leveled her bright brown eyes at Chen Yu Hua. The lady's eyes were not as brown as her own dark Chinese eyes, but were eyes flecked with gold and rays of amber that once belonged to an ancient culture in the Near East.

"They said he was caught stealing from someone's home and the police beat him. He was too sick … he just … died." She drew a deep breath as if she needed the pause to go on with the story. "I know he would never steal, even if he was starving he would never steal."

Chen Yu Hua felt sick. A flood of memories came back to her, so vivid and appalling. She was once again in the kitchen of her Aunty Chen Fugui's house. She could hear the storm, feel the icy wind and see the young man's ghostly face, thin from starvation.

"Is something the matter, Teacher Chen?" The woman lightly touched Chen Yu Hua's arm. "I'm sorry if I upset you. It was a long time ago … seven years ago actually."

Chen Yu Hua steadied herself on one of the shaky desks. She was shocked to think she had been witness to this young woman's unfortunate past. She had filed away the horrible events of that night in some dark crevice of her mind, never to be brought back. Until today.

"I'm very sorry to hear such a sad, sad story." Chen Yu Hua's voice was so low the Salar lady could barely understand her. "It reminded me of another story, that's all. I'm fine now."

The schoolroom was becoming murky; as gloomy as her thoughts in the fading light. Chen Yu Hua sat at the small desk alone with her memories. Over and over again she recalled that frightful night. Asking herself questions. "Why did I meet this lady? Is it fate? Should I tell her the real story?" At least, now she knew her intuition had been right, the young man was good and honest. She gave him food. Or? She frowned ... "If I had not given him food would he still be alive? If he had not come to the door? If? ... If?"

She put her head down on her arms and stayed at the desk not moving, until the last shreds of sunlight had gone.

"Northwest China is a hard sell," said Bill, arriving home from an especially trying day at the Foreign Trade office. "Can't get any spark of interest from the letters we've sent out. Got one reply, it was from McCain's saying they just *might* be looking at Ganzu for the potato business and would keep Qinghai in mind for the future ... maybe."

He sat on the chrome and red plastic chair in the kitchen. It didn't soothe his mood when, every few minutes, delicate pieces of whitewash came fluttering down, settling in our coffee mugs and sticking to our hair and eyebrows. Now that the cold weather was upon us the paint decided it was time to free itself from the ceiling.

"And then Mr. Cheng made a remark about how investment should be pouring in all over the place. I told him not to expect instant miracles ... right now just a few replies to our letters would help. He can't seem to understand foreign companies need deep pockets to consider investing in China, and a lot of patience to wade through the ever-changing regulations ... there's certainly nothing cast in stone in this country when it comes to regulations. It would also help to understand how the Chinese business mind works. But I know one thing for sure: the investors who get into China now will do very well in the future."

Bill spooned a fat paint flake out of his hot coffee before it melted. "I told him I read in the *China Daily* that Coca Cola is opening 16 plants in Ganzu and we should be inviting them to visit Qinghai."

"That sounds good," I agreed.

"But do you know what he said? We can't do *that* ... we have to protect our local soft drink company. Now I'm really confused ... we're supposed to encourage foreign trade but all he does is put up roadblocks. Protectionism is all very well if you never want any new business development. I really like Mr. Cheng but he doesn't think free market economy".

Bill sighed, pulled his hand across his forehead and leaned on the table, "I also told him what I've heard lately ... the 21st century belongs to China. I don't think he believes me."

"Never mind, I have good news," I said cheerfully, "today we received an invitation for both of us to attend the Symposium on Economic Development and Capital Marketing. And guess what? *You* are to give a speech."

The symposium was held in Victory Park, a convention center in the Qinghai Hotel complex. The chairs were full when we arrived. There were economists, bright young lawyers and dynamic cadres, all from Beijing and all prepared to speak on the development of this area of Northwest China.

On the rows of seats at the back of the room, farthest from the speakers, slouched the older Qinghai cadres. The ones on the verge of retirement, eyes half closed, cigarette smoke blurring their faces and shielding them from the new unfamiliar dialogue of the young moderns. These men were not interested in change whatsoever. Change was a threat. Who could blame them? They were resentful of criticism and only hoped to finish their careers and be pensioned off with minimum stress and problems.

One after another, the speakers highlighted the importance of the very changes that alarmed the old cadres: the need to open trade links with Western countries and gain economic, scientific and technological knowledge; to build an ideal socialist market economy with Chinese characteristics; and to have the spirit and ambition to modernize and bring about periods of rapid growth with good economic returns. But the main theme running through the exchange of ideas was simply one of peace and development for the country.

Bill was asked to speak on the problems Western companies experience when establishing businesses in China and to present ideas regarding economic development for Qinghai. He and Miss Chen did a clever thing, instead of Miss Chen trying to interpret his words as they went along, usually resulting in errors, they spent a week formulating the exact translations which Miss Chen read after subsequent paragraphs read by Bill. It worked very well as the transcripts were accurate.

"Doing business in China is very difficult for foreigners," said Bill, beginning his speech. He emphasized the need for finance and accountancy to be more understandable and transparent and, although China was immensely attractive to Western investors, it seemed the country was littered with failed foreign companies.

He told the audience that one way Qinghai should consider to attract foreign money would be by encouraging Eco Tourism. It was hard to convince the Chinese government that the Tibetan-Qinghai Plateau, with all its beauty and mystery, would hold any interest for foreigners. But the opportunity for well-organized and controlled trips to the plateau should have been high on their agenda, as well as the need for clean and comfortable accommodation.

As far as expanding and developing the rich Qaidam Basin, Bill recounted how Northern Canada initiated a Mining and Resources Conference that was held every two years. This brought together governments, environmentalists, prospectors, engineers, investors and other interested parties to discuss the problems and potentials of the resources sector. In this way China could initiate a similar gathering of invited guests. "When I hear officials tell me there is no money to establish a forum, I realize they aren't aware that delegates will pay their own expenses to come here," he said, and explained about registration fees, hotels, food and publicity for a Western-style conference, which must be organized at least two years in advance.

His closing remarks, once again, stressed the old case for the importance of good interpreters. "Without well-trained interpreters there cannot be accurate discussion and complete understanding."

"Very good speech," said our lunch table partner David Ma, a sharp young lawyer from Beijing. He spoke English flawlessly, having spent seven years in various US universities studying business law.

"Everything you said is true. Venturing into a business here is risky but worth the while if persevered … and new laws, although perhaps not fully tested, are on the books. China is a developing country, not what the West refers to as a Third World country. It's different, you know. China feeds itself … has its own stock market and our currency is fixed to the US dollar. This, perhaps, is not favorable to the US but is positive for China. Remember also, we are fast developing a middle class … we are heavily into global trade and have a booming market economy. Of course, along with this new found freedom comes problems. In 1949, when the Communist Party came to power, they changed the social fabric of the country, not only with laws … there were always laws, but by making the use of opium and other drugs … prostitution … gambling, all socially unacceptable. Like an old-time religion there were boundaries between right and wrong and people kept within these boundaries, not because it was against the law but because it was the proper thing to do. Can you understand what I mean?"

We nodded.

"But the bad old problems of mankind are fast returning. Prostitution … new drugs in different forms, corruption … and AIDS, another scourge we did not have before. Also, they say men are not smoking as much as they once did, but now our young women are taking their place. Western tobacco advertising that target young girls, making it sophisticated to smoke, have a lot to do with it. So you see … the freer people become the more they embrace different rules. You can't *make* people have good morals if they don't want to … even with strict laws. It has to be a social thing."

I knew Miss Chen was not happy to hear such talk. She always put aside the fact that China had an AIDS problem and would never discuss drugs. And as for prostitution ... what woman would want to do such a thing? This was all unbelievable to Miss Chen, who was as "square" as a box and at times wore blinders.

Our new lawyer friend in the Yves San Laurent designer suit poured a round of tea.

"The younger Chinese generation is not political. Not at all. They will not dedicate themselves to try and make any political changes ... they just want to get on with their lives ... making money and educating their children. My age group is more interested in politics and we know we're not yet ready for Western democracy. We can't be like you in Canada and the US, so I wish the Western world would quit focusing on democracy for my country. We'll do our best to over-haul our human rights issues ... and with discipline we'll bring modernization to China ... I hope it will be with your help and not only your criticism."

David Ma turned to Miss Chen ... "And *you* Chen Yu Hua, did a superb job of translating."

Boss Liu was excited when our office received an invitation from Senior Director Manager Li Tie Zhen to bring the Foreign Experts for a tour of the great Longyang Gorge power station, one of several large power stations built on the upper reaches of the Yellow River eighty miles west of Xining.

Everyone had the good fortune to go but I couldn't believe my bad luck; the dry dusty November air became my nemesis and, suffering from laryngitis, I had to decline the invitation.

"It was like riding to the ends of the earth," said Bill, "we turned off the Xining-Lhasa highway before the Sun and Moon Mountains and drove down this narrow road. We were totally alone." He told me how the scenery changed from cultivated fields to smooth rolling hills and then to golden sand dunes. The road had a thin coat of pavement dissolving dangerously into deep potholes and in some sections the granite hillsides had crumbled down, forcing Driver Zheng to skirt the very edge of unbounded drop-offs. They arrived at Longyang in late morning and stopped on a hill overlooking the massive site. Bill said the scene below overwhelmed him ... the great curving dam with the huge reservoir stretching as far as he could see. And, to his surprise, at the bottom of the hill was a large modern town.

Lunch was served in the home of the director, followed by a tour beginning in the conference room where walls of exotic Tibetan art were mirrored on the highly polished wooden table. After the briefing they walked down the long steps to the viewing galleries and watched sightseeing boats on the great lake. Hotels and other tourist facilities were being developed and Longyang would soon become a destination resort area.

The enormous turbines hummed several stories underground. "I was surprised how quiet they were for the size of them," said Bill. "And you should have seen the huge mural that ran along one wall. The director told us the mural had taken years to compose and was created inch by inch in a mosaic of natural semi-precious stones and minerals. It was a tribute to the many thousands of workers who labored on the project. We were then invited into the nerve center and I had the privilege to sit at the main control panel ... I realized the feeling of pride the young engineers must experience every time they're in charge of that giant power station. But poor Young Liu, I felt sorry for him, he made the mistake of taking out his camera and all hell broke loose ... two scary soldiers sporting AK47s came running over and read the riot act to him ... I guess he should have known better."

seventeen

中国

For the next two days Chen Yu Hua thought of little else except the meeting with the Salar lady. But tonight was Saturday and she had asked Teacher Zhang Qi to come to her room for noodles. She bought fresh Chinese greens and steamed buns from the meal hall and asked him to bring his own bowl and chopsticks and a cup for tea. She had been saving the small bit of tea her mother gave her for a special time and the special time was here.

She brushed her hair in front of the round mirror, pulling strands up on each side of her head and securing them with clips fashioned in the shape of butterflies.

There was only one chair in the room, her guest would have that, and she would sit on the bed. She dragged the desk over to the dining area directly under the dangling bulb. This would be their table. She wrapped up the mirror, the picture and her small assortment of toiletries in a cloth and stowed them in her traveling bag.

The aluminum kettle was boiling on the coal stove. Everything was ready when Teacher Zhang arrived right on time and handed Chen Yu Hua four bright juicy oranges. Brought up much like Chen Yu Hua in a family of teachers, he was a thoughtful man. His uncle once taught at the University of Chengdu but, during the Cultural Revolution, he met the same fate as many educators. He was thrown from a fourth story window, "jumped" they said, but everyone knew what happened to intellectuals; they were either pushed to their deaths or sent to prison for long terms. His father went to prison as a counter-revolutionary in 1955 and died there, and his mother still lived and worked at the rehabilitation camp where she had been sent to in Sichuan Province.

"Tell me about your family, Teacher Chen."

Chen Yu Hua thought about her family for a moment before answering. They were Han people, the largest of the 56 ethnic groups in China. One billion strong, they shared common traditions and language, and were allegedly the descendants of Emperor Huang Di, the mystical Yellow Emperor who ruled China around 4,000 BC. The Chens were a scholarly family, known as *Men Di Shu Xiang*, and one of the most notable families in Xunhua.

"My parents are both teachers," said Chen Yu Hua, "they wanted me to be a teacher too and here I am, a primary school teacher." She frowned and made her voice firm. "But one day I will go to college to further my education."

It wasn't that she didn't want to tell him that before liberation in 1949 her uncles were involved in political and financial affairs, or that one of them advanced to the post of Secretary General of the Qinghai Provincial Government under the warlord Ma Bu Fang; or that later, after liberation, he became mysteriously ill and died from a fever. It was just that she was not yet ready to accept the facts about people being thrown from windows, or being buried alive, or just plain murdered. She never wanted to write anything down about herself or her thoughts. Nothing on paper. Someone might see it. And then what? She had been too close to horrific events in her life and her mind was loath to re-examine the past.

When the noodles on the stove were tender, Chen Yu Hua put the pot aside and fried the finely chopped onions in a small hot pan with a touch of rapeseed oil and aromatic spices. The oil, onions, and the spices instantly released a mouth-watering fragrance into the room. She sprinkled the mixture over the noodles and the simple meal was served. Teacher Zhang closed his eyes and breathed in the pungent odors.

"It's true," he said, "the smell of delicious food brings back happy memories."

"Do you really have happy memories, Teacher Zhang?"

"Yes, of course, don't you?"

Chen Yu Hua was quiet. "Perhaps I was too poor for happy

memories."

"I think we must dig deep for good memories, you and I and all Chinese ... especially in these times."

"I have some good ones," she said, "but more bad ones."

They sat together, bent over like two old friends under the circle of faint light, bowls close to their chins, enjoying the delicious steaming noodles. Chen Yu Hua was comfortable with this man. She trusted him; he made her laugh and told her interesting stories. But tonight she was troubled. Should she tell him about the Salar boy in Xining? She still wasn't sure if she should keep the incident to herself; forget about it and not bring back sad memories for the lady. But under the light in such a cozy place, alone with her friend, she made up her mind to share her secret.

"What do you think I should do?" she asked Teacher Zhang, after relating the story of Xining, her aunty, the Salar boy and the meeting just two days before with the young man's once promised bride.

He listened intently, not speaking until long after she had finished. He sat still, with his hands holding the empty bowl. The room was silent; the only sounds came from the soothing, monotonous tumbling of the boiling water in the kettle and the gentle steam escaping from its spout.

"I'll get some tea," said Chen Yu Hua taking the bowl and chopsticks from his hands.

"I think ... you should tell the Salar lady the whole story, Chen Yu Hua." At first he hesitated, as though he was not sure what advice to give her, but then he became more definite. "Put yourself in her place. Wouldn't *you* want to know the truth? Just think ... she still believes that her young man did not steal the food but she doesn't know exactly *what* happened. It must be terrible to always wonder."

He took the mug from Chen Yu Hua's hand, touching her fingers lightly. It was like a shock of electricity for him, but she never even felt it.

"Do you really think so?"

"Yes ... and the fact that you were the one person to have talked with her young man, to know how lovingly he spoke of his girl back in Hua Long County. I think this would give her great comfort."

He blew gently at the large green leaves floating round and round on top of the hot water in his cup until they settled to the bottom. "I hope you're not thinking all this was your fault."

She was now looking straight into his eyes. He knew she was searching for answers. He wanted to touch her hand, to take away the guilt she was feeling, to hold her in his arms. He just wanted to touch her but he wouldn't dare.

"I feel so bad," she whispered, "I keep seeing him running out into that freezing cold night ... the Salar lady might blame me." She shivered slightly, just thinking about it.

"If I were this lady." He stopped talking in mid-sentence, enchanted by the young teacher. Light from the tiny 15-watt bulb illuminated her beautiful face and, like the subtle glow of a candle, spilled along her black hair, catching the butterfly clips, and caressing the amber skin of her cheeks where the shadows of her lashes lay. She moved her head and licked her lips ever so slightly and with her dark eyes stared, he felt, into his soul. He leaned forward and said softly, "I would never blame you ... I would only think how compassionate you were towards a stranger ... that you tried your best to save my young man."

He couldn't help it; he reached over and smoothed her hair. She did not move or blink. He doubted if she even noticed he was reaching for her. Touching her. Loving her.

"Perhaps you should tell her everything you just told me," he sighed.

Chen Yu Hua nodded and sipped her tea.

"Thank you," she said, "I'm glad I have you for my friend."

They sat for another hour drinking hot water and gossiping about school, and the plans each one had for their future. They even did a few lessons in English ... *cha*—tea; *kuai-zi*—chopsticks and *shu*—book, and laughed together until it was a sensible and respectable hour for Teacher Zhang to leave.

We had such a wonderful evening. I love you and want to marry you. I want to kiss your mouth and hold you in my arms and take care of you. I want to be with you forever. You are my idol, my soul mate. You are so clever and beautiful and full of ideas and versatile. You are honest and straightforward and I know we would be happy together ... is what Teacher Zhang really wanted to tell Teacher Chen as he said goodnight at the door. But he just said goodnight, and went home to write his thoughts in a letter instead. Tomorrow, he told himself, he would deliver it to her room.

The next day Chen Yu Hua decided she must talk with the Salar lady.

There was no trouble finding the house. A surprised LiLi answered the soft knocking; could she please come in and stay for awhile, LiLi had asked, but Chen Yu Hua declined the invitation, being in no mood for chit-chat. She only wanted to talk with the lady who had visited her school a couple of days before.

What a strange situation. She did not even know the name of the Salar lady yet they were about to share a tragic story of sadness, love, horror, death and guilt.

"I'm here." The Salar lady appeared at the door. "My name is Xia Lan."

"Could you please come for a walk with me?" said Chen Yu Hua, "I have something important I want to tell you."

Together they followed a well-traveled path along the riverbank, winding their way under trees heavy with fresh new buds.

"I love spring. Don't you, Xia Lan?" At least now she could call the lady by name.

They walked slowly over a footbridge spanning a swift narrow stream, past an outcropping of ragged granite rocks, and paused to bow three times at a tiny wooden prayer temple that had an offering of cut flowers, still fresh and blooming, lying at its base. Reaching a stone bench positioned for the best view of the river, they sat down together; two young women bonded forever by a tale of woe.

"I'm so glad you told me," the Salar lady said, through tears streaming unchecked from those strangely beautiful eyes. She did not bother to wipe her cheeks as she spoke. "Both our families will be happy to hear this ... we knew he was no thief and could not understand why he was in that house ... unless, he knew someone who lived there. Now we know it was you. Thank you for trying to help him and thank you for clearing his good name. We're so grateful to you."

The Salar lady by the name of Xia Lan hugged her new friend. "We will always remember you," she promised.

That evening when she returned home, Chen Yu Hua found a letter pushed under her door. She looked at it, puzzled at first, as it bore no stamp, but then she recognized the graceful handwriting. She put it carefully on her desk and started the stove fire for her evening meal. Chen Yu Hua had never received a letter in her life. She was hoping her father would write to her before she had to leave Dong Feng, but she supposed they were too busy at home. She looked at the letter again and wondered why Teacher Zhang was writing to her.

She poured the hot noodles into a bowl, opened the letter and started to read.

To My Darling Chen Yu Hua

We had such a wonderful evening. I love you and want to marry you. I want to kiss your mouth ...

It was a few minutes before she realized what the contents of the letter meant. She read it again. She sat down on the bed, with the letter dangling from one hand, unable to believe what Teacher Zhang had written. It was awful. A sick, perverted, obscene letter and she threw it into the stove fire at once, and lay on her bed and wept.

How could he have written such filth? How could he?

She did not understand they were words of love. He loved her and wanted to tell her how he felt.

Back home in Xunhua she had lived a very sheltered life and didn't realize how immature she really was. She knew nothing of love, sex or men, or the feelings men and women could have for one another. As a young child she was undernourished and delicate, substantiating the fact she hadn't even started to menstruate yet and wouldn't do so until she turned eighteen, another year away.

Middle school had also left its imprint on her. Any relationship between a boy and girl was regarded as indecent; in fact, they were told if a girl shook hands with a boy she would become pregnant. Boys and girls did not even talk with one another for fear of being accused by other students of having loose morals.

So here she was, perplexed and humiliated, her emotions running wild, blaming herself for enticing, even encouraging Teacher Zhang to feel free to write those lewd words. But what disheartened her the most and made her truly sad, was having to end a relationship with a good friend, one she thought she could trust. Chen Yu Hua did not touch the bowl of noodles, did not take off her clothes, she just turned over in bed and slept. It was a fitful sleep and once during the night she thought she heard knocking but she ignored it. "Whoever it is … they will go away," she thought.

She never spoke to Teacher Zhang Qi about the letter or their friendship for the rest of her stay in Dong Feng and, indeed, never heard from him again.

I always regretted missing the Longyang trip, not so much for the power station but for what happened afterwards. On the way back to Xining, someone pointed to a Tibetan yurt, a brilliant white tent with broad black stripes, on the distant horizon. Bill described how secluded and lonely it seemed, framed against dark clouds while the wind curled around it, ripping through the prairie grasses, driving dust into the air. "Let's take Mr. Weigand to visit the Tibetan home," said Young Liu. Driver Zhang bounced the old station wagon across the rough field to the yurt, startling the herder and his family and a vicious looking mangy black dog straining at its collar on the end of a long chain.

"I told them there was no way I was getting out of the car," said Bill, "the one vaccine we didn't get before we left Canada was a rabies shot!" After some persuasive talk in Tibetan dialect from

Miss Chen, who was frightened to death of animals, the snarling dog was dragged back and tethered closer to the post.

The yurt was a network of poles and ropes supporting felt panels of woven yak hair assembled into a tent structure large enough to house a Tibetan family. The herder coaxed his shy young wife to come out and be introduced to the unexpected guests. She was dressed in a long black skirt, white blouse and a white-fringed scarf pulled back and tied at the nape of her neck. Two long braids of black hair, held together on the ends with ribbons, flung down her back and fell over one shoulder. At first she was nervous to meet a foreigner, but soon smiled and held the door flap open.

"The lady wants you to enter. Tibetan women keep very clean homes and are proud of them," said Miss Chen.

The roomy yak hair yurt was indeed clean and tidy. The black stove and its steaming aluminum kettle were polished to perfection. It was hard to believe that the dirt floor, brushed smooth as wood, had been rough prairie not long ago. The atmosphere relaxed as the hostess passed around bowls of boiled yak milk. Miss Chen translated stories about the foreigner and his distant land called Canada and Bill asked questions about life on the rugged plateau.

Miss Chen told me later that when they left the tent and waved goodbye to the lady, she was reminded of a song written by the famous Beijing composer, Wang Luo Bin, who had spent many years working in Qinghai. He admired the Tibetans and wrote songs reflecting their way of life.

"He was even put in jail in Qinghai after Liberation," she said, "where he wrote these words,"

In a land far away

On the grasslands of Qinghai

Lives a beautiful girl

When he passes her tent

He turns to gaze at her then leaves with a heavy heart

Her small round face is like the morning sun

Her bright eyes are like the silver moon at night

He would give up his wealth to become a herdsman
to be near her
He would look into that beautiful face each day
And caress the golden hem of her robe each night
He would be a lamb and follow her to the ends of the earth
Let her touch him gently with the thongs of her small leather whip
On the grasslands of Qinghai
Far away lives a beautiful girl
He turns and sighs and in his heart remembers

Chen Yu Hua knew Bill and I were fascinated with Tibetan culture. One day she surprised us by bringing a young English-speaking Tibetan man to our home. He was born in Tibet but took his schooling in Xining and we spent the afternoon entranced as he told dramatic tales about the history of his people.

"We have lived on this land forever," he said. "We called ourselves Tibetans and our land Amdo. Later, when foreigners arrived, they called us Golocks. They even named our beautiful horses … Heavenly Horses. He told us how these horses had been at the heart of poems and paintings ever since, and about the most famous horse sculpture in China, found in an ancient excavation in Xian. It was a magnificent racing stallion, its head up, tail flowing in the wind, balanced perfectly on one rear hoof, and riding on the back of a small fish.

"I have a story about a Han invasion deep into the heart of the Tibetan-Qinghai Plateau that happened at least two thousand years ago," said our new friend, "Do you want to hear it? It's a bit of a sad story."

"Of course," we said. In this part of the world legends and myths were plentiful and intriguing, as well as questionable.

"They came to conquer the Golock Queen and her lands. When she realized her people were not strong enough to defend themselves against the powerful Chinese invaders, she devised a plan. She knew the only way to destroy the advancing soldiers was to lead them up Kunlun, the sacred mountain. The Chinese army followed closely behind the queen and her small group of guards, up, up to the snows of the mountain, never once suspecting she was on her own mission of doom. The higher they climbed, the deeper the ice and snow became. The colder the winds. When the Chinese general suddenly realized his men would perish if they went any further it was too late. They had gone too far. Every last person froze to death. The sacred mountain claimed them all … the queen, her guards, the general and his army and, although the Queen of the Golocks met a sad fate, she had saved her people."

"Is this a true story?" we asked.

Our friend flashed a great wide smile of satisfaction like "you can believe it or not." I couldn't find anyone to verify or deny the story so it must remain his legend.

Compared with the isolation of the plains in the past, ongoing changes have created better living conditions, health standards and education for the Tibetans of Qinghai. They are less nomadic, building permanent homes for their families and shelters for their animals. The Tibetans we met had television and rode motorcycles, but they were happiest when driving their herds far afield, living in their yurts, and attending grassland gatherings, horse racing and feasting, drinking Qinke wine and, above all, singing and dancing.

A lovely line from a Tibetan folk song says it all, 'Mountain, please move back one step to give us enough room to dance.'

eighteen

中国

Chen Yu Hua was floating on air. She was going to live her dream. After passing her entrance exams for Qinghai Normal School, she was settling in for three years of intensive study in Xining. Chen Yu Hua began classes in September, 1978.

She majored in English, and was taught by Chinese "English" teachers who could barely speak the language. The students learned from textbooks filled with words and sentences about revolution and politics. They recited pattern drills over and over again, concentrating on the grammar structure of sentences, taking each one apart and analyzing it for adjectives, verbs, pronouns and prepositions. She also studied five other subjects: Chinese language, politics, calligraphy, music and physical education.

Xining had grown in the eight years since she first arrived to live with her aunt. Apartment blocks were springing up in a beehive of reconstruction. The terror and fear of Mao's China was steadily giving way to the optimism of a New China and the country was stabilizing and rebuilding under Deng Xiaoping's guidance. It was exciting for Chen Yu Hua to be young and living in Qinghai's capital city. When she found out that Uncle Xiao Zhan had moved his family to Hunan province she was glad. Her heart was filled with bittersweet memories and she never really wanted to see them again.

College life in Xining was the same as college life anywhere. Girls and boys were well aware of each other and dating and friendships were blossoming on the campus. With thoughts of Teacher Zhang still fresh in her mind, Chen Yu Hua repelled any advances made by young men harboring romantic ideas. She was going to wait until she finished her education and had her life in order before she would find a mate. He would have to be a scholarly man, sophisticated, thoughtful and caring, with a good sense of humor. She would choose him and he would choose her. There would be no room for matchmakers or interfering parents in her life. Chen Yu Hua was pretty and intelligent. She did not go unnoticed by men, especially the ones looking for these qualities in a wife, for it was not only the young women who felt pressured to get married. Every family wanted their young men married and settled down by the time they were twenty five. Since the One Child Policy had been put into effect, the desire to have that special *little pearl* for a grandchild couldn't come soon enough.

But, before long, Chen Yu Hua was being courted by a handsome Fine Arts student, who had a rather distinguished reputation in school for enjoying the company of women. He was confident and very fond of himself and had never been rebuffed by any of the young ladies he desired. When he offered Chen Yu Hua a ticket for a movie film she took it. Of course, he knew she would. Every girl liked to see a movie at the downtown cinema, especially when being escorted by the Fine Arts Man.

Later, Chen Yu Hua thought about the upcoming movie. It was definitely one she wanted to see, but … "I'm very sorry, I can't go to the cinema with you," she told her surprised admirer, stretching her small hand toward him with the ticket standing straight up between her thumb and forefinger. "It was very thoughtful of you to ask me, but really, I'm too busy."

She knew if she had accepted the invitation, her name would be romantically linked to the artist and she could not bear the thought of students gossiping about her. They might even suggest she would speak of love with him and that would be embarrassing. Besides, she didn't trust him.

Chen Yu Hua's way of turning a cold face to male students made trouble for her when a teacher named Pei, a graduate from the prestigious Lanzhou University in the next province, came to teach at the Normal School. He was creative and had new and imaginative ways of teaching English. Chen Yu Hua found his classes stimulating and his oral English far superior to the other teachers. She asked questions every chance she got and challenged him on pronunciation and grammar. Teacher Pei was soon attracted to the studious girl who had spent a year serving in a country school and, at eighteen, was one of the oldest students in his class. At first Chen Yu Hua was naively unaware of the subtle changes occurring in their relationship. It was a normal teacher-student association as far as she was concerned. But as time went on she realized she was being singled out more and more with questions and discussions directed her way. His suggestive eye contact was becoming unnerving. Perhaps her classmates didn't notice but she most certainly did and began feeling ill at ease with Teacher Pei.

One day the leaders notified the students they were all going to be sent one hundred miles from Xining to a school-farm for one month. Teacher Pei was put in charge of assigning jobs to the students. Only three out of the thirty five students would be assigned to the dining hall, cooking meals for the group, and the rest would work in the fields.

Chen Yu Hua was disappointed when she heard she was chosen along with two other girls to do kitchen detail. This caused grumbling among the students. Perhaps it was a real grievance or simple jealousy but they reminded the new teacher that Chen Yu Hua was a leader, a member of the School League Committee. They said because of this she should set a good example by being sent to the fields to labor in the sun and rain with other students. But Teacher Pei would not change his mind and insisted she work in the kitchen.

Chen Yu Hua soon found out why.

He took every opportunity to be alone with her, stand near her and try to corner her and make suggestive remarks. She wondered if the other two girls were going through the same thing. She was miserable to think of her classmates toiling in the fields while she dodged Teacher Pei around the kitchen. She worked hard, making delicious meals for the students, trying to appease them as well as her own guilt for not being with them in the fields. Teacher Pei never let up, confronting her boldly every chance he got and going so far as proposing marriage.

"When you graduate we can go back to Lanzhou together," he told her, "it's only a few hours away and we can live at the university. You could easily apply for a job as a middle school teacher."

He stood with his arm across the open door, blocking her way as she tried to carry a tray of bowls to the dining room. She was disgusted with him. His grinning, swarthy face was only inches from hers and if he thought she would hang her head and avert her eyes, he was mistaken. She was angry.

"Excuse me!" she said defiantly. Slowly, he took his arm away.

That afternoon he left the farm and went back to Xining. Chen Yu Hua was sent to the fields to work in the hot sun for the rest of the month, but not before a meeting was called and all her classmates unfairly criticized her for having a bourgeois attitude and avoiding heavy work. She could say nothing, not even to defend herself. She could only stare at the floor and keep silent. This was the way in China during the Cultural Revolution.

Three years passed quickly and her schooling was finished. Now she would be going to teach somewhere in the province. In theory, teachers were expected to go back to their hometowns to work, but some found ways to beat the system and choose their own schools, usually by *guanxi* (back door). Someone who needed a favor, perhaps a better job or help for a relative, waited until after dark to go to the back door of the home of the person expected to give the favor, usually a cadre or some other official in power. Gifts of money, liquor, jewelry, clothing or anything of value would be presented in secret.

Chen Yu Hua had no back door money and no one to help her stay in the capital city. She wanted desperately to teach in Xining, but knew it would be impossible. On the eve of declaring her name for the list assignment, she was surprised with a visit from the wife of a very important leader.

"I understand you want to stay in Xining, Teacher Chen," said the older woman pleasantly, removing her new grey wool coat with brass buttons back from her shoulders. "I have a proposal for you and if you do what I ask I will make sure you will stay in Xining …

and teach in any school you like."

Chen Yu Hua was skeptical but listened to what the woman had to say.

"Would you come with me to meet my sister's son?" she asked, nodding her head questioningly. "I'm sure he would like to meet a girl but he is just too timid. You won't be expected to marry him right away or anything like that but perhaps just keep a relationship going with him for a time ... to get him out of his shyness. You know."

Chen Yu Hua was curious, and went to the flat with the woman. If she didn't go she would forever wonder about the young man and it might be worth her while to meet him. This is how much she wished to stay in Xining.

The flat was quite modern. There were lace curtains on the windows and a coat of dark burgundy paint covering the bare concrete floor. A beige wool rug with a floral border pattern lay at the entrance to the sitting room. This intrigued her. She had never actually walked on a soft rug before and could not imagine how it felt. She hesitated for a moment, then stepped lightly onto the red and cream, purple and pink flowers lying at her feet. It was springy and pleasant to the senses.

"Come ... come," beckoned the cadre's wife and Chen Yu Hua followed the lady into one of the bedrooms. "We have to visit him in here," whispered the lady, "he refuses to come out to meet you."

A young man, who looked no more than seventeen, sat on the edge of the bed. Chen Yu Hua could hear a swishing sound as he rubbed his hands together anxiously. There were no lights and it took a few moments for her eyes to get used to the gloom. The room was clean and exceptionally neat. A small poster of Mao hung on the wall near two large calendars, both of fluffy white kittens playing in wicker baskets, one from the previous year.

The aunty introduced the nephew, giving his name and age. Surprise! He was twenty-three.

"Hello," said Chen Yu Hua, but he never responded.

She thought, poor man, how unattractive and shy he looked, with his puckery pink mouth, little round glasses and his soft round face. He did not stand up to greet her and she wondered how tall he was. Then she noticed that the soles of his slippers barely brushed the floor as he swung his legs back and forth.

"Sit down, please," said the woman, "here beside my nephew."

She sat on the bed beside the young man. He flinched. She thought it was probably the first time he had been close to a girl who was not a member of his family, and he shifted away slightly, never once looking at Chen Yu Hua. She felt sorry for him; he must be embarrassed and want no part of this business for sure.

Another woman came out of nowhere and introduced herself as his mother. The two women took turns expounding the finer points of the nervous man, who looked very much like he wanted to bolt. Acting as though he wasn't in the room, they gestured toward him. They listed his amazing qualities like an object put up for auction, and talked about his responsible job, what a fine honest person he was, and his great strength of character. "But ... he has one small fault ... maybe, just a little too shy ... I'm sure that is not a *bad* fault," cooed his mother, hesitantly patting the top of his stooped head. They assured Chen Yu Hua she would have a secure future if she considered this unappealing, shy little man for a husband. "She could work in Xining and later they would be married."

"With a big dowry," clicked his mother, nodding her head and raising her eyebrows. Surely this was an offer no woman in her right mind could reject.

Both women paused for a breath and smiled. They reminded Chen Yu Hua of a couple of Cheshire cats, like the one she once saw in an illustration. She pictured it in her mind, "Alice in Wonderland". Yes, she liked that book.

It was getting hot in the bedroom and the women's high-pitched voices irritated her nerves. The young man was sweating. She imagined him sitting there like a fat little pot bubbling away with unpleasant liquids running out of every pore.

It was time to go.

She abruptly stood up.

"I'm sorry," she announced, " I don't want to marry anyone right now ... I plan to go to Beijing in a couple of years, to the Foreign Languages University."

The two women stopped talking. The young man twisted his head towards Chen Yu Hua and for the first time he stared at her. A startled look crossed his red face.

The women followed her out of the dark room, crossed the polished burgundy floor and the springy cream floral rug with the beautiful flowers, and stayed close behind as she left through the front door and out to the busy street.

"I hope you will reconsider our proposal," pleaded one.

"We thought we gave you enough security for your future," whined the other.

"We thought you wanted to stay in Xining," they both shouted after her. "It doesn't matter," Chen Yu Hua threw back. "Besides, I don't think your nephew even likes women."

The next morning she was presented with her assignment sheet and the words *Assigned to Xunhua* were stamped clearly across the top. "My hometown," she exhaled.

She packed her simple bedding in a wooden box along with her clothes and school books, and caught the long distance bus for the wearying trip back to her father's house. What a pity, she thought. Her chance to work in the city had slipped away from her. Would her future always be under the control of her strict father?

Unhappy and dispirited, she stared out the bus window through trickles of rain crossing the glass in diagonal streams. She closed her eyes.

"Now I will jump into the fire pit again," she sighed.

She didn't feel the rocking, grating motion of the bus as it passed the airport, then the Muslim section of the city with the Great Mosque, and turned sharply onto the highway heading due south to Xunhua. She didn't know that the rain had stopped. She only knew she was heartsick.

A few miles from the turn-off the bus was flagged down and pulled over to the side of the road by army personnel. Chen Yu Hua soon realized what was happening. Charging out of the haze of road dust and framed in the eerie orange shafts of the morning sun came army stake trucks loaded with soldiers. They stood ramrod straight in the speeding vehicles. From under black-visored hats their eyes were shielded from the world by dark glasses. Cross-belts dazzled white against their dark formal uniforms, and white-gloved hands clutched long rifles. The first trucks raced by as she realized the next vans in the convoy were filled with prisoners. She could see them, sitting close together, stiff and fearful, with eyes cast down. They were going to Xining to be sentenced for their misdeeds; some to jail and some to the place of execution. The last truck to pass held more soldiers. As fast as they came they were suddenly gone, leaving a peculiar stillness and a soft cloud of powdery pink dust drifting across the road and into the fields.

She thought sadly about the young Salar boy and the tears came again.

Our favorite retreat in Xining was the Botanical Gardens. Whenever we wanted peace and quiet, we hailed a taxi, showing the driver a card with the address of the gardens in Chinese characters and off we would go for a few hours of solitude.

Bill always carried a series of "get there and get home" cards. They were the size of a business card and spelled out in Chinese and English the addresses of our bank, post office, department stores and favorite hotels and restaurants. Miss Chen never missed the chance to have Bill show off his string of "get there" cards to the amusement of the leaders.

Soon after our arrival in Xining we had been invited to visit the gardens and have lunch with Deputy Director Yang Ming Da.

"The architecture of the Xining Botanical Gardens is modeled after the 'Su Hang Style' of Suzhou and Hangzhou Cities," translated Miss Chen as we walked along a stone path through the Moon Gate to a small luminous lake. Surrounding the lake were flowering shrubs and smooth topped Karst rocks looking every bit like a Lilliputian mountain range.

We stopped in pavilions containing hand-stitched silk tapestries and Chinese potted landscapes called Penjing, an art similar to Japanese Bonsai.

Famous in China for centuries, ingenious craftsman create what is described as "soundless poetry"; miniature reproductions of scenes from nature in a rhythm of plants, rocks and water, all living in a small pot.

The lunch table was laid with plates of fresh lettuce, tomatoes, cucumbers, Western bread, margarine and chopsticks. Tender eight-inch long mutton ribs were stacked on a platter.

"Please, please," said our hosts, smiling and waving toward the food. They handed Bill and me two dripping wet plates. It wasn't until much later we learned it was good manners to serve guests wet dishes to show they had been freshly washed.

"They say this is for a Western sandwich," said Miss Chen, sweeping her hand over the bread.

"Yes, I know, but I think I need a knife," I whispered.

"A knife? For what?" she burst out.

"I need to spread the margarine and cut the tomato."

Mass confusion. No one had a knife. A young man suddenly jumped up from the table. He dashed across the grass and disappeared behind perfectly trimmed shrubs bursting with red blossoms. He was back in a flash, holding a yellow Exacto knife. "OK?" He grinned.

I cut the tomatoes, ignoring the faint smell of gasoline from the knife and shook untreated water from the crisp lettuce, praying we wouldn't get "Asian stomach". I remembered the dire warnings we received before we left for China: "Don't drink the water and don't sing in the shower." The tender mutton was delicious, after we mastered the art of eating the long ribs which almost curled up to our ears, and the sandwiches were pretty good, reminding us of home.

Like a lot of things I didn't know about the Chinese people, I didn't realize how much they loved to dance. Kids in school are taught traditional folk songs and folk dances, but when they're older they learn to dance to Western music. Ballroom dancing was taken seriously, as were the rumba, tango and cha-cha. Rock music, as in the West, was all the rage with teenagers in China. Their music idols were from Hong Kong and Taiwan, and once when I showed the students pictures of stars in a magazine from Hong Kong they reacted as kids do anywhere ... "oh, I love Liu Dehua ... oh, Li Ming." And the girls would swoon.

Waltzing under the afternoon sun in People's Park was something we had never experienced before. The English teachers from Number Fourteen Middle School invited us to join them as music blared from giant loudspeakers and men and women of all ages danced the day away.

Bill was hugely popular. He danced with teachers, young ladies, old ladies, and anyone who wanted to fox trot around the concrete floor while I relaxed under the trees. I wasn't prepared when one of the teachers, Miss New York, asked me to dance. I stammered, "I'm not a very good dancer and I'd rather just sit and watch," so I realized that women dance with each other. I often thought about that afternoon when I didn't want to dance with those gracious ladies. Did I believe I was too sophisticated? In Canada I hadn't seen women dance together in years, probably since some wedding or country school event. So why was I so prudish? After all, in the early 50s I "Rocked Around The Clock" with my girl friends. Perhaps it was my age or Protestant upbringing, but I showed poor judgment that day.

There was a lovely naiveté surrounding the people we knew. Young men often walked down the street with their arms entwined or holding hands; women danced together and were not embarrassed to ask men to dance. In fact, they would go down the line asking each one in turn until a willing partner was found. They didn't take offence or feel rebuffed. No one in China thought anything different about such things, but I had been sensitized and politically corrected and now, wearing my hang-ups, I had missed an afternoon of dancing in the park. But I had learned my lesson. "Never again," I told myself and, at the next Commission staff party, I had a fun time dancing with the women as well as the men.

Also puzzling for me, was the habit of students searching out English names for themselves. At first I discouraged them, until I realized it was like a game. One day in class some students asked me if I'd take time to listen to their new names. Most names were the standard everyday Susans and Peters but when the boys came up with Satan, Dogma and Danger, I knew their knowledge of the English language was severely limited.

I once asked Miss Chen if she had an English name.

"Yes."

She surprised me with this answer, as she never referred to any nickname other than Jade Flower. "My husband sometimes calls me Scarlett," she said, alluding to the Gone With the Wind heroine. "You know who I mean by Scarlett?"

"I can see why he chose the name," I smiled. "She is very beautiful and a strong character in the book, but you certainly aren't so spoiled and self-serving as Scarlett O'Hara."

When we went for dinner at the home of Lian Hua, one of the managers of the Qinghai Machinery Co., we met a pretty fourteen-year-old girl who was starting English classes at school. She fairly begged me for an English name and, before the evening was over, I had to think up an appropriate name for our young friend.

"You look very much like a lovely Jennifer," I said proudly. "It's one of my favorite names."

"Chjen ... Jhen ..." she stammered.

Great, I thought, I gave her a name too hard to pronounce. After that I was smarter; when I was asked to bestow an English name on someone, I wrote down five or ten and let them choose their own.

nineteen

中国

In the summer of 1981 Chen Yu Hua returned to her hometown and reported for work at the new Minorities Girls' School. Of the many minorities in the area, it was mainly the Tibetan, Hui and Salar farmers who sent their daughters to attend high school. Previously it had been either too costly or against the wishes of the village elders, but when the government initiated a program to subsidize food, lodging and tuition, many more young girls were allowed to attend classes.

Although she lived in school residence, Chen Yu Hua visited her family home as often as she could. One day, after she had been home for almost a year, she was walking up the path to her father's house just as a man and woman were leaving. They looked vaguely familiar and she casually nodded her head in polite greeting as they passed. But the older couple took more than a casual interest in Chen Yu Hua. They smiled at her and looked her over closely, memorizing every little detail about the twenty-two-year old teacher. Her hair, her teeth, her eyes and how tall she was. The size of her feet. Everything!

"Mother, who were those people I met leaving the courtyard just now?"

Jia Ying never looked up. She was too busy mixing dough for the *baozi* and steamed buns. It was Ching Ming, the festival of grave sweeping, and she was preparing a feast for the family. Ching Ming fell on the fifth day of the fourth month of the Chinese calendar. The festival would mark spring and re-birth, when the land covered itself with a carpet of green, and honorable ancestors lay in waiting for praise and prayers. It was the time for the families to visit the gravesites early in the morning, sweep the graves clean, and place a shovel full of fresh soil on each one. They would burn incense and yellow papers symbolizing money and leave offerings of food. From old to young, all generations took part in this kowtowing ceremony, spending the day praying, crying and bleating poetic words in praise of the admirable deeds once performed by their illustrious ancestors.

Jia Ying never stopped mixing and kneading the dough as Chen Yu Hua went on questioning her.

"Who were those two people?" she asked again.

"I think ... they are friends of your father," said Jia Ying, still not bothering to look at her daughter.

Chen Yu Hua thought for a moment; she had seen them before. Her face lit up briefly and then she scowled.

"Those people are go-betweens, aren't they?" She confronted her mother. "What are they doing here?"

Over the past year, the conversation in the family had centered on matchmakers and marriage. After Spring Festival a few weeks earlier, she thought her father had eased up his search for a mate for his strong-willed eldest daughter, but she had resisted all the local boys and now her father had a new idea. Perhaps if he brought down a "city man" she would be more amenable to, or at least think about, marriage.

Chen Yu Hua was furious. She hurriedly left the house with her mother calling after her, pleading for her to come back. "Your father will be angry if you do not come to the grave sweeping. It will spoil the day for all of us, not having the whole family together."

Chen Yu Hua, who wanted only to be well educated, choose her own partner and career, and be the independent woman her father had raised her to be, never turned around.

When an angry Jian Pin heard about this incident he sent his youngest son to demand that Chen Yu Hua behave like an obedient daughter and come home. She must go with them to the graves of their honorable ancestors. No one had ever dared to disregard their duty to attend grave sweeping, but the pleading fell on deaf ears and the family went without her.

Later in the evening, long after the families had finished brushing branches and leaves from the worn headstones, Chen Yu Hua walked in the moonlight to the hillside. There was not a whisper of wind on the night air, and remains of food and drink and pale ashes lay unmoving on the ground. Following the ancient path, she came to the Chen family's ancestral graves, washed in shadows, solitary and still. This ghostly place gave her no fear. She put steamed buns, some gruel, a cup of alcohol and pieces of dried fruit on the freshly swept graves, and she burned the yellow fake money and incense sticks.

She stood alone, a tiny figure with eyes closed and hands pressed palm to palm. Bowing three times to the silent graves, she prayed to her honorable ancestors. A vaporous light seemed to pour over her; she felt serene and in harmony with herself and the world around her. This young woman's life was not wrapped up in a structured religion ... not Christian or Muslim or Buddhist. Not pagan or cult. Chen Yu Hua's religion had no formal name. Within her soul was an overwhelming belief that she should lead her life with as much goodness as possible.

Slowly, she walked back to her room in the school dormitory. Tonight she had spoken to the spirits of her family ... her people ... her honorable ancestors and she knew in her heart they understood.

Chen Yu Hua never planned to stay in her hometown for more than one year but she found herself starting her second year of teaching at the Minorities School. She enjoyed her work; it was interesting and the students were fun, but she was still determined to go back to Xining. It would be almost impossible to transfer; even married couples that lived in separate towns had little chance of being assigned to work together. Her only hope would be by the "back door" but still she had no money or expensive gifts for that approach. She would have to wait.

"Chen Yu Hua," said one of her father's close friends. "I have someone I want you to meet. The man is from Xining; I think you will like him. His name is Gu Yong." Her father was nowhere to be seen this day. He didn't have the nerve to suggest the name of one more eligible bachelor to his daughter, so he asked his friend to do it for him.

In the second year of living in her hometown, the "city man" came into her life. She was told he worked for a district government. He was one year older than she, had two younger sisters and was the only son of a widow. "Of course, his education is high school graduate," said her father's friend, smiling with a cigarette between his teeth, "and he does have a very excellent position with the government ... no doubt someday he will be a cadre ... and earn much money."

The city man came to the house to meet Chen Yu Hua. She scrutinized him thoroughly, looking into his fat round flat face. He was slightly taller than she was, and a bit overweight. He wasn't exactly the man of her dreams but he seemed very self-assured, with good manners and a cheerful disposition; most respectful towards her parents. She never got the chance to say a word to him directly. Her father and other adults did all the talking: the questions, the answers; all done around her and over her head, and she felt invisible. She wanted to scream and point at herself and say, "I'm here. You can talk to me. You don't have to pretend I'm in the other room. I'm right here," but she smiled and gritted her teeth and reminded herself she would always have the last word no matter what.

Gu Yong spent the next few days visiting as many relatives and close friends of the Chen family as he could. He was not shy in mentioning the fact that he was looking for a wife and Chen Yu Hua was high on his list. Soon people took it for granted that Chen Jian Pin had finally found the right man for his oldest daughter, and a wedding was just around the corner.

Gu Yong sent a matchmaker bearing gifts of cakes, candies, walnuts, Chinese dates, liquor and a block of tea, appropriately called "matchmaking tea" to Chen Yu Hua's parents. He knew they would be pleased and he waited patiently for their answer. Soon he received a gift of dates and walnuts confirming their acceptance of him.

Again, Gu Yong sent the matchmaker to the Chen home with gifts of clothes. A red wool sweater, the color of the Chinese flag, a blue padded vest, embroidered slippers and a scarf to match the vest. Chen Yu Hua was impressed but she left the clothes folded neatly in the box. She was not jumping into marriage just because her father was partial to this man.

A second private meeting was arranged for Chen Yu Hua and Gu Yong to get to know one another. They spent the afternoon together, walking and sitting on a bench overlooking the *Huang He*. They talked generally about their hobbies, their likes and dislikes and their families and jobs.

Chen Yu Hua was disappointed when Gu Yong told her he greatly admired the leaders and cadres; she admired intellectuals and professional people. She began to realize he was a show-off and a self-serving man with a huge ego, and she hated the way his mouth turned down at the corners when he mentioned people or situations that irritated him. He tried to touch her hand once but she quickly drew it away, repelled by his short thick fingers; nails buffed to perfection. He reminded her of a spoiled child that pouted when he didn't get his own way.

Inside the house, the family tittered and gossiped and began putting together big plans for the first Chen wedding. It would be splendid. Jian Pin had money set aside and he would use it for a grand party. All the relatives and many friends would come. There would be food and drink and he would hire a Tibetan carriage with red and gold ribbons to carry the happy couple to the local hotel. He would even pay for the best room for his first daughter on her wedding night.

"I'm happy they're getting along so well," Chen Yu Hua's aunt speculated, "They make such a lovely couple." She sighed, clasping her hands together under her chin, thinking about the marriage plans.

The aunt did not know and neither did her mother or Jian Pin or the matchmaker, but after the visit and all the talking was over, Chen Yu Hua had to admit … she just didn't much like the city man.

The next day her father sent word to the school asking her to come for a visit after classes; he wanted to talk to her. It was a busy day and she was giving important exams to the students. What did he want to talk with her about? Now she had to rush home early to see him. It was an inconvenience but she would not disobey her father.

When Chen Yu Hua arrived home that afternoon she found fourteen people, mostly family and a few good friends sitting around chatting, playing Mahjong and drinking alcohol. It was a festive atmosphere and her mother was setting out a huge banquet table. She was puzzled and wondered what the celebration was all about. Gu Yong was seated comfortably with a glass of liquor in his hand and he raised it in salute to Chen Yu Hua as she came into the room. He went over to her saying he wanted to talk seriously.

"We must plan a formal dinner honoring our engagement," he said confidently. "Many things have to be arranged, the Chinese calendar has to be consulted and a favorable date set for the wedding."

Chen Yu Hua was too surprised to answer him. She hurried out to the kitchen where her mother was cooking vegetables in a large sizzling pan.

"What's this all about?" she yelled at Jia Ying, "No one told me I was to be engaged today ... no one asked me if I was satisfied with this city man. Don't I have a say in my own life? Am I just supposed to love him? Well I don't even like him."

Jia Ying put the hot pan aside and turned to her daughter. It was the first time she showed sympathy for Chen Yu Hua's frustration.

"I'm sorry," she said softly, and pulled back a strand of hair from her daughter's cheek, "I'm not the head of this house ... I must keep silent, you know that."

This is what Chen Yu Hua did not want. She did not want to be like her mother; forever working, with no say in the lives of her children and no say in her own life. No fun, nothing to look forward to, ever accepting her fate ... *Just keep quiet until life is over and you are buried with your honorable ancestors.*

She hugged her mother and took a long breath. "I know, " she said, "I know."

Chen Yu Hua behaved herself through dinner for her mother's sake. She didn't smile or engage in any conversation with the city man, and she was barely civil to the happy gathering that was having great fun celebrating her engagement.

After dinner Gu Yong asked to walk her home and she agreed. Before they left she thanked her mother for the evening meal but never once did she look at her father; she was so hurt and angry with him for what he had done.

The "engaged couple" walked the fifteen minutes to the gates of her school dormitory in silence. Here Chen Yu Hua stopped and asked him to return the picture her father had given to the matchmaker. Gu Yong was surprised and fumbled in his leather bag, taking it out and holding it in his hand but not offering it to her.

"Why do you want it back?" he mumbled, afraid of what was coming next.

"Because I'm breaking off this relationship," she said forcefully, snatching the picture from his hand. He looked hurt and very sad. "We just started a relationship," he said, "how can you break it off so soon?"

"Because you and *my* parents have decided to arrange my life ... just like that," and she snapped her fingers in his face. "No one asked *me* if I wanted to have a relationship with anybody ... let alone *you*."

She ranted on and on about how she wasn't an object to be handed from her father to a city man, how she wanted to find her own husband and that Gu Yong should be looking elsewhere for a wife; they had nothing in common.

He followed her to her room and, as she unlocked the door, he stepped in with her. It was his turn to rant. He had come on a long-distance bus all the way from Xining. He thought she wanted to live in Xining. His mother was waiting to hear the good news that everything was arranged. His mother was happy with Chen Yu Hua. This would make her life easier as mothers-in-law had a lot to say about future daughters-in-law. Did she not think this was good? He had a good job, he had some money. What was the matter with her? She must have some feelings for him. How could she not have a little sympathy?

Chen Yu Hua was getting exasperated and beginning to dislike this man more and more. She wondered what she could say to convince him to leave her alone.

"I'm sorry, sympathy is not love," she said dramatically, "and I have to love a man before I marry him."

Suddenly he fell on his knees before her, he was pleading with her, his hands clasped ... *asking for mercy in that wheedling voice?*

She couldn't believe it. What kind of a man would get down on his knees and plead with a woman after she rejected him? Rejected him with as much energy as she had done. He looked foolish.

"I despise you," she shouted in embarrassment and fled out the door.

A few minutes later the city man had composed himself. He joined her outside. "We'll see how you explain this to your father." His voice was low and menacing. "I can't wait until he hears about this stupid tirade of yours."

He brushed by, trying to intimidate her. She stood straight with arms folded in the cold night, and met his scornful gaze without fear or shame or remorse at losing him. She decided she was a woman in control of her life and she was not for sale by her father or anyone else.

Before he turned to leave, he waved a threatening finger at her, hesitating for a moment as if he was too angry to speak. She squared her jaw and steadied her fiery look at him sensing his sudden uneasiness. He never said a word. There was nothing more he could say.

The next day Gu Yong left for Xining but not before he told the story of being rejected by a girl too proud and headstrong for her own good. He also asked the matchmaker to urge Chen Jian Pin to pressure his daughter into changing her mind and, "Oh, yes ... would they please return the gifts."

Chen Yu Hua was summoned to her father's house.

He flew into a rage when he saw her and scolded her the whole evening. Neither of them had dinner. He reminded her again and again what an ungrateful daughter she was and how the Chen family had "lost face" in the community. And she would have to return the gifts without his help, as he wanted nothing more to do with her or the matchmaker.

The angry embarrassing harangue was done in front of her mother and her siblings and she could only sit and listen in silence. It was the Chinese way.

When Jian Pin was through shouting, Chen Yu Hua carried the gifts to her dormitory and unpacked them. She was sick to find that a bottle of liquor had cracked and flooded the bottom of the box, soaking the expensive candies. Now what would she do? She had to return them to the matchmaker. She peeled the shiny gold paper imprinted with miniature exquisite scenes of happy lovers from each one, and set the candies on the back of the stove to dry. When they were not sticky anymore she smoothed out the papers and re-wrapped the candies. They looked like new, almost. She really didn't care. Chen Yu Hua was so sad and despondent at her father's words that she just left the gifts in the box and never touched them again.

Two months went by and one day her mother and father came to see her. They realized that Chen Yu Hua would never marry the city man and it fell on them to return the presents to the matchmaker. But before they left, her father told her there was a rumor that Gu Yong would seek reprisal. "I hear he is not a man to give up easily," said Jian Pin, "and I would keep my eyes open if I were you. He is still furious that he has lost face."

Although he warned her about the city man, Chen Yu Hua knew her father still blamed her for not accepting the proposal of marriage. He was angry with his rebel daughter and would remain cold to her for many years.

Not until she was married and had a child of her own was there a warm love between them again.

Our Miss Wei was in love.

She came to the house and in her wispy soft voice explained her feelings for a certain young man. Mr. Right, as she called him, was Zhan Jie and he worked at the Qinghai Electric Power Bureau.

He lived alone with his mother and was her sole supporter.

"You are the first people to hear about my husband to be ... yeah." Her smile was glowing.

"You're getting married?" I asked, surprised, "I thought you only just met him?"

"Yes ... since two months ... but now we have become engaged." She couldn't contain her happiness. "I will not have a diamond ring, of course, like you do in your country but I *feel* engaged."

We hugged her and wished her a long life with Young Zhan and said she would make a lovely bride.

"When will the wedding be?"

"I hope before you leave China. I want you both to be there."

The very next day I went with Miss Wei down West Street; she couldn't wait to show me a particular camera shop known for excellent wedding photography. She had this odd habit of walking with her shoulder pressed securely against my shoulder like she was giving me support as we strode in perfect unison.

We came to the newly renovated department store and stopped to look up at the second story windows. Several Western mannequins dressed in beautiful bridal gowns watched over the streets of Xining; frothy visions in creamy white lace and satin, with pearl beadwork, ribbons, rhinestone tiaras and veils with yards of netting. Each adorned with a bouquet of red roses.

All the mannequins looked like Western women and, even in the up-scale shops of Beijing, they had blonde or red hair.

"I'm going to open a new business here," I said, "I want to manufacture Chinese mannequins to show off Chinese clothes." But Miss Chen had once told me no one would buy them. Apparently the merchants wanted only Western mannequins in their windows. They even dressed them in the traditional Chinese *qipao*. In a country filled with beautiful women with lush black hair, the stores are decked out in rows of blonde and blue-eyed dressmaker's dummies.

Featured in the front window of the camera shop stood a blond mannequin wearing an elaborate white bridal gown.

"Does the camera shop sell wedding dresses too?' I asked.

Miss Wei explained that brides-to-be rented their gowns and fake silk bouquets and everything needed for a Western get-up. "But of course, we must wear red shoes," she added. "We always wear red shoes no matter what the dress looks like ... it is for good luck. I'll rent my gown at another shop closer to my home, but I want to have our photos taken here."

The walls in the gallery were filled with spectacular photos of brides and grooms in Western-style dress. This was a relatively new phenomenon. Although brides wore traditional red dresses for their Chinese ceremonies, they always posed for photos in Western dress about two weeks before the wedding. These impressive photos were then hung above the bed or some appropriate place in the young marrieds' new apartment.

Miss Wei planned her wedding according to Chinese tradition. Her parents would choose the month and day. But before this happened we witnessed a minor crisis in their love life when she visited our house one afternoon.

"Young Zhan and I aren't talking," she sniffed, tears welling up in her eyes. "We had a fight." She told us his mother didn't like her and made her nervous each time they were together. She would stare at Miss Wei's hands and feet, even her hair, ears and nose, studying them to find fault.

"In China the mother-in-law has a lot of say about the choice of woman her son will marry and his mother is making my life miserable ... she is making me feel second best. So I told Young Zhan that we were through ... I love him but I don't want to see him any more." By now she was sobbing. "If I don't come first in his life then I don't want to marry him." She blew her nose on the tissues I gave her. Appropriately, the box had a cartoon drawing of fluffy cotton balls with huge eyes dripping tears. "I saw him waiting for me on the street across from my office. He was staring at my window but I didn't let him see me ... I left by a side door and came straight to your house." More blowing. "What can I do?"

After consoling our friend as best we could, Bill sent her into our office to phone Young Zhan. "You won't sleep tonight if you don't talk this out with him."

A few minutes later she returned to the living room all smiles.

"Young Zhan says he will tell his mother that he loves me and I am number one. He says he has been waiting for someone just like me … he says I am half his soul," and she ran off to meet the love of her life for a noodle dinner in the market.

When we did meet Young Zhan, we were impressed. He was handsome and shy, and only had eyes for our Miss Wei. They made a perfect couple and we knew when the mother got over her initial fear of another woman in her son's life, they would all get along fine.

Unfortunately, we left Xining several months before Miss Wei had her wedding but she sent a letter with a detailed account of her big day.

"I was married on December 21," she wrote. "It was very early … 6:30a.m., when Young Zhan and his best men came to my home. They lit firecrackers and knocked on my door pleading to be let in. Young Zhan called my name and then my mother's name, saying he was cold and hungry and too tired to stand outside and knock. All the while he shoved red envelopes of money under the door and when my bridesmaids were satisfied with his sincerity, they let him in.

A morning feast called a half table banquet was served to Young Zhan and his family and friends. This included six cold dishes and six hot dishes. The other half of the banquet was given later in Young Zhan's home. The feast was then a full table banquet, like a full moon, symbolizing our love for each other."

She described her wedding dress, a short red velvet gown with a flared skirt and a sweetheart neckline and of course, high heeled red shoes for happiness. A pink net veil covered her face and she carried a silk bouquet of red roses. Before being driven to Young Zhan's home, she said she cried and was sorry to leave her mother and father.

"I was very sad and my tears came easily … and my mother cried too, but Young Zhan promised to care for me always and we wiped our tears. Then I couldn't find one of my shoes and Young Zhan had to produce another red envelope to buy my shoe back from my bridesmaid. This made everybody laugh."

The letter said it was good luck that the bride and groom's car drove over three bridges on the way to Young Zhan's home. The master of ceremony was waiting. He read the marriage license out loud to confirm the marriage to be legal and then extolled the virtues of the new bride to the groom's parents. Young Zhan raised the veil from his bride's face and slipped a gold band on the third finger of her left hand, Western style. She didn't mention if they kissed but I presumed they did. They bowed three times to the parents to show respect and toasted them with liquor.

The wedding banquet was held at the Qinghai hotel where the couple stood at the door and greeted every one of the two hundred guests. When the wedding march was played Young Zhan and Wei Qin Hua walked slowly to the head table for toasts to the bride and groom. They shared stories of how they met, how perfect life was for them, plans for the future and how much they loved each other.

"And Boss Liu and Mr. Cheng volunteered to sing songs for us while we went from table to table thanking everyone for helping us celebrate our marriage. We had a wonderful party."

They flew to Chengdu for a honeymoon. "We had seven days of beautiful scenery, shopping and great Sichuan food ... and by the way, you will be happy to know, my mother-in-law says she really likes me now."

One day a few months after our return to Canada we received a parcel with a dozen red silk roses. Tucked underneath was a wedding photo from Miss Wei and Young Zhan showing the attractive couple in a sophisticated pose. It wasn't hard for us to visualize the large original picture hanging in the privacy of their pretty new bedroom.

twenty

中国

These were lonely days for Chen Yu Hua. Her father had isolated her from the family for having brought loss of face to the Chen name, and rarely did she see her mother and siblings. She relied on her classmates and friends for companionship and some semblance of family life.

Wang Yan, her best friend, was gone. She had married and moved to another county and would soon have a baby. Her husband was a good man and she was happy with life, but this didn't stop Chen Yu Hua from having guilty pangs of envy every time she read one of her friend's letters. They were filled with such boundless love for her husband and enthusiasm for the state of marriage and the blessed gift she would soon receive. She wanted a girl. The whole family wanted a boy, of course, but she and her husband hoped for a baby girl.

Chen Yu Hua truly wished her friend well. It was useless to compare their lives. She was much more ambitious than Wang Yan and she could never spend the rest of her life in a tiny village on the edge of nowhere. Someday she would have her own husband and little girl but not here in Xunhua, where life was hard and her father would turn his cold face to her whenever she displeased him.

Chen Yu Hua immersed herself in her teaching at the Minorities School. Her students respected her and regarded her fondly as "Elder Sister", confiding in her and expecting answers to all their pertinent questions about life and love. Sex was never discussed. Girls relied on their future husbands to teach them about this mystery and older women would tell them about childbirth, but love was a different matter.

"How does a girl know when she really loves a man," they giggled.

Chen Yu Hua answered their questions, perhaps not always giving the best answers, as her opinions often varied from tradition. She knew most of these young women would have no choice in their marriages. They were "spoken for" as children by families with young boys. Their future was sealed and true love or love of any kind may never enter their lives. They would move from their childhood home to live with their husband's family, sometimes never seeing their mother or father, sisters or brothers again. If they were lucky, their husband would be kind and love would grow, but if not, these Minorities women were doomed to a life of drudgery. Cruel mothers-in-law could enslave them; some wives may commit suicide; some would exist in misery and some, like Wang Yan, would be happy.

Chen Yu Hua hoped that with education their lives would improve. At least they might, just might, have the choice of a life partner. "And look at me," she thought, "an educated Han woman, who is supposed to have more freedom, more choices, and more independence, yet look at the bitterness surrounding my life."

One night an unscheduled party was planned in the food hall and all the teachers were invited to come. There would be food and music and singing.

"Chen Yu Hua, you must sing tonight, we can borrow an *erhu* for you to play," said one of the teachers at the girls' school.

"I hope we have fun," said another young teacher, "we need some fun, especially you." Her hand playfully bounced the back of Chen Yu Hua's hair. "Let's get ready. I have a new blouse to wear."

It was a wonderful night. The hall was full of new faces, and there were teachers Chen Yu Hua had never met. She sang for the crowd and played the two-stringed *erhu*. She sang Tibetan songs and danced by herself and with other people. While she was performing a traditional Salar song, she found herself singing the words together with the handsomest man she had ever seen. "That was beautiful," he was saying over the noise, "My name is Yi Chang. I'm Salar nationality."

They laughed together and Chen Yu Hua apologized for not knowing the exact words and being a bit off-key.

"Not at all," he said and smiled the most perfect radiant smile ever directed her way. He was tall, athletic, spoke excellent Mandarin and had the dark European look of his Turkish ancestors. She was captivated and flattered when she found out he knew her name. "I just had to ask who the talented singer was. I noticed you the minute you walked into the room."

Chen Yu Hua couldn't sleep that night she was so excited about meeting the Salar teacher. She could not explain why she was so infatuated with him, never having these feelings before, but then, she had never met anyone quite like him. He was different from any of the Salar men she knew. He was a college graduate, and she learned he was from Xinjiang Ughur Autonomous Region, the largest province in China, far to the north of Qinghai and across the Tian Shan range. He grew up influenced by intellectual young people from Beijing and Shanghai who were sent to teach in that remote part of China during the Cultural Revolution. Students like him were fortunate to receive an excellent education from the "cream of China's youth", as these teachers were called during those years.

Chen Yu Hua sensed she had been given a new life. Something grand and exciting was opening up for her and she felt like she was seeing things for the first time. The pain of being ostracized by her family and the fact she was not going to Xining were washed away as her friendship with Teacher Yi Chang developed.

They never saw one another alone. They were always with people. It was usually in the library or eating a bowl of noodles in the food hall. She watched him play basketball and cheered for his team, and the table tennis games were thrilling as long as Yi Chang was playing. Sometimes she played against him and won. She was good at table tennis. Every game they shared, every meal, every word they spoke to one another was new and electric.

One day he asked her to visit his room at the school dormitory where he taught. She was nervous; old feelings came flooding back about becoming a topic for gossip, but she could not say no.

"And why should we care?" he said cheerily, "We live in a new

China, you know."

His room was tidy and he had several small pieces of art pinned on the walls; ink drawings of Genghis Khan and his warriors mounted on fabulous "Heavenly Horses" as the Chinese called them in the thirteenth century. There was a desk piled high with papers and a table with two chairs. A kerosene lamp burned between them as they sat facing one another, their elbows squarely on the table.

When she showed interest in the ink drawings, he could not help himself; he was such a history buff he had to tell her the story of the famous Heavenly Horses. He told her about ancient times, long before the Tubo era, when the Tibetans lived a spiritual life on the high plains with their holy mountains and holy waters. They rode beautiful Heavenly Horses, which flew like the wind and galloped on floating clouds. The progeny of wild Arabian horses, these runaways from the early travelers of the Silk Road were given their divine name when first glimpsed in Qinghai and Xinjiang. Eventually, word of their existence reached the ears of Emperor Wu Di in Chang'an.

"And do you know what the emperor did?" asked Yi Chang, leaning across the table.

"No," she said.

"The emperor sent thousands of soldiers to find these legendary horses and wage war, if need be, to bring them to the capital city. The war lasted an incredible four years before he could secure some of the powerful ponies ... and do you know why he was desperate to have them?"

"No."

Teacher Yi Chang gestured at the ceiling. "Because the emperor knew if he had one of these horses he could ride up to the Gates of Heaven."

He leaned closer to Chen Yu Hua staring into her eyes, "And would you be frightened if I told you the terrible name of the horses he wanted most to own?"

"No." She smiled.

"The most famous horses of all," he lowered his voice to a dry whisper, "were called Blood-Sweaters."

He threw himself back in his chair and laughed like a man who loved humor; loved life. They both laughed. "You should be in drama," she fondly indulged him. This would not be the last time she would enjoy his story telling.

Together they looked through his collection of history books that had been saved during the tragic years of the Cultural Revolution; precious books, many with titles unfamiliar to her. They spoke about their past lives; about their friends and families, some good, some bad. Their hobbies, the sports they enjoyed best and, in particular, their dreams for the future. They couldn't get enough of each other's words. They memorized poetry, re-hashed history, discussed difficult school lessons but never once did they speak of politics or love.

It was very late when Yi Chang took Chen Yu Hua home on the back of his bicycle. She loved to ride with him, to wrap her arms around his lean waist and careen through the dark streets, dodging water-filled potholes and rocks. She said goodnight and they waved to each other as he sped away. She hurried to the locked gates. A gust of wind swept through the tops of the trees and she looked up at the night sky, happy to know that summer was almost here. For a moment she didn't notice the dark figure step out from the shadows of the school compound wall.

"I have been waiting for you, Chen Yu Hua."

She instantly recognized the devious looking matchmaker.

"What do you want?" she asked.

His oily voice said quietly, "I think you keep very late hours for a young ... unmarried woman." He emphasized unmarried, sending chills up her spine. "I'm here to tell you that I received a letter from Gu Yong in Xining."

"So?"

He paused, taking his time to light a cigarette, sucking in his breath and blowing streams of white smoke into the air. He stepped solidly in front her and barred the entrance to the gate. "He begs you to change your mind and accept his generous offer of marriage. In fact, Chen Yu Hua," he said with scorn, his threatening gaze directed right at her, "in his letter he also warns you that if you do not agree to marry him you will regret it." With these words he spat deliberately and spitefully on the ground at her feet. "He is not a man to trifle with."

Chen Yu Hua was shocked. She tried to choke back her panic. Her father was right, Gu Yong was mean-spirited and someone to fear.

"Go away!" She heard her voice rising. "I'll never marry that man. You can write a letter and tell him for me that I never want to hear his name again … ever."

"Chen Yu Hua, is something wrong?" The gatekeeper called.

The matchmaker seemed to melt into the wall shadows with only the tip of the disembodied cigarette glowing bright red and swinging in the dark. She thought she heard him say, "Very well … I hope you won't be sorry." But she wasn't sure.

One of the tall wrought iron gates that protected the compound partially swung open and she scurried through, half running and half walking down the lane towards her dorm.

"Thank you, it's nothing," she called back over her shoulder to the gatekeeper, "goodnight."

Chen Yu Hua soon forgot all about the matchmaker and Gu Yong and the letter of threat, as she and Yi Chang began to enjoy their relationship. He stopped by her dorm every evening after dinner on his way home. She opened her wooden chest where she kept food and carefully took out two pears or two apples and they would sit and talk while eating the fruit. One night there was only one apple left in the box. She told him she didn't have a knife and he could have the apple. He smiled at her and took the apple and, to her great delight, he broke off pieces with his fingers.

"Open your mouth," he coaxed, and placed a bit of the tasty apple between her lips.

He was so thoughtful, so strong and beautiful. She knew the whole world could hear her heart beating. She wrapped her fingers around his hand and held it steady. She looked into his eyes and for the first time in her life, she heard herself say, "I love you." She couldn't stop the words. For a moment neither of them moved. Would she ever breathe again? He was just staring at her.

"We should have known this would happen," he said quietly, slipping his hand from hers. He kept looking at her. She expected him to say something more, that he felt the same way. Even kiss her. He had never tried once to be intimate with her, never once touching her, but she knew their relationship was far more than studying ancient history or eating fruit together. She knew he must feel the same way she did. Why didn't he say he loved her? That was all she wanted to hear.

"Come and sit by me," he said, taking her hand and guiding her to the edge of the bed. "We must talk. I want to tell you why we cannot ... must not, give this love a chance to grow."

Slowly he told her the story of his favorite sister, the eldest girl in his family. "So full of life and very beautiful," he said, "and she caught the eye of a young man studying at the university." Yi Chang told how the two young people fell deeply in love. He, being Han nationality and she, Salar minority, they knew it would be difficult to marry but they made plans anyway. "They could not live without one another," he said. Yi Chang stopped to take a breath, stumbling on the dry, brittle words, barely forcing them from his throat.

"They were separated by the parents. Neither family could bear the shame of an inter-racial marriage. Not the Salar people, who insisted she marry a Muslim and certainly not the Han people who didn't want a minority woman in the family."

He stopped talking. Chen Yu Hua saw the tears in his eyes.

"It was awful," he continued, "she screamed and wept day and night ... and threatened to run away with her lover ... even take her own life. My father and mother locked her in the house for months until they found a Muslim farmer, twenty years her senior ... a crude man ... who would marry her and take her off their hands."

He paused again and looked sadly at Chen Yu Hua.

"She was educated and lived in a well-to-do home," he went on, "now she is living ... no, slaving, on a peasant farm ... she looks old and gray and I don't mean only gray-haired ... I mean gray-spirited. I have never once seen her smile." His voice trailed off and he leaned his head against Chen Yu Hua and held her.

Chen Yu Hua knew what he meant. She began to cry silently, tears dropping freely on her hands, folded on her lap. This story would be their story. They would bring disgrace on their nationalities and she knew in her heart that if he were brave enough to make an offer of marriage to her, she would not have the courage to say yes. Their lives would be an impossible mess, her father could die of shame and she might not be able to adapt to Muslim life. It was all too hopeless. Such would be the consequence for a mixed marriage in Northwest China in the summer of 1982.

She never saw Yi Chang alone again. He never came to her room to share fruit or read history. They met often at the food hall or at games or school activities, greeting one another casually, showing the world their smiling faces, like happy superficial masks hiding two broken hearts.

One evening Chen Yu Hua was preparing exam questions for her students when Yi Chang called softly at her door, so softly she thought she imagined it.

"Chen Yu Hua can I talk to you?"

They exchanged unimportant pleasantries for a moment. No, he couldn't stay; he only came to say goodbye, he was leaving in the morning.

"I had to see you. I've been assigned to a teaching job in Urumqi, in Xinjiang where my people live … I'm going home."

He held his arms wide to hug her. He was warm and strong and Chen Yu Hua felt old feelings rushing over her. He kissed her forehead and smoothed her black hair.

"You and I will never meet again but this I will tell you." His voice was soft against her face, "you will always be my first love … I will never forget all these lovely days we spent together." He took her small hands in his and held them tight against his heart. "I will keep the memories of you here forever … until I die." He smiled at her briefly, afraid that if he touched her anymore he would never leave.

"Goodbye, Chen Yu Hua."

Every word tore at her heart.

She watched him walk away. "Please don't go," she whispered. She wanted to call him back. They could make it work; they just needed time. But instead, she sat down on the chair and started to sort the school papers.

Her students were having exams tomorrow.

Planning a cocktail party was a new experience for our Commission staff. They had never heard of such a thing and couldn't imagine having fifty people standing toe to toe, eating and drinking in our little house.

We sent gold-embossed red invitation cards to mayors, cadres, Commission staff, our Chinese and foreign friends and to the highest official in town, Mr. Liu, Communist Party Leader.

You and your spouse are invited to a cocktail party

at the home of Mr. & Mrs. Weigand

Saturday, December 9 from 6:30 to 10 PM

No.83 Nan Guan Road

R.S.V.P.

"But ... you know ... our leaders want to sit down at a party," insisted Young Liu.

A vision came to mind of China's cadres sheathed in plumes of choking cigarette smoke, perched on over-stuffed chairs draped with lace doilies and parked along walls facing into the center of a wide room.

"This will be a new experience for them." I said confidently.

"Where will they smoke?" The ugly smoking question was asked by Miss Wei.

"Outside in the courtyard."

"But ... our leaders ... yeah ... are not so ... so flexible."

"We won't worry about that now Miss Wei." I buried the

smoking debate yet again. "Let's see ... what are we going to eat? We can't give everyone a plate and chopsticks so I think we'll have finger food."

Mr. Cheng looked at me. "Ughhh," he said. I knew he was mentally filing "finger food" in the "mashed potato" category until I had Miss Chen explain finger food is nothing more than small bits of food to be eaten with the fingers, not with utensils. This was still a mystery for the seven faces listening to me.

"We'll go to the hotel and order small pieces of food like lemon chicken, tomatoes and beef ... shrimp ... foods easy to pick up." I wiggled my fingers in the air and pretended to eat.

"We'll also need glasses for the beer and other drinks ... and maybe small plates," Bill suggested.

"Throwaway plastic plates," I added, "and a few chopsticks for serving."

The staff was becoming enthusiastic, caught up in the spirit of another party. They loved a party, but were apprehensive about a party at the foreigner's house. The idea of mixing with their leaders on the same level was new and a bit intimidating for them.

"Don't worry, it'll be lots of fun," I said.

We drove with Driver Zhang to the Qinghai hotel where the manager introduced us to a thin, very short Head Chef, wearing a tall crisp pleated white hat. Everybody was talking at once but eventually we made it clear to him that we needed trays of small juicy tidbits of meat and fish for fifty people, some sliced veggies, like tomatoes and cucumbers and, of course, lots of glasses for the booze.

We wondered if the tiny chef understood what a cocktail party was, but overflowing trays of food, surprisingly close to what we ordered, showed up right on time for our party.

Our house was buzzing the week before the event. Someone, perhaps the mayor, sent ten soldiers to clean our windows, sweep the walks and wash the steps. Two large porcelain pots set with tall Cyprus shrubs were placed on each side of the front door.

I started thinking about our grand idea. What if it was a complete failure? What if the leaders were insulted by having to stand to drink liquor, eat food with their fingers and, horrors, smoke outside? Maybe they didn't want to bring their wives. And maybe it wasn't right to expect them to mix with junior cadres and foreign schoolteachers? After all, if this party was a bust it wouldn't be Bill or I who would suffer the scolding; the ones to bear the criticism would definitely be our Commission.

"Did you say something?" asked Bill.

"Yes," I answered thoughtfully. "I said ... poor Miss Chen, and poor Boss Liu, poor Commission if this party doesn't work."

Our foreign friends arrived shortly after six. In the kitchen, Julie and Carol sorted trays of food, along with paper plates, serviettes and chopsticks, to be delivered to the main room. Our two interpreters came a little later. Miss Chen, very chic in a new black suit, was beautifully done up with mascara, *Chinese Red* lipstick, glowing cheeks and hair pulled back with a fancy rhinestone clip. Miss Wei, her hair long and shiny, was equally glamorous in a white sweater trimmed with gold and a black ankle-length voile skirt that swirled around her slim legs.

Eight red candles were lit, the beer was cooling in the fridge and Erin lined up tiny shot glasses for Qinghai Barley and Mao Tai. The sofas and chairs were pushed back to make room for our guests. I looked at my watch ... it was almost 7:20. Where were the people?

"Perhaps they didn't get the time right," said Keith.

"Humm ... and maybe they don't like Western cocktail parties after all," I said, looking anxiously at Bill. Just then a chorus of loud voices rang from the courtyard.

We rushed to open the front door. "Hello," smiled Liu Guang Zhong, number one mayor of Xining, holding a huge plant. Our fifty guests were lined up behind him, along with three children whose folk singing and dancing turned out to be the evening's entertainment. The guests carried bouquets of roses, plants, small gifts, and bottles of alcohol. One person gave us a wool wall hanging of a Tibetan lady wearing large oval copper earrings, and Mr. Cheng presented an oil painting he had done of a scene from the grasslands.

On this night we learned something about Chinese protocol; no one ventured to the party before the mayor. The group had congregated down at the guardhouse gate waiting patiently for him to arrive.

Behind them, filming every small detail, trailed the TV crew.

Boss Liu and Miss Chen need not have worried about Xining's first private Western cocktail party. It was a roaring success! The mayor and leaders relaxed with glasses of alcohol and seemed at ease mixing with their subordinates and foreigners alike. They brought their spouses, stood face to face with one another, smoked outside and seemed to enjoy the unusual experience of a stand-up party.

The Chinese are truly averse to eating with their fingers, so we were relieved to find fifty pairs of wrapped chopsticks popped in with our order. The tiny chef had been on the ball. Now everyone happily jabbed and stirred through the loaded trays, picking out their favorite juicy bits of meat and fat nuts. No need for plastic throw-away plates. Certainly no need for the pretty drink napkins sent by our family back in Canada.

"Nice ... parteee," Driver Zhang grinned in newfound English; his two words had been tutored by Miss Wei.

"Now Driver Zhang can speak English ... yeah?" She smiled.

After the guests left, Keith made a remark about a subject neither Bill nor I had thought about. The fact that so many senior officials and important cadres and leaders were together in a private home for a party amazed him. He wondered about security, but we knew that just outside our courtyard walls there must be guards and police patrols nearby. It was their responsibility to know everything about Bill and me and the visiting foreigners ... everything.

Like the time Bill went to an export company without the knowledge of the Commission.

Shortly after we had arrived in Qinghai a smart young businessman named Patrick heard about a Canadian Expert living in the heart of Xining. He phoned and invited Bill to visit the prestigious offices of his company. Bill enjoyed the meeting with Patrick and the other young men and promised to help them connect with Canadian firms.

"Very Western-looking offices," Bill told me later, but when

Miss Chen found out he had visited strangers from another company without registering with the Commission, she was not pleased. We were soon to learn this was a "no-no" and it was Miss Chen's job to lecture us about fraternizing with complete strangers.

"You don't even know this *Patrick*," said Miss Chen, surprising us with her bluntness. "You must realize that our Commission is totally responsible for your safety ... if anything bad were to happen to you ..." She stopped for a moment to catch her breath, "if you were *used* (we weren't quite sure what this meant) by another Commission, or say ... kidnapped or anything like *that*." Her eyes grew wider as she lectured on, "our Commission would be in a lot of trouble ... we would have to answer to Beijing. I would be in trouble. Miss Wei would be in trouble. And Boss Liu would be in *big* trouble!"

"Sorry, Miss Chen," said Bill, "I didn't think it was so serious. I thought I could help any companies that wanted to trade with Canada."

Apparently not. Bill never again went visiting with smart young cadres; in fact, the word must have spread rapidly as there were no more spontaneous invitations.

Oddly, the Commission seemed to have no problem with us roaming the streets of Xining on our own. We sought out historic sites near our home. The crumbling wall that once ringed the city was still visible in places, and a high mound of earth stood nearby where some long-ago general rallied his troops. We looked for antiques in the Muslim shops, went to the Bird market on a street where old men walked with cages of treasured songbirds, and bought house plants in the Flower Market. On weekends when the interpreters were busy with their families we taxied off to the Qinghai *Binguan* and drank Heineken beer in the lobby in hopes of meeting an English-speaking foreigner. We only met one: a crusty old Danish matron, conscientiously following in the footsteps of the English adventurer Alexandra David-Neel. In the early twentieth century, this mystic traveler spent years wandering on horse, sedan chair and foot through China, stopping for three years at Ta'er Monastery, south of Xining, to study. The Danish lady was disappointed to find there was no mention of this famous explorer, no museums or books honoring her name, and when we explained that we lived in Xining, she made it clear she was unhappy, as if we were responsible for this oversight.

We hosted a second large party later in the year. A gathering of performers from the local theater company rocked our little house with folk singing, balancing acts on the arms of chairs, juggling, dancing and magic tricks, and the ear-splitting baritone voice of a Beijing Opera star rang out for all to hear down Nan Guan Street.

Bill and I were invited to a neighborhood theatre featuring the same baritone in a Beijing opera stage production. Unlike the harmonic and melodic style of European opera, Chinese opera with its blend of screeching falsetto singers, loud clanking of clappers and banging of drums, seemed noisy and disaccorded to our Western ears. But it is the beautiful artistic costumes, expressive eye movements and spectacular dance that attract a Western audience. The face painting alone is fascinating. Heroes are mostly portrayed in simple colors, whereas the villains are painted with complicated designs. Colors are used to distinguish characteristics of the actors: red is for courage and loyalty, black for impulsiveness, blue for cruelty and white for wickedness, except when you see a white nose, which signifies humor and joviality.

Beijing opera, dates back two hundred years to 1790 when four famous Anhui troupes arrived in Beijing to perform before the imperial court. It further developed under its powerful patron, Empress Dowager Cixi and, by the end of the Qing Dynasty (about 1911), two things happened; the opera became more accessible to the common people and women were allowed to act on stage.

Miss Wei's Western wedding photo.

English teachers Julie Cox and Carol Ames.

Midwives CIDA Project announcement. Vice Governor A, Mayor Liu, Vice Governor Bai Ma, Jerrine, Bill, Miss Chen.

Gathering of Muslim children, Datong County.

Knowing Miss Chen

Midwives Project meeting at a Muslim farm home, Datong County. Madam Yang, Miss Chen, Bill, Jerrine, Vice Governor A, Mrs. Ding, Tian Sheg Hua.

Designer seamstress, husband and sleeping baby, Datong County.

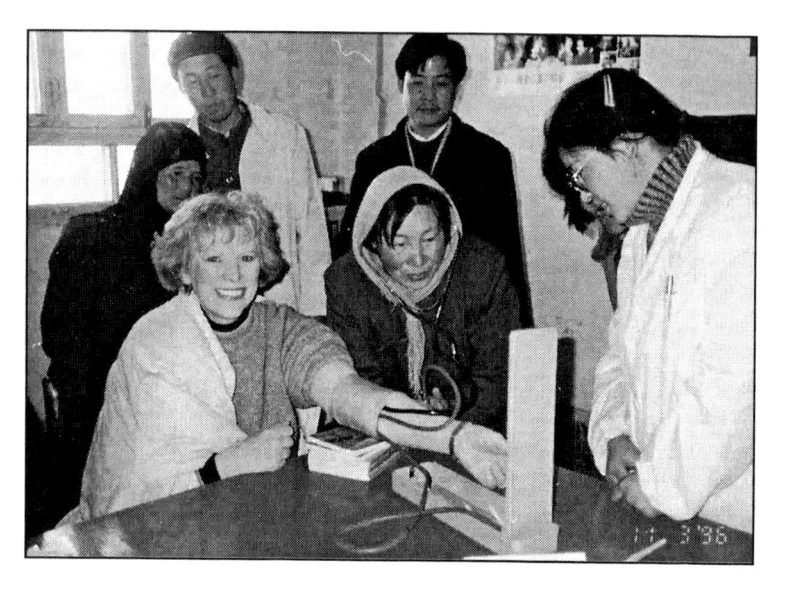

Midwives learning to take blood pressure, Datong County.

Midwives arriving at school on Mechanical Buffalo.

Attending symposium on economic development.

Murray and Lynda with curious onlookers.

Living Buddha at Tongren.

Jill Gillett makes friends with children.
Westgate Market, Xining.

Knowing Miss Chen

International Women's Day.
Nicole Archer, Miss Wei, Jerrine, Jociane Archer, Miss Chen.

Norman Ross tours Xining after visit with
Gold Commissioner.

Tibetan midwife graduates with her Canada Satchel.

Tu lady, Li Fa Xiu and family, Huzhu County.

Knowing Miss Chen

Mr. Bai, aged 80. An Old Soldier; a veteran of The Long March with Mao Zedong, wearing his Yukon pin and holding a City of Whitehorse flag.

Teacher Chen at the gate of the Beijing Foreign Studies University, before the Tiananmen Incident.

Jiang Pin at home in Xunhua.

Boss Liu, Bill, Jerrine, Acting Ambassador Sunquist.
Canadian Embassy, Beijing.

twenty-one

中国

A third year of teaching began at the Minorities Girls' School for Chen Yu Hua.

Nothing could take away her emptiness and sad feelings since Yi Chang left, and she was still suffering from the family's unfair punishment for her stubbornness. She buried herself in her work, keeping herself inundated with students' problems, exams, extra studies and music. She never let her mind wallow in old memories, good or bad, nor let it dream. In this way Chen Yu Hua got through the days, living in limbo and living for the moment.

She accumulated enough money to buy herself a secondhand bicycle. Now she had the freedom to visit friends across the city or shop at any of the markets, bringing home food in the wire basket mounted on the front of her bike.

One of her favorite markets, sprawling and bustling in the center of Xunhua, was called Little Hong Kong. Chen Yu Hua loved to browse through the colorful stalls where ethnic people stacked their tables with exotic foods, silver jewelry, beadwork, wooden carvings, paintings, all kinds of clothing and animal skins, bejeweled hoary yak skulls and Tibetan daggers.

At one of the Tibetan stalls Chen Yu Hua ran her fingers over some turquoise bracelets; small beads twined together with braided black horsehair, crafted skillfully in some far-off yurt.

"This is a very pretty one," she said to the Tibetan girl.

"Yes, it is. It will look beautiful on your wrist."

The girl was young. Large silver and turquoise hoops dangled from her ears, and her thick waist-length plaited black hair, like a tail from one of their magnificent horses, was adorned with circles of pounded silver and colored beads. She wore a plain black pleated skirt, a finely striped turquoise, black and white apron and a bright red satin blouse clasped at the neck with a gold brooch. She was very beautiful. Her skin was flawless and Chen Yu Hua remembered some of her students telling how the young girls would rub their faces with butter or sour cream and wash with yak milk. They used a silk thread technique to pull away fine facial hair before applying a thick honey mask. Keeping faithful to this daily routine ensured that Tibetan girls, living in the harshest weather on the high plains, would have smooth skin and retain a youthful appearance.

Perhaps the girl was turning seventeen, thought Chen Yu Hua.

She knew this year of life was the most cherished and memorable time for young Tibetan women, celebrating what was known as dressing the seventeen-year-olds. It would take place at the Tibetan New Year in the same year as the young girl's birthday. She would be pampered and fussed over, excused from hard work and given more than her usual share of nourishing food.

In the "dressing up" ceremony, married women rubbed yak butter into the long black hair of each girl and braided it into nine thick glistening pigtails. They adorned her hands with rings and bracelets of gold, silver, and ivory and draped strands of exactly one hundred yellow agate and red coral beads around her neck. Next came the robes of red and green shimmering satin, embossed with motifs of gold and lined with soft white sheepskin. A huge fluffy red fox hat was placed on her head and the finished effect was stunning.

It was the time for expensive gift giving: furs, garments and jewelry worth tens of thousands of yuan were lavished on daughters by their doting parents. In fact, the entire family savings could very well be squandered for this ruinous and excessive once in a lifetime coming-out party. Their mothers tutored them in fine manners with wise words, "walk slowly, speak softly and be more considerate of your family as well as other people."

Chen Yu Hua knew the celebration would come to an end with a sumptuous, extravagant banquet and dance held in their honor, and she thought how wonderful to be so pampered at seventeen.

"I'll take this one, thank you."

She smiled at the young girl, paid for the bracelet and slipped it over her hand. It seemed foolish to spend so much money on vanity but she had never bought jewelry for herself before and it made her feel good.

The bicycle basket overflowed with apples and pears and one valuable juicy peach as well as the staples: bean curd and Chinese greens. It was a sunny day and she decided to take the back road to the school. It ran on the outskirts of the city and was much longer, but it would give her time to enjoy the vibrant autumn colors. She thought about the Tibetan girl again. If she really was seventeen she would have enjoyed an unforgettable rite of passage, probably the happiest time in her life. The Tibetans would tell their daughter that she was no longer a girl, she was a woman, and was allowed the independence to live apart from her family and have as many male friends as she wished until she married.

"Lucky girl," grumbled Chen Yu Hua out loud.

Riding smoothly along the road she thought about her life. She had to renew her plans to go to Xining for further education and must overcome the void left by insensitive parents and lost love.

There were several cyclists on the road, mostly students, who greeted her as they passed. What a terrific feeling she had, sitting straight and tall and free with the crisp air cooling her face, in complete control of her "new" old bicycle. Life would change for the better. She was sure of it now. She hummed to herself.

Chen Yu Hua was unaware of the man following her on a bicycle, hanging back pacing her speed over the last mile. The young man saw his chance. The road ahead was empty of traffic as far as the next turn. He pulled his collar up around his face, yanked his hat low over his forehead and sped to overtake the pretty teacher.

It happened in a second.

He brought his bicycle parallel with hers and jabbed his foot hard at her front wheel. Chen Yu Hua's eye caught the moving image and realized in a flash she was being attacked. Losing control of her bicycle as it hit soft dirt, she was thrown into the shrubs and gravel by the side of the road.

"Compliments of Gu Yong," shouted her assailant as he sped off down the road.

Chen Yu Hua lay for a few minutes, dazed and angry. Two young students from her school came to her aid. Her hands were bleeding and one side of her face was scratched and bruised, as were her knees and elbows. Fruit and vegetables were strewn everywhere and the precious turquoise bracelet had been torn from her wrist, scattering the little beads of blue in the dry yellow grass. The expensive peach lay squashed against a huge rock, its sweet juice draining away into the gravel. She looked at it in horror. "That could have been me," she wept.

"Where is father?" called Chen Yu Hua angrily, pushing open the door to the family home. She saw her mother in the kitchen, bent over as usual, this time over the old Flying Man sewing machine mending trousers. Will she ever finish her work, thought Chen Yu Hua scornfully. Will they ever give her time for herself?

"Chen Yu Hua … what happened to you?" Jia Ying was shocked, not only by the battered look of her daughter but that she was actually standing in the house. It had been so long. Tired of pleading with her husband to heal the shattered relationship he had with their oldest daughter, Jia Ying was disheartened and only wanted peace in her family.

"I've come to see father." Chen Yu Hua was terse and never properly greeted Jia Ying or said she was sorry for the unexpected intrusion.

"Can I look at your cuts? I have some Mercurochrome … "

"I just want to talk to father," interrupted Chen Yu Hua, ignoring the sympathetic gesture by her mother. Jia Ying was uneasy with the stern tone of her daughter's voice.

"Come in here, Chen Yu Hua," called Jian Pin from the other room. "There is no need to be rude to your mother."

Chen Yu Hua was suddenly anxious at hearing the cold voice of her father. She went cautiously, almost timidly through the open door to his private place.

He was sitting by the window reading the Tang poet, Li Bai.

There were stacks of old books on the shelves: history, poetry and the great Chinese classics ... *Journey to the West* and *A Dream of Red Mansions*. He once told his sons he was glad he had saved them from the "book-burnings", risking his life by hiding them behind a false wall in his home. Now he could enjoy the books again, just as much as he did when he was headmaster at Gandu Normal School.

Chen Yu Hua had not visited the house for over a year and was surprised to see how the once tiny room had been changed. How big it was. Long scrolls of calligraphy signed by her father and dated before she was born hung high on the walls. Jian Pin was once a Master Calligrapher; she knew that much about him. There were black and white pictures of him in college before 1949, a picture of his mother and father in unfamiliar wedding clothes, and a picture of him with his siblings at his mother's knee.

There were two more pictures that caught her attention. She looked upon a small finely carved shrine, its tiny doors open and, for the first time, observed a picture she knew must be her great-grandmother. She stared into a sepia-toned ancient world she could never imagine. Another old photo with a black onyx frame bordering the sober face of a very young Jia Ying leaned against the shrine.

Four satin brocade cushions were puffed up on a long bench, and a desk ... where did the desk come from? A Calligraphy stone, smooth and delicately carved with flowers and birds, sat on the desk, surrounded by various inks, pens and brushes.

Her mind slipped back. She was suddenly a child again.

The carved bench. The half window. The three lovely ladies on the curtain. The airless room ... it had once been her classroom! Now she understood. This clever man had hidden his precious treasures all these many years safely behind a false wall. The pictures. The scrolls. The books. And she never even knew.

"Why are you here, Chen Yu Hua?" Her father's crisp starchy voice, detached and bitter as she had ever heard it, brought her back to reality.

"Do you see me? Do you see this?" And she pointed to the broken skin and blue smudge on her right cheek.

"I see you ... what happened?"

"Gu Yong sent a man to kill me. He knocked me from my bicycle and I landed in gravel … I'm sore and stiff. Look at me … I look terrible … I feel terrible."

"What makes you think Gu Yong had anything to do with this? Maybe it was an accident." Jian Pin's voice hinted that he had little patience for this outburst today from his daughter.

"Because … the man said it was compliments of Gu Yong."

Chen Yu Hua was as calm as she could be, keeping her frustration and disappointment in check. "It was no accident, father." Her voice started to quiver and she told him about the threatening visit from the matchmaker late one night at the school gates.

"Well then," said Jian Pin carefully, "I suppose all I can say is … *I warned you.* I told you to keep your eyes open." He was getting bored with the conversation and picked up his book to find the page where he had left off. "Li Bai was a wonderful poet," he said autocratically, "he described the Yellow River as spilling out of the heavens on its way to …"

Chen Yu Hua's mind exploded. She was tired and sore, sick and hurt by his indifference. It wasn't fair. She screamed at her father. "You are going to see to it that it all stops."

Jian Pin's face clouded as his book slipped to the floor. He had never been spoken to like this in his life, not once, by any of his family.

Chen Yu Hua hit the desk with the flat of her hand. Jian Pin jumped to his feet as she picked up his heavy jade signature chop, holding it defiantly. "You are going to use this to write to the matchmaker and tell him that Gu Yong must leave me alone … I'm afraid of this dangerous man. I will *never* marry him and you know it."

Jia Ying's frightened face appeared at the door. "Chen Yu Hua … please," she pleaded softly, only to be ignored.

It was suddenly quiet … not tranquil-quiet, but the electric quietness that lies on the land before a storm comes crashing.

No one moved.

Warm tears burned her bruised, flushed cheeks while she focused on tiny crystals of dust in the air, playing on the stream of sunlight, giving it movement and life as it poured into the room through the large window. Did I do that when I hit the old desk, thought Chen Yu Hua? Her father was so angry he refused to look at her. She stood very still, watching the way the dust danced in the sunlight. How absurd! She was hurting, frustrated and sick at heart and here she was watching meaningless atoms of dust.

Jian Pin slowly picked up the fallen book from the floor and placed it carefully, almost tenderly, on the window casement. He turned away from his daughter, spaced his legs apart, folded his hands behind his back and stared with an impassive face out to the courtyard.

She was crushed.

A slight motion of his head indicated their meeting was over.

Jian Pin wrote a letter to the matchmaker stating emphatically that his daughter would not consider marrying Gu Yong of Xining and, whatever else he wrote, Chen Yu Hua was never harassed again.

The Christmas season was just around the corner and Miss Chen and the Commission staff were all caught up in our plans for a Western celebration. They surprised Bill and I with a tall fir tree firmly planted in a ceramic pot, compliments of the Botanical Gardens. It was delivered to our house by two husky soldiers. Traditional Christmas decorations were non-existent but strings of tiny white lights and reams of red crepe paper were readily available in local department stores. We bought as much as we could carry home, for the tree-dressing party with our three English friends, some of the Commission staff, the Chinese English teachers and as many kids as we could invite. Julie, Miss Chen and Miss Wei organized the food and wound the tree in a myriad of lights while busy little fingers folded and shaped delicate red roses, securing each one in its precise place on the thick green branches.

We stood back and someone flipped on the electricity.

Everyone gasped. The tree lights filtered through the crepe paper roses and cast a soft crimson glow on the delighted faces of the children. They weren't noisy or rowdy, but quiet and lost in thought as they stared at the tree. Bill and I were touched. At home our grandchildren would be having fun, laughing, bouncing around the room playing games, too excited for bed. But for these Chinese children, who had never before seen a tree from the forest decorated in lights and flowers, it was a spiritual time.

"It's most beautiful," sighed Julie. We all agreed and sang "Jingle Bells" and folk songs and sat on the floor in the dark room, bathed in the warm magic of the fairylike Christmas tree.

Bill had the forethought to bring his Santa suit to China, and now, a few days before Christmas, there would be a Santa Claus in Xining. I spent hours sewing red hats trimmed with fake white fur and pom-poms for Driver Zhang and the crew, and we decorated the Commission station wagon with gaudy crepe paper streamers and bows. Our Santa was scheduled to make an appearance in the lobby of the Qinghai Hotel for a "Meet Santa Claus" afternoon. Everyone was welcome.

We dressed Bill in the suit, packed pillows around his middle, painted his cheeks bright pink and fastened a beard to his chin. He pulled on a borrowed pair of extra large shiny black rubber boots also trimmed in white fur, and we were ready to go. We drove through the streets of the old city with Driver Zhang leaning hard on the horn. It was an astonishing sight for people who had never seen or heard of Santa Claus. Here was a crazy Western fellow in a red suit, his face wrapped in a curly white beard, shouting over and over from the car window ... *Sheng Dan Kauai Le* ... Merry Christmas! His fancy-hatted helpers also yelled and waved greetings while colorful streamers rippled in the wind, and one big red flower bobbed up and down on the grill of the old station wagon.

We arrived at the hotel the same time as the TV cameras. Santa Claus made his grand entrance through the four hundred or so well disciplined children sitting cross-legged on the floor. Their eyes were glued to the bizarre-looking fat man in a red and white outfit who shuffled in boots too big for his feet and continually yelled Ho! Ho! Ho! He was escorted to an armchair in the center of the lobby while TV cameras rolled, the manager beamed and a giant Christmas tree blinked on and off.

"Let's get the children to sing," said Santa in a muffled voice, "these children are too quiet ... we need some Christmas Spirit." He waved his arms eagerly like a choirmaster and sang, "*ding-ding-dong ... ding-ding-dong ... ling er xian ding-dong*": "Jingle Bells", in Chinese.

It wasn't long before everyone was singing and swaying. "Aren't these kids well mannered?" he smiled from his armchair, "they're so cute."

Suddenly every little kid wanted to touch Santa Claus. They wanted to sit on his knee and stroke his beard and let their adoring mothers take photos. They touched his big tummy and patted his pink cheeks. In the crush of kids, I heard a muffled "help" coming from Santa Claus, who was slowly falling backwards in his chair. Miss Chen and Driver Zhang rescued him. They pushed his chair upright and Miss Wei tossed handfuls of candy into the bedlam just in time to distract the mob and give Santa a chance to get his breath. He straightened his beard, which was dangling on his chest, and pulled up the slipped pillows. One fuzzy white eyebrow had dislodged itself and was gone forever, and the tousled white wig had pitched back, exposing a fringe of short brown hair on his forehead. All the while, the little kids shrieked and laughed and scrambled on the floor for the candies. A decision had to be made: it was safer for Santa to mingle with the crowd than sit in the chair. Miss Chen clapped her hands. She yelled over the commotion and lined up the kids behind a bedraggled Santa. They squealed and sang "Jingle Bells" and snake-danced all around the lobby of the Qinghai Hotel that memorable winter day in China.

There never was a more popular Santa Claus *anywhere*.

"Would you like to go to church?" Miss Chen asked. We had been in Xining for six months and had never heard of a Christian church, but on Christmas Eve we went to a large, old Anglican Church that was enjoying a popular revival, and sang Western carols with a thousand Chinese. They poured out the songs in their language and we in English.

Earlier in the day we exchanged gifts with Miss Chen, her husband Mr. Liu and their daughter, nine-year-old Si Xian. We had met Mr. Liu several times and, although he was curious about us, he was still shy. Si Xian was never shy. She called us gramma and grampa and loved the whole idea of celebrating a Western Christmas. We weren't sure what she would think of the blonde Barbie Doll sent by our daughter Nikki from Canada, but it turned out to be a huge hit.

Julie came for Christmas dinner. She would be leaving the next day for England, perhaps drifting out of our lives forever. Keith and Erin also came. The five of us ate the inevitable chicken legs in gravy, mashed potatoes, vegetables and salad and Julie's wonderfully light bread rolls. For two weeks Driver Zhang had been kept busy delivering Christmas cards and heavy gift parcels of magazines, CDs, decorations and food from our friends and family at home. Our friend Sandy sent us a throw rug wrapped around a bottle of champagne! We had butter, cheese, chocolate, real coffee, a plum pudding with brandy sauce and sips of Grand Marnier.

We talked about life and told funny stories. "Will you ever come back to China?" we asked Julie. She didn't think so. Eight years was long enough. "There are new countries to see." We also wondered if we would ever meet Keith and Erin in the US. "Of course," they assured us, "we're only across the border in Seattle."

The long red candles burned down and carols from the Beijing CD player drifted through the rooms. "Silent Night, Holy Night" ... Bing Crosby. All of us felt nostalgic; we were so far from our homes. Christmas 1995 with our three new friends would soon be a pleasant memory.

twenty-two

中国

"Teacher Chen," said a young student, as she poked her head around the corner of Chen Yu Hua's classroom door, "the headmaster wants to see you in his office."

Chen Yu Hua could not believe her good luck; the headmaster wanted to send her to buy musical instruments for the school, and the very next day she was on the bus to Xining. "I can't think of anyone more knowledgeable than you to go in my place," he had said, giving her self-confidence a boost. She was happy to have a much-needed break from the monotony of life in Xunhua.

The long-distance bus to Xining had never improved. It was still dusty and grimy and the engine threatened to expire with every small grade in the road. As usual, the roof of the bus was overloaded with goods, causing it to sway dangerously on the curves. Black smoke belched from the rusty exhaust pipe, the tires were worn and the driver had a heavy foot, but through some miracle, the bus made the scheduled run twice a week with no mishaps.

It was early in the spring of 1983. Money was available in the school budget for new books and musical instruments and the teachers had been given a small raise in pay. Deng Xiaoping, designing and re-designing plans in his Blueprint for a New China, was calling for more development and reform. He told the people that it would take a long time to change the country, but it would be done. "China is like a big ship, it must be turned slowly," was his creed.

Chen Yu Hua finished shopping for the school instruments the first morning in the city, finding herself with free time. She was invited to visit the office of a former professor from her Qinghai Normal School days. Over steaming tea they conversed about Chen Yu Hua's life and career at the Minorities School, and he showed her the latest teaching instruction books. He was asking her about her future plans, when a man walked into the office holding a book under his arm.

The professor nodded his greeting. "If you don't mind I must speak with Liu Hao for a few minutes about a special book," he said to Chen Yu Hua, motioning the young man to sit down. "This is Chen Yu Hua ... she is one of my former students," he said proudly. "She speaks excellent Mandarin and teaches English in Xunhua at a minorities girls' school."

Chen Yu Hua sat quietly, pretending to study a trade magazine on teaching techniques, all the time observing the young man. He was about her age, tall and handsome, and had an angular face and straight European nose. She thought he looked shy and honest, that he was an intellectual and she felt an immediate attraction to him. He spoke softly to the professor and acted a little self-consciously. He did not glance her way once except when he was leaving, and then all he did was avert his eyes and mumble something that sounded like "nice to meet you."

When she got home to Xunhua she told her friends, "all the nice young men live in Xining."

She never expected to see the handsome man again and was pleasantly surprised when a letter arrived from the professor asking permission for Liu Hao to correspond with her. She was delighted. Soon she received her first letter from him and their relationship began. He wrote to her every week, recounting his life. He was a teacher, born in Xining and, although he worked on the grasslands of the Qinghai plateau when he was a student, he had never been to Xunhua. He would enjoy meeting her again, he said, and hoped she would someday come to work in Xining.

Chen Yu Hua noticed an advertisement in the *Qinghai Daily* newspaper:

> *Middle school teachers having two or more years experience and*

passing the required entrance exam will qualify for a two-year further studies diploma at the newly established Qinghai College in Xining.

It was September and finally her life was coming together. She told her friend, "there's a light at the end of the tunnel."

"I know," said the teacher, "and make sure you only walk down the part of the street in the sunshine." She laughed, giving her own version of the adage about the sunny side of the street.

Chen Yu Hua passed the entrance exams easily, returning to Xining, where Liu Hao was waiting. She was delighted with life at the new college. It was different than when she was a naive and vulnerable seventeen; she was mature now, appreciating the chance to further her education.

She was assigned two surprising positions at the school. One was Chief of the Recreation Division of the Student Union and the other was the coveted position as announcer for the college broadcasting system. With this job came special privileges, including a large private room in the living quarters of the administrative building, away from the college dorm. She had never before lived in such a bright place. There were clean white tiles on the floor, a table with four matching chairs, and a bed tucked out of sight behind a screen at one end of the room. Filmy yellow curtains adorned the big windows and a brand new desk sat under the blue-tinged light of a long fluorescent ceiling fixture.

In her new room were tools of her broadcasting trade: a radio transmitter, cassette player, record player, tape recorder and microphone. Every day from Monday to Saturday at 7:15a.m., her job was to turn on the radio and play music for morning exercises, followed by the news from the Central People's Broadcasting Station. Chen Yu Hua enjoyed her duties and boomed her recognizable voice out of loudspeakers around the college several times a day, giving her a certain prestige.

Liu Hao came to visit often. They walked through People's Park, climbed the mountain to Beishan Temple and sat on the grassy slopes overlooking Xining. They mingled with large crowds as they roamed through the night market, stopping for noodles or, when they could afford it, a small delicious steamy hotpot of beef or mutton, swimming with vegetables, noodles and tofu. Every time they ate this dish she would laugh and repeat the tale of the dead sheep washed down from the plateau.

They enjoyed one another's stories and this night, as they sat in a hot bustling tent sharing kebabs of chicken and pork, and bowls of white rice, he reminded her about the legend she had promised to tell him; the one about her ancestors arriving in Xunhua valley.

"I find it strange that your people have lived in what was once part of ancient Tibet for hundreds of years," he said. "It seems unusual that Han people found their way to that primitive part of China ... unless they had a good reason to go."

"Yes, they had a very good reason ... an unusual reason ... and surprising! Would you like to hear about it?"

"Of course," he said shyly. "Perhaps one day I will see Xunhua." And he mumbled to himself, "If I ever get invited."

It was a peculiar tale, wrapped around the big feet of an empress. It happened many years ago during the reign of Emperor Hong Wu of the Ming Dynasty in a place in Nanjin City called Thuzi Lane. It was a moment in time when fate, twisted and unexpected, decreed a harsh punishment upon hundreds of people.

"It was Lantern Festival," began Chen Yu Hua. "The lane was teeming with happy revelers watching the parade. There was no room for a drop of water to trickle between the people, it was so crowded, and the night was turned into day with the light from the lanterns ... hundreds of lanterns, each painted with scenes of local everyday life. The story goes that one very special lantern stood out from all the others and drew much attention. It was a fine painting of a beautiful peasant girl riding a magnificent horse. The girl was smiling, dressed in traditional costume, holding a watermelon in her arms and, in the stirrups hanging from the saddle of the great horse ... rested her big feet."

Chen Yu Hua paused and drank from a water bottle.

"There was much attention given to the big feet," she explained. "As well you know, in those times high-class women had their feet bound into very small golden lilies, and it was unthinkable to dare portray any woman, rich or poor, with big feet in a painting."

Chen Yu Hua told about the Emperor's wife, Empress Ma, and how she had been born into a poor family and had much in common with the ordinary people of Thuzi Lane. She enjoyed the celebrations of her youth and found it hard to forget the good old days. On this night as with every other Lantern Festival, she was drawn to the excitement of the parade in Thuzi Lane.

"As our Chinese saying goes," murmured Chen Yu Hua in a soft cautionary voice, "if you are doomed, you are doomed ... and there was no escape. The happiness of the people in Thuzi Lane was coming to a quick sad end and no one could have imagined the tragedy about to befall them. You see ... Empress Ma kept a shameful secret all her life ... she did not have golden lilies."

Chen Yu Hua told Liu Hao that she was fascinated each time she listened to her father telling the legend when she was just a child. He told her how Empress Ma had seen the beautiful lantern. At first she admired it, which pleased the local artists who designed it, but then her suspicious mind began to conjure up something sinister in the picture and she complained to the Emperor that the people were mocking her; insulting her. She became paranoid and likened herself to the common girl on the lantern. She thought the watermelon referred to her young life in her home village called Huaixi in Anhui Province. The word *huaixi* could also relate to watermelon, her surname Ma could also mean horse, and the big feet were of course, in her troubled mind, her own big feet. Even the eunuchs of the palace did not know about her feet, but after she had been overheard telling the Emperor about the lantern, everyone found out her secret and gossip flew around the court. She felt humiliated; her dignity bruised.

"The Emperor was furious," said Chen Yu Hua. "He executed the poor artisans responsible for the offending lantern and decreed the banishment of hundreds of families living around Thuzi Lane to the furthermost region of China, to live in penal servitude in a remote place called Tibet. And guess what? When you come to my beautiful Xunhua you will realize it was actually a kind of freedom given to my ancestors and now their descendants are enjoying a good life."

Liu Hao was oblivious to the relentless noise of the passing crowds. He sat and listened, spellbound by every word his lovely friend was saying.

"An amazing story," he said. And then he heard something else that made his heart sing.

"I want you to see my home for yourself. Soon." Chen Yu Hua smiled.

Going to Hong Kong for New Year's Eve sounded like fun but after a hassle at the Public Security Bureau over exit and re-entry permits, and the hefty fees levied, we changed our minds. Nothing seemed easy, no matter how much patience one had.

"That's a lot of money for permits," Bill said on his third frustrating visit to the Bureau to speak with the young lady who looked more like a teenager than a P.S.B. officer. "Miss Chen, please tell the lady we did not hear about such big fees until today. She never once mentioned them on our last two visits. She should really tell people the cost of the fees *before* they start making preparations for a trip. It's only a matter of courtesy."

He promised himself not to get steamed up. This was China. Be reasonable.

The dialogue was long and intense between Miss Chen and Miss Teenager. They took turns eyeing Bill with Miss Chen pointing at him from time to time.

"She says she doesn't care, these are the charges and she knows for certain that Chinese people pay the same fees when they exit and re-enter Canada. So you may pay now for your permits."

Bill took a deep breath.

"That's not what I'm complaining about, Miss Chen. I know I have to pay the fees but I'm just not in the habit of carrying 1,200 yuan in my pocket at all times ... I don't think it's very fair that she did not tell us the amount on the first visit. It's a real inconvenience having to make a fourth trip out to this office."

Miss Teenager shrugged and turned back to her daily reading, ignoring everyone.

"Miss Chen, will you please tell the lady I would like to speak to the supervisor?" He knew he was nitpicking but he didn't care. "I want to lodge a complaint."

A few more words. A few more hand gestures.

"She says, please tell the foreigner ... I am the supervisor."

So instead of another trip to the P.S.B. office we arranged a New Year's Eve party at the famous Legend Hotel in Lanzhou, 185 miles away. Our friends Shirley and Bill Read agreed to fly down from Korea to meet us, and we would go with the Chen family on the train. Keith and Erin would join us later.

"Now that we're all going to Lanzhou," said Bill, handing Miss Chen the phone directory, "I think it's a good chance for you to learn how to make reservations."

The bookings went smoothly; four non-smoking rooms close together. It was only when Miss Chen described the evening's events at the hotel that *Chinglish* slipped into the conversation.

"Mr. Weigand, your tickets for the midnight party include two cups of alcohol and some *snakes*."

"Snakes?"

"Oh, so sorry ... I mean *snacks*."

The morning we were leaving for Lanzhou we stood on the dark street, with suitcases at our feet, for over an hour waiting for a ride to the station. "See you in the morning," Miss Chen had cheerily told us the night before.

"It's seven thirty," Bill stewed, "she was supposed to be here to pick us up at six thirty."

Just then a taxi careened around the corner of Nan Guan Road and screeched to a stop. Miss Chen and Mr. Liu jumped out of the car and ran to us, picked up our bags and threw them into the trunk.

"Get in! Get in!" yelled Miss Chen, "we have only ten minutes to get to the station."

We piled on top of one another in the back seat. Si Xian was scared by all the commotion, and half asleep. She sat on my knee uneasily watching her mother.

"Where have you been?" demanded Bill. "I hope we don't miss

the train."

I glanced at Miss Chen. By now she was hyperventilating and a few tears dribbled down her cheeks. Mr. Liu rested his head on the back of the seat, closed his eyes and took a deep breath.

"We all slept in," she sniffled, "please don't be mad ... I'm really sorry."

The taxi suddenly slammed to a stop in front of a flight of endless stairs leading up to the station.

"Hurry! Hurry!" Miss Chen was pushing us.

I watched as Mr. Liu sprinted up the stairs two at a time, his new black fedora tilted forward on his head. One moment his long coat clung feverishly to his legs, and the next moment it swirled and whipped like giant black wings caught in a gale. The two heavy suitcases seem to float straight out from his sides. This is a movie I thought, we're in a slow-motion movie.

"Hurry!" yelled Miss Chen again.

"Ridiculous," growled Bill, and Miss Chen kept running and crying and dragging little Si Xian by the hand.

When we got to the train platform we could hear the whistle blowing. A guard waved and shouted for us to run. She had taken the stairs away leaving no choice but to heave our suitcases through the open door of the coach and literally crawl up on our knees, pushing one another aboard the train as it began to move.

Bill was still grumbling under his breath, saying, "I was really looking forward to a relaxing trip."

But we made it. The whistle blew one last time and we settled into the hard seat section with a car full of Chinese faces peering curiously at our impressive entrance. Mr. Liu left to find our reserved soft seats.

Miss Chen quit crying and wiped her face with a damp washcloth I had given her and Si Xian smiled.

"I hope you're not mad at me, Mr. Weigand."

She was all bright and happy, humming and blowing her nose as though she hadn't caused us all a few heart palpitations. "We had relatives over last night and we didn't get to bed until two o'clock. I was so tired." She sighed a long sigh.

"No, I'm not mad," mumbled Bill, "I guess I just don't like

missing trains."

"I'm so glad," she smiled, looking very wise. "You must always remember a saying we have in China ... when you get angry, you only hurt yourself."

It wasn't long before Mr. Liu returned and herded us back through the crammed coaches to our reserved seats. Someone forgot to tell us that in China it was a must to be on time to claim reserved seats. If people are late it's assumed they are not going to show and the seats are up for grabs. Ours had been grabbed. Three men were occupying our places and they were not about to move or be intimidated by Mr. Liu or Miss Chen or any old foreigners.

"You should sit down," Bill said to me, pointing to the one empty spot by the window, "If we don't jump in there now someone will take it."

The men looked so sullen that I couldn't bring myself to push by them. I persuaded Bill to secure the seat while I smiled as broadly as my face would allow and listened to the argument rage on around me. A guard wearing what looked like an army uniform was practically rubbing noses with me, leaving little doubt he had no use for foreigners. I kept smiling. He kept on scolding me. I looked at Bill for moral support but the coward was reading the *China Daily*.

"What's the guard saying, Miss Chen?" I was almost afraid to ask.

"I told him we were sorry to be so late but we all have to sit together because you don't understand the language. I told him that you are Foreign Experts and I am your interpreter."

"And?"

"He says foreigners should obey rules the same as the Chinese do ... if they are late they should take the seats that are left over even if they are in the hard seat section."

This made me mad, which gets you nowhere in China.

"You tell him we always obey rules but this isn't fair ... we paid a lot of money for these tickets just to be assured of having seats." Just then Bill popped his head out from behind the latest news from Beijing and produced the five tickets.

The guard glowered at both of us, unsmiling, unmoving.

"He says, he doesn't care … rules are rules."

It seemed that everyone was in on the big argument. Passengers became totally engrossed by what was going on, and were hanging out of their seats or standing in the aisles tossing in comments for what they were worth. I thought perhaps they were taking sides and wondered if anyone was on our side. Maybe they were betting on who was going to win and maybe they wanted us out of their coach. Bill stood up and insisted I should take his seat. I knew he didn't think I was being diplomatic enough.

"We had better find other seats. Perhaps back where we started," he said, matter-of-factly. "We really should have been on time."

"Not yet," insisted Miss Chen.

Our saving grace came in the form of a stocky little lady in a dark blue railway uniform. She had an unusually soft, persuasive voice. It didn't take long before the men reluctantly moved to other seats and the battle was over.

"I feel bad about this," I said sheepishly, referring to the uproar we had just caused. "I hope no one's upset with us."

Miss Chen looked surprised. "Of course not, why would anyone be upset?"

Within minutes the whole incident was forgotten as though it was never hugely important in the first place.

The train steamed on to Lanzhou, the noise level rising steadily to full volume. People visited with each other, slept, read or just stared out the windows, but whatever they decided to do, it was done in a thick fog of strong smoke from Hong Ta Shan cigarettes or the popular Ashima, which sounded to me remarkably like *asthma*.

In one of the most polluted cities in China, the four-star Legend Hotel was an oasis. It became a private make-believe fairyland for Si Xian. She rode the escalator up and down and took endless hot bubble baths. She dressed in the tartan outfit our daughter Teri had sent from Canada and posed for photos in front of the huge Christmas tree in the lobby. She was in heaven and the only nine-year-old in the entire place. In fact, there were very few guests in the hotel December 31, 1995.

Bill and Shirley came all the way from Korea. Among the gifts they brought for us were a Pyrex pie plate, coffee and, of all things, Canadian bacon. Erin and Keith arrived in the afternoon. We drank champagne with our good friends and enjoyed Western food in a dining room blazing with lights from a dozen crystal chandeliers.

"Happy New Year, Miss Chen!" I said. "Are you enjoying your first turkey?"

"*Xin Nian Kuai Le* ... Happy New Year, Jeri! It tastes *a lot* like chicken!"

twenty-three

中国

Eighteen months of Chen Yu Hua's two year program had raced by and she wanted to know more and more about Liu Hao. They had much in common and she would miss this shy, polite and caring man when the day came for her to leave.

She thought about going home to her family, but the mixed feelings she had about them made her sad. If only they would forgive her for disobeying her father, instead of making life miserable and isolating her. But now she enjoyed Liu Hao and the hustle and excitement of the city where there was always a surprise around every corner. Like the day she spotted her first real Western foreigner walking down Xi Dajie, one of Xining's main streets.

The young foreigner had very blond hair and round blue eyes. His skin was *white*. She had seen foreigners on TV before but never up close and her curiosity got the better of her shyness. Most Chinese, even if they wanted to, were afraid of being denounced for speaking to a Westerner. During the Cultural Revolution, which was still very real in their memory, people who had any conversation with foreigners or merely had overseas relatives could be thrown in jail. The concept of the "open-door policy" was not yet believable in this remote part of China, far away from Beijing.

She also remembered the story of a young interpreter, assigned to a doctor from America while he was working in remote parts of the province. They went everywhere together, from small mountain villages to banquets with the leaders; she was his constant companion. When his term was over and he left China, the gossip began. Cruel and scandalous rumors. The poor girl could not bear the pressure; she and her family had to move away all because she knew a foreigner.

Chen Yu Hua joined the tag-along crowd that followed the foreign man. When he stopped to look in the window of a shop, they stopped to look. When he walked up to the third floor of the department store, they walked behind him and, when Chen Yu Hua had her chance, she moved up beside him and said, "Hello, can I help you?"

He answered her in English.

It was the first time she had ever spoken English to anyone other than a Chinese English teacher. She was intrigued by his facial expressions and couldn't take her eyes off his huge nose, huge by her standards anyway. He told her that he was from Sweden and worked for an oil exploration company in Golmud, near the Qaidam Basin, 500 miles west of Xining. She helped him purchase a leather suitcase and a sheepskin vest in the Big Cross Department Store, while the curious crowds regarded the two ... the strange looking foreigner and the pretty Chinese lady, as afternoon entertainment.

She found the foreigner easy to talk to and he seemed especially interested in her childhood. "When I was a little girl, sometimes foreigners would visit Xunhua and although we were very scared we chased after them, staring at them. The foreigners kept calling ...Hello! Hello! And of course, we didn't know what the strange words meant ... I remember when they looked at us with their blue eyes, we were frightened to death of those big people."

They both laughed at her stories and soon it was time for him to leave.

"Thank you, Chen Yu Hua," said the man from Sweden. "It was such a nice afternoon and you speak excellent English ... perhaps you would accept a tip for all your help." She was perplexed when he held out twenty yuan to her. She had never heard the word "tip" before. Refusing the money, she thanked him and explained that Chinese would never accept money for advice or work freely given. This was considered a good quality in a person.

"I am proud to know I have been of help to you," she said, making sure her grammar was perfect.

Several foreigners visited Xining that year and if Chen Yu Hua thought any of them spoke English she would boldly approach them for a conversation. She was eager to learn the correct pronunciations and study the gestures and expressions peculiar to her chosen second language. It was important for Chen Yu Hua to be the very best at whatever she did in life. If this meant speaking with complete strangers on city streets to learn their language and customs, so be it.

"My term is almost over ... another couple of weeks and I'll be on my way home," said Chen Yu Hua. She was walking across the soccer field with Liu Hao towards the school dormitory, admiring a large full silver moon hovering just above the horizon.

"I read somewhere when the moon appears big like this it's an optical illusion," said Liu Hao.

Chen Yu Hua was only half listening.

"It's really the same size as it always is. If you look at the moon through your legs like this ... " Liu Hao bent his tall frame in two and peered through his legs. "You see ... the moon is normal."

Chen Yu Hua could not keep from laughing. He was always telling her some useless information, making her laugh. She was going to miss him and was in no hurry to rush back to her family in Xunhua. She had written to her parents faithfully every two weeks since she came to Xining. Never once had they penned a reply, not even a small note, so bitter and resentful and unforgiving were they; still punishing her for making the family "lose face".

"Will you write to me?" asked Chen Yu Hua.

Of course he would, but she wondered if her relationship with Liu Hao was going anywhere. He was too reserved and shy to say he would miss her when she was gone. Again, her future seemed bleak. She could see herself doomed to teach at the Minorities School forever and ever, growing old, and bent over her cane, still talking about English verbs and singing Tibetan songs.

They were coming back from the night market where Liu Hao bought a turquoise and horsehair bracelet, "I was thinking about the bracelet you lost and I want you to have this new one," he said shyly, slipping it over her hand. "I hope you remember me every time you look at it."

He suddenly bent over and kissed her, just like that, squarely on the mouth. She was so shocked. It was her very first kiss and she was weak at the knees, trembling with excitement, and not knowing why she felt this way.

"I must go in now," she said, her heart was beating so fast it made her feel faint, "See you tomorrow." She hurried away leaving Liu Hao alone. He felt lost and a little confused by her sudden departure. What happened? Perhaps he had been too forward ... too soon. He certainly would have enjoyed a second kiss, but maybe another day.

That night Chen Yu Hua decided to marry Liu Hao. She turned the bracelet round and round on her wrist, studying each small turquoise gemstone. They felt warm and sensuous to her touch and little shivers of ecstasy tingled along her spine. She knew life was good and Liu Hao would make a fine husband.

On January 3, 1996, at the Canadian Embassy in Beijing, the Canadian ambassador signed the contract for our Midwives Project.

We had waited for the snows of winter but they never came. A light dusting fell in November and we were told to expect more in April. Xining's air was too dry to produce snow, but it was a different story in the high mountains of Qinghai and Amdo County in northern Tibet. It was one of the severest winters the Tibetan herders could remember. According to government figures, over 6,000 people fell ill from starvation and disease, and one million animals, sheep and yak, perished in the deep snow. Forty severe blizzards pounded the area without mercy from September through to the end of January.

Relief from the Chinese government and around the world was immediate. They opened roads and distributed food, tents, fuel and grain to forty thousand people in the stricken regions. The snow was so deep it took the army several days and nights to clear the way for the convoys of supply trucks to inch along mountain roads in blinding storms. In one village starving yaks began tearing and eating the tents of the herders. The families, unable to drive the frenzied animals away, huddled in small government buildings with no heat or food for over half a month until rescue came. In another tragic scene in Yuqag Township, 300 emaciated villagers, without food of any kind, sought refuge in the newly built HOPE School, ripping the wood from their homes to fuel the fires.

People starved and froze to death in the snows of the high mountains that terrible winter while we lived in the dry atmosphere of our city.

Scot Slessor, from the Canadian Embassy, brought money to Xining to buy grain. He personally supervised the loading of trucks and watched the convoy leave for the stricken villages. We had lunch with him at the hotel and talked about our project. It was the second time we met; the first was back in October when he blew into town with Phil Calvert and visited our little home. "You *do* have a house ... a *real* Canadian house," he had said, and they dropped cheese, chocolates and wine on the kitchen table.

A Xining winter was not the best place in the world for lungs. I coughed and hacked in the cold air laced with coal smoke and Bill suffered from sinus problems. It didn't help when most of our meetings were held behind tightly closed windows in the milieu of a factory chimney. Every cadre was a chain smoker. Statistics showed one in three of all cigarettes manufactured in the world were sold in China, and we inhaled most of them second hand.

People on the streets wore white surgical-style masks made from layers of cheesecloth. Miss Chen bought us a couple, then stood back and laughed as we tried to stretch them across our noses from ear to ear.

"Your noses are too big!" She loved it when she had an opportunity to point out our over-sized facial appendages. "You should have a Chinese face. We say our face is like a flat board with seven holes!"

Our chosen project had been passed by CIDA.

The next month was busy. We had meetings with various cadres and officials from the Health Bureau, had our books and blue bags printed, sorted boxes of equipment arriving from

Shanghai and organized the money from Beijing. Our little Bank of China around the corner, the one that always burned dozens of candles when the power went off, received the bank transfer of 26,000 Canadian dollars, or 159,000 yuan, for our project.

The day came for our press release. We were pleasantly surprised and honored to make our announcement about the Midwife Project together with Number One Mayor Liu, Vice Governor Bai Ma, Mayor Yang and other dignitaries. Our friend Ms. Chen Jing Jun was all smiles as were the ladies from Datong and Vice Governor Mrs. A (pronounced "R").

There was more pomp and circumstance than we expected. Young Liu had spent two days constructing a long red banner with Chinese and English lettering heralding our project, and seven members of the press and TV were there for the photo op. We shook hands with one another, opened a bottle of wine and proposed a toast to a successful training program. Mrs. Ding agreed we had come a long way since our first meeting in August and soon we would be out in the townships.

Our first trip began on a bright cloudless day.

We were heading for Hao Jila, a small mountain village beyond Datong. It would be a long bumpy ride, the first of many to visit the teachers and pupils involved in the training course. When we reached Hao Jila it was snowing. The village was only a cluster of buildings springing from the milky clay soil it stood on. There were mud walls for houses and mud walls for the courtyard; the whole scene melted tone on tone into the landscape.

The village was desperately poor, hovering ten thousand feet up the side of a mountain trail. Not a soul was visible, not a bird or animal, as Driver Zhang drove our station wagon through Main Street to the nursing station where the Public Health staff was expecting us.

"Driver Zhang says welcome to paradise," chuckled Miss Chen. "Hao Jila means very excellent, the best or perhaps … paradise."

"I'm glad we wore our heavy coats," I griped, "Jeeze, it's cold."

We waited, watching big snowflakes mixed with rain falling on the windshield until the door of the little building opened and a very young lady greeted us. She was one of the nurses, sent to work in the remote parts of Qinghai, usually for several years at a time; a particularly monotonous, lonely existence for a young Han woman from the city.

The chilly classroom had a large clear light bulb dangling from the center of the ceiling as the eight women, wrapped in coats and shawls, crowded around us, curious to see foreigners and eager to begin learning. The teacher was serious about her lessons; she clapped her hands for the women to sit down and asked Miss Chen to begin.

"You must always speak first," Miss Chen reminded me, "I'm only the interpreter. The directions must come from you." So between the two of us we informed the women about the money they would receive and the graduation at the end of the term, showed them the sample kit and described the proper use of its contents. Miss Chen held up the small weigh scale and performed some elaborate demonstrations with her hands. The women laughed.

"I told them when they put the baby in a scarf to weigh it they must hold it over the bed," she said, "I don't want the baby slipping out and falling on the floor."

We stayed and watched the teacher instructing her class, writing with chalk on the battered blackboard. The students became engrossed; they had note pads, pencils and bilingual books in Chinese and Tibetan. There was more technical knowledge and plain information about midwifery available in front of them that day than they had ever seen.

When we left the classroom we were surprised to find a group of locals waiting patiently for us. We could see they were poor, not thin and starving poor as they were well fed, but poor in material things. One lady pushed her small son towards Bill, obviously wanting him to shake hands with the foreigner. What an uproar he made, screaming and clutching his mother's leg and hiding by wrapping himself in her coattail.

Miss Chen interpreted. "He says he is not going to let that foreigner touch him!"

The other children weren't so vociferous. They stood quietly and timidly shook our hands, and stared at us like we were aliens from Mars. One young boy had a very distinct cleft lip. He smiled at me and I thought if he lived in Canada he would receive a simple corrective operation. I asked Miss Chen if this was common, she said there were many children in this part of Qinghai with this condition as well as enlarged thyroids.

"Although all commercial salt sold in China has Iodine added, people who are poor get natural salt from Qinghai Lake ... it's cheaper but not as good for them."

When we were leaving I looked for the boy with the deformity and, whatever the reason, perhaps embarrassment, he had disappeared and we never saw another like him.

A real treat always waited for us after the morning classes. We drove to selected farm homes for delicious luncheon meals prepared by the family; pork and chicken dishes, noodles, peanuts, breads and steaming tea. If it were a Muslim home, we would not have pork, only mutton, and tasty bread made by rolling, twisting and braiding dough, then deep-frying the big rounds in rapeseed oil. At first we wondered how the farmer could possibly afford to supply such generous meals for our entourage until we were told the food for these visits was courtesy of the government.

We spent two months touring remote villages. The classes varied in size and nationality; some had only Muslim students, and others included Tibetan, Tu and Mongolian. Women came to classes any way they could. They walked for miles from remote homes high in the mountains or rode donkeys and the lucky ones were driven on Mechanical Buffalo tractors. They had one thing in common: they were dedicated to learn.

In one village, much to my shame and regret, I displayed my frustration.

An astonishingly beautiful young nurse, with smooth skin, delicate features and full black hair swept back with tiny seed-pearl combs, met us on the clinic steps. She took us first to her sparsely furnished quarters to see the usual hard dirt floor, the narrow bed, and the small coal stove filling the air with biting odors. She was very proud of it all and told us she had been there for several years. On a dressing table she had laid all her worldly goods: an oval hand mirror, her toiletries, a small vase with mauve silk flowers, and an array of hair combs. Hanging on the wall was a large gold-framed photo of herself wrapped in blue silk in a collage of various poses, confident, young, sexy, spirited. It was as though she was preserving the aura of this beautiful person. As though she was saying, "this picture is really me ... not the poor girl standing before you in this dark room."

We visited the birthing room where she had just given a lecture to fifteen students on the method of examining a pregnant woman. The class was still there and so was the noticeably expectant mother. I looked around the room. A birthing chair sat in one corner. Had it ever been cleaned? Dried blood was sticking to the cracked old leather. The examining bed was equally soiled with a once-white sheet stained with grime and brown blood. I couldn't contain myself. It wasn't fair. It just wasn't fair. The beautiful nurse who had never been trained properly, the smiling, glowing, mother-to-be who didn't realize the danger that germs presented for her newborn, and the serious students taking in every word of the lectures; all were unaware of how ignorant and lacking in pertinent information they really were.

"Miss Chen, please ask the nurse if this village has water." I tried to sound cheerful but couldn't.

"Why do you want to know this?"

"Please ... just ask."

"Yes they have lots of water ... they say it's the best in Qinghai."

"Ask them if the nursing station is supplied with soap," I said, not looking at Miss Chen, who hadn't caught on to my questions yet.

While she was talking to the nurse I couldn't help but think about an article I once read regarding high infant mortality rate in poorer parts of the world. 'If only midwives would wash their hands before delivering an infant it would cut down the death rate,' it stated bluntly.

After we had discussed the water and soap issue with the nurse, I asked calmly why no one washed the examining room and especially the birthing chair. I pointed to the sheet.

"And this must always be clean," I said, my voice a little more agitated. "This is precisely where disease starts."

Miss Chen stared at me. A suffocating moment passed. I could hear my own shallow breathing. At first I thought she wasn't going to say anything, but then she launched into her own campaign against dirt. She flipped the soiled sheet with all the theatrical aplomb of a stage actress while the startled nurse grew rigid and the students looked as though they couldn't believe their ears. As for Mrs. Ding and Mrs. Yang, who appeared to be somewhat confused about what was going on, I was hoping I hadn't gone too far; I didn't want to anger them.

"OK, Miss Chen, I think we've said enough," I smiled weakly at the nurse. "Tell her I'm very sorry but she should teach the students to use hot soapy water often and explain that the reason we're doing this project in the first place is to try and cut down the number of infant deaths."

The group seemed to be in a surprisingly good mood as they followed us back to our station wagon. Not a total loss of face for the young nurse. She smiled and shook my hand and waved as we drove away but I was still unhappy about the meeting, especially when Miss Chen said, "Imagine ... today she met her very first foreigner only to get a scolding."

"I can't help it," I said defensively, feeling I was about to cry, "It just takes some soap and water ... a little work and it saves lives. The Chinese always admire Dr. Bethune ... always saying how wonderful he was ... well, did you know he was very strict with the hospital staff where he worked? He insisted they must be clean and never perform operations without sterilizing everything."

I could tell Miss Chen was starting to feel bad for me. This I didn't need. She straightened up and folded her arms like she always did when she wanted to say something reflective. "You must understand ... the nurse probably has never been shown what to do, there are many things we don't know ... have never been taught. You have to think about that." She sighed and looked thoughtful. "Perhaps they're too busy or it's like, maybe a traditional way of life."

"Well then, it's a tradition that should be changed, Miss Chen," I said, a little too harshly, "I don't like a lot of so-called traditions, especially the terrible ones tolerated against woman in the name of religion or certain societies or certain rites ... female circumcision, bride burning ... just to name a couple of ghastly ones ... and countries where women have no say in their own lives, no say regarding their children or divorce or owning property." I shook my head gravely. I had to quit. I softened my rhetoric and even managed a feeble smile. "But dancing or singing old songs or using recipes your great grandma passed down ... now those are healthy traditions."

"Yes," said Miss Chen quietly, "I agree with you."

I hoped she did.

twenty-four

中国

Before leaving Xining to return home to her teaching position, Chen Yu Hua went to visit someone she had never met. Li Wen Shi was a man who was once very important in the life of the Chen family. He was a friend to her father and uncles, and an important influence in Xunhua and Xining in the time before the Revolution. Convicted of being a Class Enemy, his youth had been taken from him, exhausted in the prison near Qinghai Lake, but now he was a notable professor living at a university, and he was free.

She took the city bus to the eastern part of Xining. An impressive tree-lined avenue led to the wooden paneled entrance doors of the sprawling Russian-built institution known as the Minorities University. She made her way to the living quarters for teachers, students and workers. Professor Li greeted her and ushered her into his large apartment. The wide hallway had a smooth concrete floor with smudges of blue enamel paint still visible in places, and doors leading off on both sides to other rooms. A faint odor of incense hung in the air.

Professor Li stood tall and straight and rather delicate, she thought. She imagined his willowy figure wrapped in the flowing silk robes of Chinese literati, standing in a place of learning, lecturing eager students in some long-ago dynasty. He would be holding a book of science or mathematics or Chinese history and embracing it with his slender expressive fingers. Small merry eyes glinted out of his smooth beardless face; good breeding and culture were evident in his every move.

"Welcome to my home ... come, come," said the soft voice,

husky with age. "I would like to show you my apartment. It is very comfortable for me and my wife … and our grandchildren visit often." He took her to a small library anteroom where shelves on one wall were crammed with old stale books. Well-worn, their covers were wrinkled and turned up from dampness and, across the room, flimsy paper scribblers and narrow brown journals lined the shelves from floor to ceiling. In front of a high window stood a decrepit desk trembling under a mountain of newspapers, books marked for further reading, bits of note paper with ink scratches, old calendars, signature chops and calligraphy ink stones. Amid the clutter sat an out-of-place blue and white Ming sleeve vase, filled with dusty dried-up flowers.

"I am so pleased you came to see me. Tell me … how is your father?"

"He is very well grandfather." She did not wish to lie but could not tell him they hadn't spoken for months.

"And your mother?"

"Very well."

A framed black and white picture of a young man in uniform caught her eye. It was obviously very old. She could see the photo paper had yellowed and faded, but the young eyes, unusually clear, watched intently from under the brim of the Mao cap with the prominent Communist yellow star.

"Please, grandfather, I must not be rude but can I ask you about this picture?"

"I still miss him … we were like brothers," Professor Li said. He took the picture from the shelf and used his sleeve to polish the dust from the glass. "He was my best friend, we grew up together in the same village in Gandu Township, went to the same school." The old man stared at the glass and the eyes stared back, "tragic … tragic," he said softly.

He told Chen Yu Hua that one day the young man, barely sixteen, made a fateful decision to run away and fight with the Communists. The professor begged him not to go, it would be dangerous, but his friend, fascinated by Mao Zedong, said he believed in their cause. Whether or not he really did believe, or was just naïve, he never returned and Professor Li never saw him again.

It wasn't long before word came that his young friend had been killed in a skirmish.

Chen Yu Hua followed the professor to the lounge. He slipped into his over-sized chair, sat upright, brought his legs together and laid his hands palms down motionless on his knees. He would never cross his legs like a foreigner or be restless in his movements: he was a Chinese gentleman, brought up with impeccable manners ingrained since childhood.

She sat on a black leather sofa across from him; a low table held dishes over-flowing with nuts and dried fruit, little cakes and cups of tea. The walls were draped with diplomas, awards, certificates and scrolls of calligraphy, and the sun filtered through the four dusty casement windows giving the room a peculiar claustrophobic misty glow. She had the sensation of thick, almost chewy air, like the air she thought she remembered once in a small room somewhere in her childhood; air so heavy it moved with you.

They talked about her family, about her young life in Xunhua. Pleasant, casual talk. Her schooling. And he was proud of her for going into the teaching profession.

"What about you, grandfather? I don't know much about your life," said Chen Yu Hua quietly, shocked by her own boldness. She knew it was impolite to ask but she was genuinely curious about this gracious old man. To her delight Professor Li smiled. "I would be pleased to tell you about my life," he said.

He told her he was the son of landowners, born in a China when wealth and privilege meant a secure, peaceful life; a time when the country was divided into regions and administered by powerful warlords. As a child he was educated by private tutors, later sent to Lanzhou to receive senior high school and university education. He spent time as a professor at the Nanjing University before returning to live and teach in Xining. In those days the city was small and remote, a trading center still enclosed by ancient walls and towers dating back to the Ming Dynasty. And Ma Bu Fang was warlord. He thought well of Ma Bu Fang and became a close friend to his son.

"Ma Bu Fang joined forces with Chiang Kai-shek in 1927," the old man went on. "He initiated good things under his jurisdiction.

He stamped out gambling and prostitution ... the use of opium. He built hospitals and primary schools in every county and opened a trade route through Qinghai to encourage business. But then, just like other warlords, he exploited the peasant farmers with heavy grain taxes and, when he instituted conscription, it was mostly young farm boys who became soldiers. Rich fathers merely hired poor peasants to enter the army in the place of their sons. He was in the midst of proposing a highway to Tibet with American support when the Communists came to power and forced him to flee to Formosa."

The old man sipped his tea and motioned gracefully with his left hand towards a cream-colored porcelain cup, as fine and fragile as an eggshell that sat in front of Chen Yu Hua. "Please, have more jasmine tea," he said.

He drew a long raspy breath and resumed his story.

"In the late 1940s, Mao Zedong sent an army north, in his words, to liberate Qinghai Province ... there was a huge battle and General Cheng from the Communist army was captured by Ma Bu Fang's men." She heard Professor Li's thin voice falter, ebbing slowly away in the back of his throat. "Ma Bu Fang phoned directly to Chiang Kai-shek at his headquarters in Nanjing asking what to do. The answer was, 'execute the Communist general at once and do not take prisoners.' General Cheng was directly taken out and shot."

Chen Yu Hua studied the professor; his head back, eyes closed, his hands knotted together as though he was praying. He sighed, rocking his lean body ever so slightly.

"And then Ma Bu Fang's troops took the three hundred or so Communist soldiers ... they were so young ... some just boys ... and they were buried alive ... it was sad," he whispered. "Sad."

Chen Yu Hua was moved, fascinated by the story. She had never been versed on the history of the famous warlord and was stunned to hear this dramatic account by a man who witnessed such brutality being done by Chinese to Chinese, in the saddest of all conflicts, a civil war.

Professor Li said nothing more. He left the room, taking a break from his story-telling. Chen Yu Hua sat in front of the delicious tea, the polished oranges and the lovely red-bean curd cakes. But she sat still and never touched the food.

The professor returned, composed and cheerful again, with many more stories to tell. About the ancient Silk Road and the brave generals who fought historic battles around Xining, but what left Chen Yu Hua in awe of this old gentleman with the sparkling little eyes that smiled on their own was the story of his imprisonment. Being too close to Ma Bu Fang proved to be his downfall.

"Grandfather," she whispered, "my father says you spent twenty-eight years in jail ... please, can this be true?"

"Yes," he said, "it wasn't so bad ... I met a great many interesting people in the prison at Qinghai Lake and, as long as there was no political talk, we were free to discuss anything. My favorite time was when the intellectuals arrived after Mao's Hundred Flowers in 1958."

The professor smiled happily and nodded his head. "I learned much ... it was like having a lot of teachers around ... and when the Capitalist Roaders came they had more interesting things to tell me. Everyone came to the jail at one time or other," he chuckled. "In a series of waves ... politicians, officials, army leaders. I met them all ... gathered infinite knowledge and skills from them. I was released in 1980."

The sun was almost gone. By now the lights would have been turned on in Chen Yu Hua's home, but here in this quiet soundless place, it would somehow be inappropriate to let artificial light invade the serenity.

"Tell me, Chen Yu Hua, are you married?"

"Not yet, grandfather," she smiled. "Soon."

"Is he a kind person?"

"Yes ... and he is a history teacher."

"Good." He handed her a book. "This is for you ... it is the story of Ma Bu Fang because you should know the history of your part of our country."

She thanked the professor and promised to read it. He walked with her to the door.

"Don't wait so long to come back," he said.

Chen Yu Hua was thoughtful. She came away from the Minorities University with the greatest admiration for Professor Li, a man she called grandfather, a man who held no grudges toward his captors and turned an incarceration, which should have crushed him, into a learning experience.

Miss Wei picked up a new saying from us. No kidding! Only she enunciated each syllable and it came out "no kid-ding" with a hesitation between *kid* and *ding*. She was fascinated with Western idioms and every morning when she got to her office downtown she phoned Bill ... "Can I please have another new idiom today?"

She kept us busy writing down every idiom and phrase we could remember and she would say, "hello, I'm in the pink today ... how about you? I hope you're not blue today," or "I painted red on the town last night."

After the idiom session on the phone she would read an article from the China Daily News. Bill would correct her pronunciation and comprehension. We learned that interpreters could memorize and write the words but didn't understand their meanings. Miss Wei's daily English lesson worked well. We also had to choose our words carefully when talking to people with limited English; nothing would confuse a new student as much as rhyming off bizarre idioms like, "I have it on the tip of my tongue."

Early one morning she arrived at our house, animated and out of breath, "Jeri ... Jeri ... I've been to the market and found some chicken *chests* for you ... we should go right now and you can buy them ... Yeah?"

I didn't have the heart to correct her. Anyway, to me chicken chests sounded more refined than chicken breasts.

The market was at its best in the morning, relatively clean and not crowded and we soon found the trader she was looking for. His counter was stacked high with white boxes, each stamped clearly with big blue letters, "FRESH FROZEN CHICKEN FROM

CARROLL FARMS—ARIZONA USA."

"Can we see what they look like please?" I conveyed through Miss Wei. The smiling trader whacked the heavy box on the concrete floor to loosen the solid block of ice. Then with a long yellow handled screw driver in one hand and a large wooden mallet in the other, he hammered away, prying the breasts and legs from their frosty prison.

I wondered what the general manager of the packing plant back at Carroll Farms would think if he could see this performance ... bashing and hacking his box of neatly packed chicken chests on the dirt floor of a market in the middle of China. But mostly I worried if these boxes of "fresh chicken" had been thawed and refrozen on the long trip from America.

The chicken turned out to be pretty good. The chests were a bit stringy but the huge meaty legs simmered just enough in the packaged gravy and beer to become tender and tasty. At least our new friends, the Archers, thought so when we had dinner together at our house for the first time later that day.

We met this delightful couple soon after they arrived in Xining. Tony was a rangeland and ecologist manager and was approached by the EC (European Community) to be an adviser to the Qinghai Animal Husbandry Department. His job was to oversee the development of new types of hardy and fast-growing forage grasses for experimental use on the Tibetan Plateau.

Josiane and Tony Archer were our age and lived in the Tian Ju Agriculture Commission Hotel. Tony was a slim, athletic and wiry Englishman and Jo, sophisticated and stylish, spoke with a lovely soft Swiss accent. It wasn't long before we learned she could whip up an apple tart in no time and even found new ways to cook the chicken legs as she had an oven, a *real* oven, in her flat.

Their young pretty daughter, Nicole, was visiting for the holidays before returning to her studies in England.

"Were the chicken chests good?" asked Miss Wei the next day.

"They melted in my mouth," I said to those big brimming-with-emotion eyes of hers.

"No kid ding ... Yeah?" she breathed.

The ancient Chinese celebration known as Spring Festival or "passing the year" is determined by the lunar calendar and falls annually between January 21 and February 19, on the date when the new moon lights up the sky.

In 1996 the Festival began officially on February 18.

Families spent days preparing for Spring Festival. They scrubbed and scoured every corner of their homes to rid them of bad luck, paid any outstanding debts, pasted gaudy banners all over the place, and they cooked.

The Commission staff "decoration squad" showed up early in the morning. Young Liu, Mr. Cui and the ladies, hung traditional large red and gold lanterns from the living room ceiling, and stuck red banners on each side of our front door with the words Happiness ... Long Life ... Prosperity, stamped prominently in flashy gold Chinese characters.

The completely dried-out Christmas tree was still standing in the corner. No one cared that the tree had overstayed its allotted time. No one said "what are you doing with a dried up Christmas tree in your living room in February," they only admired it. We had cut down the top, stripped off the brown spiky needles, wound the lights back on the bare branches, replaced each red paper flower with a new one and, voila, we had a bushy little tree, decorated for Spring Festival.

We bought a gleaming gold-colored money bank shaped like a sailor's hat and hung Happy New Year prints of plump little cartoon children on the wall. We bought fruit, candies, gold and red candles, and filled small red money packets with two-yuan notes to hang on the tree for visiting children.

That evening was spent at dinner with the Chen family. We had walked through the back lanes of the No.14 Middle School compound, acrid coal smoke smarting our eyes, and up long narrow stairs to the tiny apartment on the fifth floor. Mr. Liu led the way with his flashlight. Si Xian took my hand to guide me up the black-as-pitch stairwell. "Come gramma," she said, only it sounded like *guama*. I squeezed her hand.

They opened the door to the bright apartment, a stark contrast from the black stairs. The living room doubled as Si Xian's bedroom and was painted off-white. Even the old window casements were painted and the floor was tiled in blue and white. Two small padded blue seats sat on either side of a table covered by a white lace cloth. A daybed stretched along one wall with Si Xian's precious stuffed toys, and the Barbie Doll we had given her for Christmas, arranged neatly on pillows. Along the other wall was a portable electric organ, a cabinet with TV and video machine, silk flowers in vases, posters on the walls and a long calligraphy banner created by Miss Chen's father, Chen Jian Pin. Windows draped in blue nylon curtains separated the living room from the glassed-in porch where laundry was hung to dry, and plants, boxes and paint cans fought for space.

The cozy bedroom had storage cupboards, bookshelves and a wooden desk. It was surprisingly roomy. The small toilet closet had no shower or hand sink, but a wire stand with a colorful enamel basin filled with warm water stood in the hall. It was draped with pretty towels and had a new pink bar of soap for the guests.

When I told Miss Chen how beautifully her place was decorated, she was pleased. "I got lots of my ideas when you renovated the old house," she said, "but you know we've been promised a new home ... maybe next year."

There was a knock at the door. It was Mr. Liu's mother and father and his wide-eyed eight-year-old nephew, Si Yuan, who wanted to meet and perhaps touch a real-live foreign grandpa.

Mr. Liu set up a round dining table and served tea and beer and snacks until the main meal was ready. We enjoyed eight cold dishes as we sat close together, comfortable, like family, like we belonged. There were no strangers here. I'm sure Grampa Liu knew it was impolite to stare at the foreigners but he couldn't help it. Maybe it was because he was a doctor and he wanted to compare anatomies but every time I turned my head I felt his curious eyes on us. His wife was totally at ease, her grandmotherly plump face beaming with a warm smile.

From the tiny kitchen Miss Chen created eight hot dishes. It made me realize how time consuming a Chinese dinner could be and how little chance the cook has to enjoy the guests. Every dish was prepared separately and came to the table sizzling from the kitchen wok.

Dessert was the traditional Eight Treasure Pudding. We toasted "Happy Spring Festival" and Miss Chen played the little organ and sang while Si Xian danced. Mr. Liu hung a meter of snapping firecrackers out the porch window to scare away any evil spirits and Si Yuan got up enough nerve to sit on his foreign grampa's knee.

Later that night we went to sleep naively thinking the holiday season would last five or six days. "It might be seven days," guessed Bill. It turned out to be two weeks of boisterous celebrations.

"Surely you are not asleep," said Miss Wei when I foggily answered the shrill ringing of the office phone. Her familiar soft voice slowly penetrated my thick brain.

"What time is it?" I mumbled.

"It is now a quarter to midnight and I want to wish you Happy New Year … you should wake up and celebrate because soon you will not be able to sleep anymore."

She was right.

Fifteen minutes later the most thunderous barrage of fireworks lit up the sky, sending clouds of smoke sifting through the night air of the city. Sharp reports, like hundreds of machine guns, resonated from long strips of small red fire crackers dangling from every window in the high apartment buildings. "It sounds like a war," said Bill.

It was the beginning of a giant festival. China was on the move. Transportation was stretched beyond its limits with over thirty-five million people "going home". It was like the whole population of Canada moving back and forth across the country during Christmas week. Feasting, visiting, dancing, singing and fireworks, all day … all night … fireworks … day after day, for two weeks.

The invitations rolled in.

We dined with Mayor Liu and his wife in their spacious apartment, where a painting of what looked like a snowy scene in a Quebec village hung over his Western sofa. The star performer from the local opera company belted out traditional folk songs; he was the same baritone who shook the foundations of our little house back in November.

Knowing Miss Chen

The next night it was gourmet spring rolls, the specialty of Miss Ma, Mr. Cheng's attractive wife. Dinner with Mayor Li and wife. Dinner with Mayor Yang and family, Boss Liu and family. Breakfast with a lady from our office who gave us the gift of a calligraphy stone. And Shanghai flavor at the home of Chen Jing Jun, prepared by her husband. Many of the older men were very good cooks. Most retired sooner than their wives and, due to the lack of golf courses or the money and freedom to travel the world, they took over kitchen duties and turned themselves into market shoppers and excellent chefs.

And visitors came to our home. The Leaders came with a huge cake, which we shared with the soldier guards across the lane. Our office staff came with some of their families. Driver Zhang brought his daughter. Teachers and friends came. Patrick arrived with a Canadian who was visiting Xining. And all the while deafening explosions of fire works reverberated around our little house.

One day a stocky gentleman in his 80s, smiling broadly and looking more like seventy, walked three miles to our home to invite us for dinner. He said he was curious and decided he would like to meet some Western people. It was an invitation we couldn't refuse. Along with his family, and especially his grandson, we listened to his intriguing stories about life as a young soldier in the Communist army and how proud he was to take part in the liberation of Xining.

"Miss Chen, I don't think I can eat anymore," said Bill, "when do we go back to work?"

Miss Chen thought for a moment. "Maybe next week ... but who wants to work during Spring Festival? Besides, today we go to Miss Sun's home and all the teachers will be there. We're going to have a *jiaozi* party."

So we spent a long afternoon drinking tea with the teachers, learning to make *jiaozi*, a food very similar to Ukrainian peroghies. We mixed flour, water and oil into dough and flattened it with a long thin rolling stick. A type of cookie-cutter was used to stamp out three-inch diameter rounds and the *jiaozi* were stuffed with ground pork, garlic, herbs and vegetables. We fluted the edges with our fingers and dropped the fat little rollovers into boiling water. Mine fell apart. *Mei guan xi*, it doesn't matter; not to worry, there's lots more *jiaozi* to eat.

On a dark night, half-way through the festival, BeiBei and her parents brought over a big dish of New Year's traditional *yuan xiao*, small round starchy white dumplings with a sweet center of fruit and bean curd. They also wanted to show us how to light firecrackers and throw rockets in our courtyard. Demonstrations followed. BeiBei waved a lighted rocket that danced and sparkled over her head. With their poor English and our poor Mandarin it was a wonder we didn't blow ourselves up, especially when BeiBei's mother lit a small rocket in Bill's hand and indicated for him to throw it.

"*Fang! Fang!*" She yelled.

Bill wasn't quite sure what she was trying to tell him. He thought he should wave it around like everyone else was doing. This rocket was different. The frantic father made us realize that Bill must get rid of the thing. "Now! Now!" And his wife yelled even louder, "Throw! Throw!" Finally, he flung it toward the bottom of the courtyard, against the brick wall, beside the winter-bare lilac bushes ... just in time! *Vhroom*! It was the sports day hand grenade episode all over again, only with a real live rocket flaring and blazing in the dark.

Spring Festival was coming to an end. Lantern Festival was over and the last major event was the giant three-hour parade of stilt walkers, acrobats, military and school bands, traditional costumed minorities, young students proudly waving school banners. And there was dancing: ladies fluttering red fans, and Tibetans stretching their thin silk sleeves like the water sleeves of the characters in Peking Operas. Mongolian men, arms crossed, stomped, crouched, tumbled and kicked out their long leather-covered legs. Noisy prancing lion dancers with the feline movements of a lion, were a riot of color; great shaggy head masks swinging to the sounds of drums, cymbals and gongs. On every corner the parade would stop and a salvo of firecrackers sundered the afternoon air.

"It's been an amazing two weeks," I said, as Bill and I sat at dinner with the Archers in their apartment. "We think we've eaten enough food to last us for a year."

"I could use a good night's sleep and a reprieve from the fireworks," said Tony, rubbing his forehead. "The Chinese really know how to throw a party, don't they?"

twenty-five

中国

It was summer holidays in Xunhua.

Chen Yu Hua had been back from Xining for four days when she was invited to a family dinner at her parents' home. Her father still ignored her as she had turned twenty-five and was regarded as an 'old-aged youth'.

Everyone agreed she should have married, so Chen Jian Pin would not have to bear the shame of an unmarried eldest daughter who had refused a good man. She could be living in Xining now, in a fine house with Gu Yong and perhaps a baby boy, making her parents proud. It was too late. Nothing could be changed. She enjoyed herself with the family the best she could. Some of them were friendly and some were distant, and her mother only spoke to her when her father was out of earshot.

Chen Yu Hua's favorite aunt was her mother's youngest sister, a genuinely warm and understanding woman who chatted with her niece about college and her life in general.

"I'm sorry Chen Yu Hua," she said one day, "your father has been pestering me to ask you something." The aunt was embarrassed and fidgeted with a basket she was carrying. "This is none of our business ... but he wants to know if you have a male friend." She released her breath quickly, glad she got the words out. "You don't have to answer if you don't want to. I'll tell him ... "

"It's all right," said Chen Yu Hua, "you can tell him I do have a young man and I'm going to invite him to come to Xunhua and meet the family."

The aunt smiled and hugged Chen Yu Hua. "You poor girl, I

feel sorry for you. Your father is so unfair ... and my sister can't seem to stand up to him."

Liu Hao, carrying a small cloth bag, stepped nimbly off the long distance bus. Chen Yu Hua greeted him and took him to her parents' home. His pants, jacket and shirt were crumpled from the hot bus ride, and his messy black hair had not seen a comb since early morning. Somehow, he looked too shy, too tall, and too awkward in the presence of the Chen family. He fiddled and twisted the little bag, wrinkling the cloth until it looked worn and worthless, then opened it and presented her parents with six tiny cakes.

Jian Pin scowled at him. It did not matter that Liu Hao towered above everyone else, her father's scorching look brought him down to size, making him feel insignificant. His shoulders drooped and he looked very sad, believing his first impressions to be less than perfect in the eyes of his hopefully future bride. Didn't his mother or father tell him, thought Chen Yu Hua, to bring a brick of tea, some liquor, cigarettes or candy to his prospective parents-in-law? Something more than small cakes, dry and crumbly from a long bus ride.

Jian Pin showed his disappointment by not speaking to Liu Hao for the rest of the afternoon.

"Who is this *city man*?" he said scornfully to his daughter as he passed her in the hall. "He looks more like a peasant farmer."

Chen Yu Hua was embarrassed and could do nothing but try to make Liu Hao feel as comfortable as possible in her father's home. Later she went to the kitchen where Jia Ying was washing vegetables for the evening meal.

"Why is father acting this way?" asked Chen Yu Hua.

"He thinks Liu Hao is very cheap."

"Perhaps Liu Hao doesn't know any better." Chen Yu Hua was making lame excuses for her friend. "No one told him our ways."

"Our ways are Chinese ways," replied her mother, looking surprised to think Liu Hao had never been taught simple proper manners. She picked up a cleaver and began chopping more of the green vegetables. "Your father says if Liu Hao loved you and had any respect for us he would know how to act ... or, at least, find out from someone else what he should do."

Chen Yu Hua was crushed. It was so important to older Chinese for traditions to be followed strictly, no exceptions.

"Your father also compared Liu Hao to Gu Yong … he thinks Gu Yong is more sophisticated and experienced … and he has such a good job."

The steady chopping of the vegetables and the heat of the kitchen gave Chen Yu Hua a headache.

"He is also mean," said Chen Yu Hua as sarcastically as she could. Jia Ying shrugged and went on chopping.

The evening was spent in icy silence. Chen Yu Hua tried to make reasonable conversation but found it impossible. Her father was reading one of his history books and when Liu Hao made an inquiry about the author, a sullen Jian Pin only grumbled the answer and never lifted his eyes from the page.

The following day was easier. Chen Yu Hua and Liu Hao explored the city, walking by the *Huang He* and being welcomed at her favorite aunt's home for a delicious meal and relaxing afternoon.

On the third day, the whole Chen family prepared a large dinner in honor of Liu Hao, and Jian Pin looked slightly more favorably toward his future son in-law. Liu Hao's honesty and intelligence and his warm open smile impressed him. But there were shaded references, little hints and innuendoes that Gu Yong would have been the better catch for Chen Yu Hua.

After all the frustrations she bore, longing for her father's approval of her marriage and Liu Hao, she had to accept that all he could say was "we must set the wedding day." And before Liu Hao went back to Xining a wedding date was set for Saturday, the fifth of October.

Chen Yu Hua did not have enough time or money for a beautiful wedding. She had no chance to wear the dream costume that was popular among new brides of the day: a red satin *qipao*, matching red satin shoes with stiletto heels, and a delicate pink net headpiece, shirred and shaped like a large sensuous flower. Instead, she was grateful when her favorite aunt gave her a red blouse with metal buttons up the right side, soft brown trousers, and matching brown shoes. These pieces of simple clothing would be her wedding outfit.

Liu Hao's father and mother should have presented their daughter-in-law with new clothes, the traditional custom, but instead they gave her a piece of Dacron cloth, navy blue, to make skirts. This annoyed Jian Pin.

"A piece of cloth ... what kind of family are you marrying into?" He huffed as he gave her 200 yuan to buy some "decent" clothes.

Chen Yu Hua asked nothing from her parents but when they insisted she take the money, she bought 100 yuan worth of cheap clothes and gave the other half back, not wanting to be indebted to them ever. She was still affronted by the way the family had treated her when her older brother was married just ten days before her own wedding. Jian Pin spent considerable money, almost all his savings, on the elaborate affair for his son and daughter-in-law. A weeklong feast was held in the courtyard of the Chen home with Chen Yu Hua and the other women exhausting themselves preparing the enormous quantities of food. Talk of her own wedding was non-existent and although the date had been set, no one bothered to mention it. Only later did her mother's youngest sister ask how her plans were coming. Did she have a dress? Where would the wedding feast take place? Did she need help with anything?

Chen Yu Hua was happy for her brother and not resentful or envious of the big celebration in honor of his marriage. She only wanted the family to wish her good luck and to stop hurting her with their silly little ridiculing remarks, facetious or not, about Liu Hao and his family. The most important date in her life so far, her wedding, meant nothing to her; she was disinterested and cynical. All she could think about was getting far away from Xunhua as soon as possible and being back in Xining with Liu Hao.

A week later Chen Yu Hua and her parents and a few close relatives boarded the long distance bus to Xining to prepare for the wedding. Chen Jian Pin's eldest daughter was finally getting married.

Chen Yu Hua's dowry was taken to Liu Hao's room at No.14

Middle School where he was a teacher of Classical Chinese history. She was bringing to the marriage a pair of red suitcases, a single cylinder gas washing machine, a pair of new satin quilts, a wash basin from her time in Dong Feng, two black combs, two mirrors and two new towels. Her father in-law employed carpenters to make some simple wooden furniture for them and gave them an old fourteen-inch black and white TV.

Chen Yu Hua's mother and father chastised her for living so poorly, and accused her of getting married without a proper place to call home. They said she was settling for second best. Liu Hao was a nice man but she should have married Gu Yong or someone equal to her station in life. Did she forget that she was from the honorable and once powerful Chen family? Did she not realize she would regret the day she married the wrong man? Did her parents not realize their constant scolding and endless hounding to marry drove her away from them? She loved Liu Hao. He was kind and gentle and that was most important to her.

On the morning of Chen Yu Hua's wedding day, Liu Hao and his escorts arrived at the home where she was staying with her parents, in three rented cars. One of the cars, a bright new Mazda, caused quite a stir. It was the first to be seen in Xining and, for once, Liu Hao had impressed his future in-laws. It was ironic that he got a nod of approval from the Chen family by doing something as insignificant as hiring a flashy car. Jian Pin went so far as to pat Liu Hao on the back … "Good choice," he said.

Chen Yu Hua didn't notice the upstaging by the new Mazda. She was too busy crying honest tears, sad to say goodbye to her family. It was traditional for brides to cry when they left their parents' home, but some girls faked their tears and only pretended to be heart broken. Chen Yu Hua was truly sad and her tears were real. It wasn't a happy leaving; there was too much tension between them, too many bitter words and hurtful times. It could have been so different, if only they would accept her for being herself and welcome Liu Hao into their family.

The ceremony was simple. It was actually a celebration. According to Chinese law, the official at the registration office had legally married them a few days earlier. Liu Hao paid for the innocuous piece of paper that stated they were now man and wife and the official smiled and shook their hands. "Congratulations," he said.

The bride and groom made deep bows of respect to their parents and drank a toast of liquor to each one. Kind words were spoken and Chen Jian Pin raised a glass of Qinghai Barley to welcome his new son-in-law into his family. Chen Yu Hua sat and listened to the hollow praise, knowing it was all a glib facade, but the guests clapped and smiled, nodding their heads in approval. Like so many families, there was the face saving playacting as though the tensions between them had never existed.

After the ceremony a small banquet was held with more speeches and toasts. Lots of toasts. Some of Liu Hao's friends tied an apple on a string above the heads of the newlyweds, making them keep their hands behind their backs while taking bites out of the bouncing apple. Their friends clapped and laughed uproariously each time the bride and groom missed the apple and touched mouths in a kiss. Traditional Han songs were sung, final toasts were downed, and Chen Yu Hua's wedding day was over.

No fancy gifts had been exchanged.
No rings.
No vows.
No photos.

It was very late, after midnight, when the lovers went to their room at the school compound, and the bride, exhausted, ashamed and confused by the actions of her family, cried on her wedding night. Her new husband understood and loved her. "Everything will work out fine," he said tenderly. That's what she wanted to hear as she snuggled close to Liu Hao. She had made a very good choice for her mate.

Chen Yu Hua and Liu Hao spent ten tranquil days together before she was to return to Xunhua and the Girls' School. It was a healing time for them both. She bought traditional Happiness Candies to present to Liu Hao's leaders and colleagues. Friends had small parties to celebrate their marriage and she got to know her in-laws. Her shy mother-in-law smiled easily at everything she said and her soft spoken father-in-law, a general physician, treated her with more respect than her own father. "We are very happy," they told her sincerely, "our son has chosen a good wife."

But she was far from being happy herself. Liu Hao had to stay teaching in Xining and she had to go back to Xunhua to her small room at the dorm, where she would be lonely and miss her husband. It would be another three or four months before she saw him again.

"So now I'm married," she said to herself and repeated an old Chinese proverb: "In life every one of us has the opportunity to have the starring roll in two ceremonies ... one at our wedding and one at our funeral."

The Chinese are most sincere about observing International Women's Day.

Chairman Mao had a conciliatory saying he used often: "Women hold up half the sky." But the women had their own saying "we hold up three-quarters of the sky."

So on a warm day in March I went to a women's lunch at the school to be entertained by singers, dancers and storytellers, and an amazing lady from one of the local banks who could count money by hand faster than a machine.

Seven women sat around our table. Nicole, the young lady from England, was university-educated with an excellent future; she was free to travel and free to live in any country of her liking. Her mother Jociane, who like myself, had lived an interesting life, was well traveled and still in good health. I'm sure Miss Wei and Miss Chen considered themselves fortunate too. Both were well educated with good jobs and respected families. And the two high school girls, healthy and self-assured, looked smart with their shoulder length hair and trendy designer jeans. In the New China they would soon enroll in university and choose any major they wished, unlike their grandparents after Liberation. In those days, forming a new government was critical and people had to be moved rapidly into the work force. Every single person was slotted into a profession without any consideration for his or her skills or desires.

We asked Miss Wei and Miss Chen, as well as the high school girls, if they were in favor of the One Child Policy instituted in 1979 with the motto, "later, longer, fewer."

"Most of us are," Miss Chen said. "The regulations are flexible in rural areas. If the first child is a girl they are allowed to have a second child, and Minority women can have two children. I actually know many young career women who would rather not have children ... yet others feel one boy and one girl would be the perfect family. But we all agree that our country has too many people and cannot support any more. As for me ... I think one child is enough."

She talked about the wide gulf between urban and rural women. "Many rural women have little or no education at all, and without education they have no financial power and no position within the family unit. Therefore they go to jobs outside the home; hard jobs in the city, like construction work, to make extra money to send their children for further schooling."

We discussed women and the workplace, and the Glass Ceiling, which is no different in China than in other countries. The only exceptions are government departments and state-owned businesses, where guidelines ensure that all levels of administration have a percentage of women leaders. For example, every province must have a woman vice-governor and men are not allowed to compete for positions designated for women.

"Do modern Chinese women leave home and live on their own before they get married?" Nicole directed this question to Miss Wei. "I also wonder if most married couples have parents living with them."

"Some young women prefer to live alone if they have a good job and if they can afford it, but you know, it is very expensive to live by yourself. Also, married couples would very much enjoy the extra space and privacy without having to share their tiny apartments with parents." Miss Wei cleared her throat demurely, "and sometimes there is much trouble in the home ... like if the mother-in-law is not very nice to the daughter-in-law ... yeah?" The students giggled behind their hands and nodded to one another. "But this tradition is so deep in all of us, it is our duty to look after aging parents ... sometimes they may be sick or perhaps we need parents for babysitting ... but really, if we could, young married people would like to be alone."

"I still remember an NGO Forum last year in Beijing," said Miss Chen. "A Japanese woman was addressing our group on women's positions in the home and society. She expressed her admiration for Chinese women ... she said they are much freer than Japanese or Korean women. We agreed. This is partly due to the One Child Policy. It gives us more time to advance our careers, and women are now achieving high-ranking roles in Chinese companies ... certainly in government ... and this of course gives them more money and more independence to choose their own lifestyles."

I asked if there was a safety net for a young woman I had seen earlier that day.

"I was in the car when Driver Zhang stopped for a red light beside a young, incredibly thin girl, perhaps eighteen or so, squatting on the sidewalk. She was rocking from side to side, mumbling to herself ... her hair looked terrible, partly matted and partly flying all over ... and her poor face was covered with bruises. I wondered if she might be on drugs." I hesitated. "Or perhaps not in her right mind ... and since it was such a rare sight in Xining I found myself staring at her."

I didn't tell them about the strange spark when our eyes met. The sad girl knew I was someone different. I didn't tell them the way she kept staring back at me, unblinking, and that she raised her hand as if to say hello to someone who didn't belong in her country. I wondered what she was thinking as she looked up at me in my comfortable car from her accepted space on the wet, cold sidewalk with a little bundle of rags sitting at her bare feet. That I could help her? That she didn't like me? Was she thinking at all? I didn't tell them about the empty feeling in the pit of my stomach.

"Your young woman will have to be cared for by her family,"

said Miss Chen. "There is no other place for her ... except, perhaps, if she is lucky, a charity organization could help her."

The conversation was turning glum until Jociane asked, "With all this discussion about women's roles, I want to know who looks after the money in the family, the man or the woman?"

The Chinese women laughed in unison, "We do, of course ... just like most women in the world."

We laughed a lot that day. When we opened our gifts, donated generously by the government for the occasion of Women's Day, we found small pretty aprons.

"Aprons!" said a disbelieving Nicole.

"Aprons! Aprons!" we echoed, laughing and tying them on as we strolled back through the winding lanes to our house.

Lynda and Murray Adams, young friends from Canada, phoned that night from Beijing. They were about to board the train for the two and a half day ride to Xining. They had been planning this trip for several months, having reserved their soft seat compartment tickets well in advance.

"Guess what?" said an excited Lynda. "You'll be proud of us, we've exchanged our tickets for cheaper ones. I think we paid far too much in Canada for them. They told us here it will be the same trip ... everything's the same and we'll even get there at the same time."

"Are you sure you have a compartment in soft seats?" asked Bill doubtfully.

"The ticket lady assured us it was the same trip."

"Did she speak English?"

Lynda hesitated. "Well ... I think she understood ... we got seventy-five dollars back so we're happy."

We couldn't wait to see them.

Snow was falling and melting on the station platform when they arrived with huge backpacks I could never imagine carrying. Murray and Lynda's white-blonde hair, along with his six-foot-plus height, made them instant curiosities.

They told us later about their journey.

"It wasn't the same trip at all ... we were in the hard seat section!" They both laughed until tears squeezed from their eyes, as they related their not so wise move to exchange the original tickets for cheaper ones. There were six narrow bunk beds in each section, they said, and they took the one on the bottom and slept together crowding their big packs between them. As the hours went by they began to enjoy the camaraderie with the Chinese, who kept touching Murray's arms. "We wondered why," said Lynda, "then it dawned on me they wanted to stroke the blonde hair on the back of his arm."

Like everyone else, they ate snacks and drank beer until the bathrooms got too over-taxed. So, no more beer. They played cards with each other while the Chinese watched and smoked and hung down from the bunks above them. They were offered food, smiled at, touched, sung to, and occasionally some young student would come by to practice his limited English. The lazy, unhurried train stopped at every local station on its milk run through Inner Mongolia down to Lanzhou and over to Xining.

"Our trip was half the price, and a tiring six hours longer. The soft seats turned out to be hard seats," said Lynda. "Hey, I'm glad we did it, but I don't know if I'd ever want to do it again … I think the ticket lady back in Beijing should have told us it was a hardship trip, don't you?"

"Did the lady speak English?" Bill asked again.

"Well I think so … maybe … a little … I'm not sure."

Lynda and Murray were a great hit at No.14 Middle School. Lanky Murray towered over the boys on the outside concrete basketball court and Lynda wowed the group in the music room when she gave demonstration lessons for Texas line dancing.

"We call this *slap leather*," she puffed as she kicked, slapping her heels to the music with twenty students and teachers forming lines and following her every move while my Garth Brooks CD boomed out something about "hoping Detroit goes wild."

"What a great afternoon. These students will never forget today," said Miss Chen, who mimicked each step like a professional. That night she and Lynda and little Si Xian stomped on the black and white tiles in our large front hall to the rhythm of our one and only country CD.

The five-day visit was flying by and Miss Chen asked daily when we were going to have dinner with Mayor Liu.

"He wants to have a dinner in honor of your daughter," she pushed for the third time.

"We call her our daughter ... she's our former daughter-in-law ... this is only a private visit you know. We appreciate the invitation and we always have fun at Mayor Liu's dinners ... but we don't want to bother ... "

Miss Chen interrupted me.

"I cannot put off the mayor of Xining one more time," she almost snapped at me, "he is *insisting*!"

Needless to say, we had a fun dinner with Mayor Liu.

The next morning we packed a lunch for Murray and Lynda; hard-boiled eggs, cucumbers, tomatoes and a box of shortbread cookies sent to us in one of the care parcels from Canada, said goodbye to them and loaded them on the train to Lanzhou. The whirlwind visit was over.

It snowed that day ... all day. And the temperature dropped. The heater we bought back in November that swiveled and produced a lovely warm glow in the living room, exploded suddenly in a shower of sparks and burning wires, on what turned out to be the coldest day of the year.

twenty-six

中国

On November 4, 1986, Chen Yu Hua gave birth to her daughter in their tiny one-room home at No.14 Middle School in Xining. The midwife wrapped the crying, red-faced infant tightly in a cloth and laid her in her mother's arms. At eight and a half months pregnant, Chen Yu Hua had taken the long-distance bus one last time to be with Liu Hao in Xining. They named their daughter, Si Xian.

Chen Yu Hua had lived and worked at the girls' school in Xunhua for the past year with only one six-week visit with Liu Hao in the winter. It was common for families to be separated, husbands in one city and wives in another. Now for the first time a new policy had been issued by the Central Government decreeing that husbands and wives should be allowed to live and work together in the same area.

Chinese people, whose lives were centered on family life, had been fragmented and scattered by the Cultural Revolution, forcing families to live and work apart for years. Chen Yu Hua and Liu Hao considered themselves fortunate to be together after only one year of separation. Their future looked good. They would be assigned a larger apartment in the school compound and Chen Yu Hua would be employed as a teacher.

When Si Xian turned eighteen months old her mother had the chance to take the entrance exams for a two-year term at the prestigious Beiwai (Beijing Foreign Studies University) in Beijing. It was important for Chen Yu Hua, as opportunities like this did not come along everyday and it would be difficult to advance her teaching career without further education.

Six months later Chen Yu Hua settled her daughter in care of the Liu family and boarded the train for her first adventurous trip away from home, making the two and a half day hard seat journey to Beijing.

Walking down the lane under a canopy of large maple trees to the university entrance Chen Yu Hua felt special and privileged. This is where she always wanted to be, here in these quiet, solemn, peaceful halls of knowledge, hidden away from the rude noises of Beijing City. There were many foreign teachers at the university and she studied subjects totally unfamiliar to her and the parochial schools in Qinghai. Methodology, American and English literature, cultures and societies, and psychology, were some of the absorbing studies. She cherished the opportunity to speak English every day and to hear lectures by famous professors and scholars from other renowned universities. Her life was enriched and her views of the world had suddenly opened up to her inquiring mind.

Two of her favorite teachers, who had been at Beiwai since the 1930's, took a keen interest in the students from Qinghai Province. Isabel and David Crook, noted for their straightforward honesty and sincerity, left a deep impression on Chen Yu Hua. She admired them both and held them in highest regard. One day after finishing lunch in the small campus restaurant there were dishes of uneaten food left on their table: pieces of spare ribs, bits of chicken, several half plates of vegetables and bowls of rice.

"Let's take home whatever is left over," said Mrs. Crook, and she pulled a small container from her handbag. "It's not good to waste food. We all know that."

Chen Yu Hua and her colleagues were amazed. According to Chinese custom it was not polite to take leftovers from the dining table. It would result in loss of face for them. They hesitated, but followed suit and, for the first time, they packed up the remaining food and took it home. Chen Yu Hua never forgot this little incident. She thought about it later and mulled it over in her mind. These foreigners, who had more money than she did, felt no shame taking food that had been paid for and rightfully belonged to them. Why wouldn't it be acceptable for her to do the same? The professors dared to lose face and no one cared. Mr. and Mrs. Crook were right. The food should not be wasted. The students were poor but they thought their "faces" meant more than saving the food. It was such a sham, all this saving face.

She decided the Chinese were wrong. "Slap your face until it is swollen and you will look imposing," was the old proverb.

She never again left food on a restaurant table after a meal. When people laughed at her she told them this story. They usually agreed and said nothing more.

Not all her experiences with teachers turned out to be positive. A middle-aged British teacher called Margaret taught methodology. She was strict and unrelenting with her criticism of everyone but her classes were vivid and interesting and the students admired her teaching. They were also intrigued by the way she changed her clothes daily, and was always fresh and scrubbed looking with never a hair out of place.

"I hear she has crates of clothes," gossiped the students, "she can wear a new costume everyday if she wants to."

In class one day, Teacher Margaret announced that she was leaving Beijing and going home to London to obtain a doctorate degree. The students were disappointed as she was a brilliant teacher and they were sorry to lose her.

"I have a lot of clothes that are still new," she said to the girls in her class. "I don't want to take them home and perhaps you would like to have them."

The students were excited and grateful to be able to visit the foreign teacher in her home and to receive gifts of clothing from her. They went to her apartment where Teacher Margaret had laid out pretty clothes on a table. She handed each of the girls a plastic bag, telling them they could choose whatever they liked.

Suddenly the teacher began shouting, "what are you doing?" One of the girls had picked up some photos that were lying on a table beside her. Shocked by the tone of the teacher's voice, she dropped the pictures and sat in bewildered silence. For the next few minutes Teacher Margaret reprimanded everyone loudly, especially the young girl, for not listening, for touching things that didn't belong to them, and for being impolite and noisy.

Chen Yu Hua was embarrassed. No one spoke. The girls quietly picked through blouses, skirts, sweaters and jackets, choosing each item carefully. Teacher Margaret's voice returned to normal but not for long. One of the students had turned her plastic bag upside down and out dropped small pieces of paper and bits of plastic.

The shouting was louder this time. She accused them again of being sloppy, careless, untidy and disorderly. They were frightened by the hysterical outburst and the young offender started to cry.

"I didn't mean to do that," she sobbed, "it was an accident ... I wasn't thinking."

"That's the trouble," berated Teacher Margaret, "you people never think ... you have no courtesy ... you have no manners and you don't seem to want to learn any."

Teacher Margaret from England was usually not a mean person but what she said to the students that night was unwarranted. She had taken a two-year assignment at the Foreign Studies University and was an excellent teacher. The first year at the school went smoothly, but slowly she realized that she was unable to tolerate some customs of the Chinese. She had given them English names and expected to mold them into perfect English students and when this failed, she lost interest and resented having to go to the classroom everyday. She became frustrated and felt like a misfit in this strange country, incapable of appreciating a new culture or exploring the fascinating life going on around her. In her clouded, narrow thinking she did not want to learn from her students, she only wanted to change them. Being a perfectionist, her failure to morph each student into a mirror image of herself had taken its toll on her nerves.

When her father died in England she decided to return home to pursue further education and teach in a private school, where she really belonged. Whether Teacher Margaret would ever look back on her eighteen months in Beijing with any fondness or whether she would erase it from memory, no one would know.

China was not for everyone.

"We must go now," said Chen Yu Hua resolutely. She said thank you and goodnight and hustled the crying girl and the others out of the room, away from the frustrated English woman who, by now, only wanted to see the backs of them.

The young girl, still sobbing, said she didn't do it on purpose, never meant to be rude, and was sorry about their loss of face. They were humiliated and the fun and enthusiasm they thought they were going to have turned out to be a discouraging evening. They were only exuberant girls who had never been to a foreigner's home before and didn't understand the protocol and necessary courtesies. They would never forget Teacher Margaret and their first cultural experience in the home of a Westerner.

I never in my life expected to meet a Living Buddha but here we were sitting on small stools across from him in a spotless room in a Tongren Monastery.

Our friend Jill Gillett had arrived from London and we decided to take a trip into the wilds of Qinghai where very few Westerners had traveled. We contacted Jenny Guo from China International Travel Service. She was an attractive young woman with a lovely soft voice, who spoke excellent English and had an amusing way of asking if you enjoyed something.

"Do you like it?" She would say.

"Yes ... I like it."

She would come back with, "I like it that you like it."

Jenny arranged for a Nissan Land Cruiser, a driver, and herself as interpreter to take the three of us over Qingsha Pass and down into the valleys of Tibetan villages to Tongren and the surrounding monasteries.

"Take some lunch," said Jenny, so we made sandwiches from the last tin of Canadian salmon brought by Audrey.

Qingsha Pass, at 12,000 feet, was a bleak, stormy, gray and white world. After leaving the warm spring air of Xining, the pass was an arctic snow scene. Heavily loaded trucks labored up the mountain road, some of them spinning out and sliding backwards, skirting the rim of the precipice. No one spoke as our Nissan crawled at a steady pace on the ice. We knew it was perilous and found little comfort looking down to the canyon floor far below only to see a derelict bus lying on it side.

Soon the road widened, giving the driver a chance to stop. High above us the wind screamed like banshees, snapping tattered Sutra streamers attached to ropes that stretched from the tops of flexible bamboo poles, down to the rock-strewn ground.

It was a huge *Lhaze Mound*, a crown of arrows, spears, sticks and clubs, each one bearing a Tibetan prayer flag planted firmly on a ridge of clay and rock.

Jenny said that Lhaze Mounds went back to the time of the Tubo Kingdom. "When King Songtsan Gampo finished building his magnificent palace he placed arrows on the rooftops as decorations. From this came the practice of forming mounds as symbols of the King's authority, to honor him wherever he camped on his journeys. Then through the years, these Lhaza Mounds evolved into religious sites where Tibetans pray and place their small flags."

"It's wild," I said, the wind grasping at my breath.

"Yes, and if this is a place of worship it sure makes a cold spot to kneel and pray," observed Jill

"It looks to me like the White Pass Summit in the Yukon," said Bill.

It was at this moment I made a foolish remark. "Tell Driver Liu," I gushed to Jenny, "he's an excellent driver ... that was slippery on the pass but he was very good."

"Yes, very good," repeated Jill.

This praise was all the driver needed. He had just been granted the exclusive right to press his foot to the floorboard. And press he did. We careened down the rough road and into the lush valley, stones and dust flying, horn blowing, narrowly missing girls carrying water and donkeys piled high with dried branches for firewood. We scattered chickens, sheep and goats in all directions. The driver came as close as he could to school children without sending them flying into the weeds and Mechanical Buffalos veered out of our kamikaze charge with mere inches to spare.

"Can you tell the driver to slow down?" I raised my voice to Jenny, "he's going too fast! He's going to kill somebody! And it might be us!"

She just stared, her eyes transfixed on the road. I wasn't sure she was quite conscious. She had dozed off, then was jolted awake after crashing her head on the roof as we hit a deep pothole at top speed.

"You know," she said haltingly, "these drivers are very ... sensitive. Maybe I can ask him to stop so you can take pictures."

We were lucky. The driver stopped when we rounded a corner and found hundreds of parked vehicles in a field, and people scattered up the mountainside.

"They are tree planting," said Jenny. She explained about the re-forestation of millions of trees each year in China. This was evident throughout our travels in Qinghai, by the rows and rows of newly planted trees in various stages of growth. People in government departments, schools and factories, take turns going into the hills to plant seedlings, combining this patriotic work with a picnic and a day away from their usual duties.

Before we got back in the car the driver said something to Jenny.

"Driver Liu says he is enjoying your company," she smiled, "he took some Italians out last week and they kept wanting to stop all the time."

"I think I know why," said Bill.

The broad sweep of the valley of Huangnan Tibetan Nationality Autonomous Prefecture was home to *Regong Art*, the most influential art among the Tibetans. The monasteries engaged in sophisticated woodcarving, *Duisui* embroidery and multi-colored sculptures.

Skilled *Tangka* painters were also a major attraction in Tongren monasteries. The word Tangka refers to painting intricate Buddhist themes on cloth scrolls in lavish colors, often with liquid gold. This art has a long history, beginning with simple mural drawings on walls. As Buddhism spread and the art became more complex, it was gradually accepted and appreciated, and considered a cultural heritage, worshiped by all Tibetans.

The small monasteries were beehives of energy. Groups of young monks, eight to ten years of age, wrapped in red toga-like robes, sat on benches at outdoor classrooms. Other monks were printing scriptures on long thin strips of paper with wooden engraving plates; still others were meditating and studying.

We watched carvers, bricklayers and carpenters restoring a temple damaged during the Cultural Revolution. Jenny spoke with an eighty-year-old man working on a sculpture. He said almost every man in the valley inherits the occupation of artisan handed down from generation to generation. The women tend the fields while the men work on the monastery. I'm not sure why, but we decided to carry a few rounds of bricks and fell in behind the stream of men and women of all ages lugging their heavy loads. They smiled patiently at the foreigners as if we belonged, not even asking Jenny what we were doing there. Our enthusasm soon faded but I would always be able to say I helped build the monastery at Tongren with my six bricks.

"I have a surprise for you," said Jenny, when we arrived at Wutong Temple. "I have arranged for us to have lunch with a Living Buddha. Would you like that?"

"Of course," we said, having no idea what she meant.

"There are three Living Buddhas here," said Jenny, "the one we are going to see is my favorite, and he is also the head Buddha. He is fifty seven years old and was proclaimed to be a Living Buddha when he was only seven."

In a small shop we bought Brick Tea as a gift and, packing our bag of sandwiches, we walked up a very long passageway to a small courtyard where a monk's attendant greeted us with a smile. The tall thin young man, his feet bare, graciously escorted us into the private quarters of the Living Buddha.

The first thing I thought when I saw the Buddha was that he looked exactly what a Buddha should look like. Small and round with a wonderful calm face and gentle eyes. He wore a dark red Kasaya, the outer vestment of a Buddhist monk. And around him the walls gleamed with a type of red wood. Perhaps it was cherry wood, I couldn't tell, but it reflected the sunlight coming in from the windows, washing the room in a rose hue. We knew we were in a special place. A sanctuary. We had slipped into a world of spiritual tranquility somewhere in the heart of China.

"I told him I have some foreigners who wish to meet him," murmured Jenny, her soft voice the only sound in the room.

The Living Buddha smiled and made a sign for us to sit.

A small, black old-fashioned coal stove, the type once found in English parlors, stood on the burnished oak floor in the middle of the room. The decorative chrome gleamed with endless polishing and reflected our movements. The Buddha sat above us on his large typical Chinese kang, a thin hard mattress on wooden planks. What wasn't typical was the delicately carved headboard and enclosed sides of the bed made from the same red satiny wood that lined the walls, reflecting a soft light on the filigreed doors and screens. Three neatly folded blankets lay at the foot of the kang.

The Living Buddha never moved. He studied each of us in turn and spoke quietly to Jenny.

"He wants to know where you are from."

"We're from Canada," Bill answered, motioning towards me, then to Jill, "and our friend is from England."

The holy man tilted his head and frowned.

"He doesn't know where Canada is," said Jenny.

Three noisy young monks came to the room and stacked themselves in the doorway, chatting and laughing, interrupting the stillness of the moment. The Living Buddha turned and smiled fondly at the group, like a patient father with his lively sons. The monk who had led us to the room spoke up in passable English, "I think I know where Canada is ... somewhere near America?"

The Living Buddha and his disciples had a conversation, with the Buddha nodding slowly in appreciation of whatever the young men were saying. A lot of aah's and ooh's coming from him.

"Yes ... the Living Buddha thinks he has heard of America ... but he's not sure about Canada."

The Buddha's eyes seemed so kind and apologetic for not knowing my country, that all I could do was mumble, "we're right next door to America."

"But he has heard of England," the young man beamed and we all smiled at the gracious Buddha. I was quite envious that he recognized Jill's country and not mine.

"I'm sorry," said Jenny, "it is hard for me to understand their dialect and with only one man speaking a little bit of English ... it is very difficult to ask questions. But it would be okay to eat your lunch now ... they are going to serve tea."

"No, no," I said a little self consciously, "we can eat later."

Jill agreed. I knew she was thinking what I was thinking; that the sight of the three of us chomping on salmon sandwiches with fresh green onions and mayonnaise somehow seemed indecent here in this hallowed place, in the company of the Living Buddha.

Instead, we sipped Chinese tea, nibbled on dried apricots, raisins and nuts, and sampled bits of small cakes, yak butter and deep fried bread.

It was time to leave this gentle person. What seemed like minutes had been well over one hour.

It's hard to describe a religious feeling. It comes unexpectedly from surprising places. From a great Cathedral or a famous painting; from the faces of family or perhaps a sunset. That day in Tongren we experienced a sense of the divine in the presence of a Living Buddha who, like the monks of Shangri La, had little desire to explore a world beyond his own monastery.

Traveling back to Xining was as hair-raising as the trip out. The three of us managed to eat the warm, soggy, ever so slightly tainted salmon sandwiches the best we could while being knocked about, clutching one another in the back seat.

"Sure hope we get home before dark," I coughed out, referring to the bizarre custom of Chinese drivers roaring around in the dark without turning on their headlights. More than once we asked the reason for this peculiar motoring behavior, flicking lights on and off to signal other vehicles that they were on the same road. At home we called it 'playing chicken'.

We asked Jenny the same question, "Why?"

"They want to save the generator," she explained knowingly.

Driver Liu made a detour to a remote white pagoda, which stood shimmering like a tower of jewels on a distant treeless mountaintop. Our vehicle skidded to a stop in a shower of dust and gravel, giving an old woman the fright of her life as she circled the pagoda in a clockwise direction, weeping and praying for her soul. She prayed harder and shuffled faster when she saw a huddle of Foreign Devils roll out of the Land Cruiser.

"Have you seen the lack of tread on the rear tires?" asked Jill nonchalantly. "Oh well, not to worry, there's plenty of tread on the front ones."

It was amazing, but we did arrive home safely that night. Jenny and Driver Liu came in to settle the account.

"Did you like it?"

"Yes ... we really liked it."

"Good ... I like it that you like it."

We gave them a good gratuity, not only for the great adventure we shared, but mostly because we arrived home with our bodies intact.

After they left, Jill expressed all our needs. "Double scotch please," she said, in her fine English accent, and we had a toast. "To our health ... may we hang on to it until we leave Qinghai!"

The next day we visited the Great Mosque on Dongguan Dajie, in east Xining. When we entered the main gates we were stormed by dozens of exuberant little kids, yelling "hello, hello" over and over again. The children followed us as we wandered around a huge courtyard paved with flagstones and Miss Chen met a man from her hometown. It was someone she hadn't seen since she left Xunhua. They talked excitedly like old friends do when filling in the blank years that had flown by, and then he asked if we wished to see inside the mosque.

"He wants us to visit the prayer room," she said cheerily.

"I don't know if they appreciate foreigners going into the inner mosque," I said, not knowing the protocol. Jill wondered if women were even allowed inside.

"Yes, yes, it's alright. Come, my friend holds a very high position here, and he says we have time to see it before the five o'clock prayers."

"You girls are going to get into trouble," warned Bill, peering through the doorway, "I'll stay right here and look after your coats."

We removed our shoes and Jill and I followed Miss Chen and

her former school chum into the cool atmosphere of the palatial domed hall. Thick carpets in subdued tones of blue and dark red were spread over the floor. It was a quiet empty place, ethereal and solemn. We barely spoke above a murmur.

"Hui Muslims, spreading Islam into this part of the world, built this mosque in the fourteenth century," explained our guide in hushed tones. "They took pride in a *hadith*, a saying that began in the time of the Prophet Muhammad. It means to 'seek knowledge even unto China.' It was important for Muslims to travel to lands as far away as China to exchange knowledge and understanding of each other's cultures."

There were two architectural designs of mosques, he told us, one, such as The Great Mosque, was Arabic in style with a domed roof propped up by pillars; the other being the typical Chinese style, featuring upturned eaves, intricately carved beams and painted rafters. No matter the style, all mosques would display the crescent moon, the symbol of Islam. And pointing straight to the sky were imposing "summoning towers" waiting to call the faithful to prayer.

He told us the great hall could hold 1500 people for religious services.

"The Dongguan Masjid is elegant and attractive," said the guide reverently, gesturing around the room with his arms outspread. We could feel his pride. "It is a respectful place and enhances the city of Xining with its beautiful architecture."

The tranquil moment was not to last. A man in black clothing, black hat and a long black beard strode angrily across the stone courtyard, scowled at Bill and entered our sanctuary like he was bearing the wrath of Allah.

"I think we should go now," whispered Miss Chen as we slouched past the two men in deep verbal discussion. We could still hear the argument, or perhaps it was just a greeting, or perhaps a one-sided scolding, we would never know. We pushed our way into the hordes of preschoolers, still chanting, "Hello! Hello! Hello!"

Bill had the 'I told you so' look and Miss Chen said, "You are right, I don't think they want foreigners in the prayer room."

It was a more relaxing trip to the Xining museum.

I was always pleading with Miss Chen to tell us more about the history of Qinghai Province. Then one day we had a pleasant surprise. She hustled us off to a compound of well-maintained buildings that had once been the headquarters of the warlord Ma Bu Feng, preserved only because it was taken over by the Communist Party in 1949 and used as headquarters. It was used again in 1966 by the Red Guards.

The place was deserted but we managed to find a caretaker with a key to open the door to the gloomy assortment of low-ceilinged rooms. We entered a small ancient world of pottery, bronzes, tapestries, calligraphy and paintings, every bit as fascinating as the grandiose museum in Xian.

According to Miss Chen it was a mystery as to when the collections were organized and how they survived the Cultural Revolution and who was responsible for writing the yellowed cards describing each historical item.

Jill spotted an unusual bowl. It was very old but undamaged and had the same shape and decoration as one she had seen in a museum in Australia; the same ochre color with dark brown geometric figures, edged in tiny white dots, similar to the Dreamtime Rock Art of the aborigines. We thought how odd it was to see some of the oldest artistic images of modern Australia, sitting amid ancient Chinese artifacts, when, for years, relics and art of foreigners had been banned or destroyed.

"But when you think about it," said our clever friend, "this style of art probably did not come from Australia ... but from India, where the oldest known Rock Art originates. Possibly it was carried by people who traveled from South East Asia to northern Australia."

Later, when we put a happy but slightly over-tired Jill on the plane to Beijing, she had anything-but-boring memories of dressing in Tibetan costumes at Ta'er Monastery, catching her death of cold, and answering important questions from school children like "do teen-age British students have boyfriends and girlfriends?" and "who was the English Nobel Prize winner for Science in 1948?"

twenty-seven

中国

Chen Yu Hua missed her baby and husband but she received many welcome letters and a few pictures from home. She choked back the tears when she read, "Si Xian is talking so much now. She asks for you every time we show her your picture." Even Jian Pin was writing to her, and her rapport with the family had definitely improved. They were all proud of her now that she was in Beijing studying, now that she was married with a baby. The animosity and bitterness had melted away. It would not be good to harbor bad memories, just forgive and forget. This was not easy, but a least she forgave.

The experiences she had in the capital city of Beijing would be stories told and retold many times when she returned to her life in Xining. With China's new reforms Chen Yu Hua saw foreign investment bring great changes to the city. Prestigious hotels were being built and major companies from Europe, North America, and Japan were courted to develop modern industries. China was beginning to open to the West.

One day Chen Yu Hua was talking with Duojie, a young friend from Qinghai who was enrolled in the Central Nationalities University next to Beiwai. He asked her if she would be interested in visiting a five-star hotel. It was a good idea but how could they do this without a passport?

"I borrowed a passport from another man at the university," assured her friend, "No one will know it isn't mine. I also borrowed a Western suit, shirt and fancy tie," he added.

The next day Chen Yu Hua fussed with her hair and make-up,

dressed in her finest clothes: a navy suit with a rose colored blouse, matching black patent shoes and handbag, and off they went together to the Beijing International Hotel in the heart of the city. They were in awe of the fancy cars, the well-dressed people coming and going, and the beautiful gardens surrounding the hotel. They had never seen anything so splendid before, commenting to each other how wonderful it must be to be rich and never worry about money.

Duojie presented the passport to the security guard at the door. They were both uneasy but the busy guard didn't scan the photo closely and they were allowed to walk into the lobby.

Chen Yu Hua caught her breath. What a beautiful, luxurious place it was. She was overcome by what she saw; thick carpets on the floors and, where the carpets ended, the floors were polished like dark glass. Huge colorful bouquets of fresh flowers decorated tables, and trees were growing in a glass atrium as naturally as they would grow in the parks. The furniture looked unfamiliar to her. Large plump red sofas were covered in soft velour material so unlike the heavy Chinese wooden benches carved with dragons and flowers. Above these sofas hung a huge painting of a scene from Chinese history; multitudes of people bowing, paying tribute to some ancient emperor in his palanquin. The hotel was paradise. Even the working staff was dressed immaculately.

They couldn't find the elevators, so they walked up the stairs to the second floor, curious to experience the feeling of actually being a hotel guest. The third floor … the fourth floor … the fifth floor. A young guard appeared.

"Can I help you?" he said brusquely, looking the pair up and down.

Chen Yu Hua thought fast. "Yes, we're looking for Mr. White's room. He is from England. He wanted us to visit him."

"What is the number of his room please?" The imperious guard asked, he was getting suspicious, and Chen Yu Hua and Duojie were showing their nervousness, especially Duojie, who had sweat around his upper lip and the hairline of his forehead. He was not used to being confined in a Western suit with a Western tie strangling his neck.

"We don't remember his room number," she confessed cheekily, "Perhaps you could tell us."

"I can assure you that I have never heard of a ... Mr. White, you say? If I were you two, I would be on my way out of here as fast as possible."

"Please tell Mr. White we did try to visit him," kidded Duojie.

The guard was obviously provoked. He frowned and looked as though he might advance towards them. Chen Yu Hua pulled Duojie's arm. "Come on, before they accuse us of being thieves," she whispered, "let's go."

Later when they were walking down the street, Chen Yu Hua took a good look at her friend in the sunlight. She burst out laughing. His Western suit, which was too short, had what looked like messy food stains all down its front. There were smudges on the blue and red silk tie, and the wrinkled white shirt was not especially clean. He had no socks on his feet and wore his own black cloth shoes, linking him to the peasant farmers of Qinghai.

Duojie was confused by her laughter.

"Oh, Duojie, no wonder they asked us to leave," she smiled, "I don't think we're well enough dressed for them."

They both had a laugh at their brazen adventure in the famous hotel, so luxurious and so out of reach for two friends from the hinterland of Qinghai Province.

Chen Yu Hua never lost her fascination with grand hotels. When a girl friend asked her to go to the park one Saturday afternoon, she suggested they have a drink in the new Shangri-La five-star instead.

"We can walk to it," said Chen Yu Hua, "It's not far and it's such a beautiful day."

This time the two pretty young women were not asked for passports as they walked through the open glass doors under the nose of the red uniformed doorman, and into the lobby.

The Shangri-La was one of the finest luxury hotels built in the early 1980s. Its lavish oriental interior, decked out with exquisite silk rugs, precious porcelains, wall hangings, paintings and other treasures, was even more sumptuous than the Beijing International.

"This is Western furniture," Chen Yu Hua informed her friend as she pointed to sofas splashed with various shades of blue, mauve, pink and white. The sleek modern tables. The ornamental lamps. Her second visit to a five-star had suddenly made her a connoisseur of hotel accessories.

They sauntered casually around the lobby, letting their senses absorb the soft rugs and the color of the flowers; the ambience of this other world. They mingled with men in expensive suits and fashionably dressed women. Most guests were from Hong Kong, they assumed. There were a few Americans, and several Japanese businessmen. For a short time the two women masqueraded. They made-believe it was their world.

"Let's have a drink in the bar."

The friend followed a confident Chen Yu Hua to a table for two by the window. It was great. For the first time they were on the inside looking out. It was great until the cocktail hostess came and handed them the drink menu. The prices jumped out like neon lights.

"Chen Yu Hua," said her friend quietly, as she leaned across the table, "the cheapest drink is 20 yuan."

"The most expensive is 200 yuan ... for one glass of Napoleon Brandy," breathed Chen Yu Hua. "I only make 150 yuan a month."

They composed themselves and studiously scanned the menu, pretending to make up their minds.

"How much money do you have? And don't look in your purse."

"Six yuan," whispered the friend.

"I have ten."

"What drinks can I get for you?"

The hostess was back. The time of reckoning had come. She was dressed in a long black satin *qipao*. Her hair pulled into a loose nape-of-the neck ponytail and Chen Yu Hua found herself staring into eyes heavy with black mascara and the glossiest, reddest lips she had ever seen.

Should they have a glass of red burgundy? No, perhaps a sherry. It was late afternoon, so perhaps a white wine? The sherry might be the best after all.

"Maybe a glass of champagne," offered her friend in a

monotone voice.

"No thank you," Chen Yu Hua said unexpectedly. She glanced anxiously at her watch, closed the liquor menu and handed it to the surprised hostess. "We are too busy today ... already late for our meeting. We really don't have time for a drink." And they got up and left as graciously as they could.

Outside the front doors of the hotel, gardeners were busily digging up summer flowers, planting winter shrubs, pruning the rose bushes and covering them with protective burlap. It was unusually warm for early October and a few hardy chrysanthemums were trying to keep their yellow bloom. The two young women decided to sit and rest on a brick wall surrounding one of the rose gardens.

It wasn't long before a guard, his face scrawny and hawk-like, spotted them and hurried over.

"You can't sit here," he screeched and flapped both his hands wildly as though to chase away offensive flies. "You will spoil our hotel's image if you keep sitting here. Now, go ... go ... go!"

Chen Yu Hua and her friend laughed as they walked away in the warm autumn sunlight. They had seen with their own eyes the marvel of the new grand hotel. Maybe they were asked to leave; maybe they did not belong. So what? It was exciting and fun, and they might just do it again one day. They might even save enough money to buy a glass of champagne.

In the meantime there were other sights to behold in Beijing, and her friend Duojie always came up with original ideas. He was the organizer of excursions for the group. Just to be with this young Tibetan meant good times and Chen Yu Hua was fond of him. Like a brother.

Norman Ross of Ross Mining Corporation, one of Canada's largest private placer gold companies, was arriving in a few days and Bill decided Miss Chen should learn some gold mining terminology. She would be interpreting during their meetings with the Directors of Qinghai Gold Mining Corporation. I could hear them in the office going over the words: placer gold, sluice boxes, tailing piles, stockpiles. She said she was getting an all-round education in English words, everything from medicine to minerals.

We picked up our friend Norm at the airport. The plane was an hour late. The welcoming delegation of directors, vice-mayors and office staff who always went with us to greet our guests, probably never realized how much we appreciated this gesture.

"How was your flight?" asked Bill, when we arrived at our home where the left-over paper banners at the front door were beginning to peel and the little tree in the living room, looking dreadfully tired, was still illuminated by Spring Festival lights. "Did you have any problems other than taking the scenic route?"

"It started out pretty good," Norm smiled. "The gate numbers at the Beijing Airport were in English, thank god. After a half hour or so there was a lot of chatter over the intercom and most of the people in the waiting area got up and started to leave ... so, having some experience with traveling, I picked out certain people waiting at the same gate and followed them. In other words I made sure I didn't lose sight of the purple sweater or green hat or yellow shirt," he laughed.

Apparently this all turned out to be nothing more than a gate-change and soon he boarded a Russian plane equivalent to a Boeing 737. The proposed flight time was one hour thirty minutes non-stop to Xining, but one hour out there was a series of announcements and the plane suddenly changed direction.

"The Chinese people seemed quite excited, all talking at once, throwing up their hands and some were even standing in the aisles," he said. "When the confusion settled down I hailed one of the flight attendants ... I knew she could say "hello" in English so I explained that I was trying to get to Xining ... she said, 'we have problem, but no problem ... Lanzhou.' Lanchow, I thought. What does lanchow mean? Then I realized it was a city somewhere near Xining. I started to worry ... like would you people know what happened to me? Or what if I had to get off the plane, could I be sure I would get back on another one bound for Xining? Would I ever see my luggage again? And, oh yes," he began to laugh, "I wondered what was really wrong with this experienced airplane and would we actually land wheels first? Anyway we landed safe and sound at Lanzhou but weren't allowed to get off the plane so I stopped memorizing every feature of the purple sweater, green hat and yellow shirt."

Norm told us about watching from the plane window as a mechanic crawled up inside the front of the engine.

"It wasn't long before the mechanic jumped out of the engine, walked forward and signaled the pilot to fire up ... sure enough the engine started, belching thick black smoke all over some of the poor passengers coming out of the plane next to us. Then off we went ... hopefully, I thought, for Xining."

"Well you got here," said Bill, only an hour late. Mei guan xi ... no problem. We find there's always lots of excitement when you travel in China."

Norm noticed the wall clock. "How come we're still on Beijing time?" He asked.

"All of China's on Beijing time. Smart idea, don't you think? Great for doing business."

In the Gold Commissioner's smoke-filled office Miss Chen excelled with her new mining terms. We learned that gold mining in Qinghai was no easy matter. The mines were located primarily in the mountains around Qaidam Basin at altitudes of five to ten thousand feet and, other than the high Andes of South America, this was the only mining done in such harsh conditions. Not even Yukon mining, north of the sixtieth parallel, was as formidable.

There was the usual round of dinners and factory visits during the week Norm was in Xining. At one factory he wanted to buy two or three glorious Qinghai rugs but decided against it when he was informed he could only purchase one hundred at a time ... or at least a container of fifty. He said he had no idea what to do with fifty carpets. He was a gold miner not a rug dealer.

Since the Archers were also leaving the same day as Norm, we decided to have our last supper together. Seven of us, including John Davis, who worked with Tony Archer, gathered at our house for one more repast of traditional chicken legs and French apple tart with walnuts, all washed down with Tsingtao beer.

"Everybody has to sign the wall," said Bill.

Tony studied the two hundred or more names. "There's not much room left," he said.

Norm laughed and jumped on a chair. "Sounds reasonable to me." He stretched his arm up as far as he could and scrawled Norman Ross Was Here across the top of them all. "I'd say I can't get much higher in life than this!"

Our one-year stint in China was sliding by too quickly. There were still projects to finish before Bill and I had to leave the country. May 4th was the date set for the midwives' graduation. The ceremony would be held in an old theatre in Datong where four hundred midwives would be presented with their birthing kits.

twenty-eight

中国

In the winter of 1989 there was an uncalm feeling on the campus. Talk of democracy and human rights, and anger that dissident student Wu Jianseng still languished in prison after ten years, rippled below the surface. Chen Yu Hua was aware of the rumblings but she refused to recognize them and shied away from zealots who stirred up angry thoughts. She wanted only education. She had a life to go back to, a loving husband, a new baby and she did not want to see any more turmoil in her country.

"But life has definitely improved," she said to several fellow students one day when the conversation drifted to lack of freedom in the new China.

"Do you want to be told what to do all your life?" attacked a woman with round glasses and unbecoming chopped hair. She directed her question, along with a scornful gaze, at Chen Yu Hua, who was at once too intimidated to defend her statement.

"That depends what you mean by improved," sneered an intense young man she had never seen before. "Yes, we have more *things*, but there's more to life than things. We have to get rid of Deng Xiaoping. He is too old. You know what happens when old people govern a country." He waved his finger at Chen Yu Hua as though she was the errant child in the class.

"I don't think age matters," she rallied, trying to sound convincing but in truth she was feeling trapped.

"Mao was old," he shot back defiantly, "they say he was too old … that he was not responsible for the mischief he caused. What do you think? Do you think that's right?"

Chen Yu Hua could hear no more. She left the small gathering in the lunchroom, frightened and confused; being apolitical, she had never been witness to such talk. As far as she was concerned life in China was getting better. They should give Deng Xiaoping and his reforms a chance ... the "big ship" thing.

The sheltering halls of learning were suddenly not so tranquil anymore. She knew something was coming. Fear crawled into her mind, the same frozen fear that haunted her through the Mao years. "Surely, we won't have another upheaval in our lives. Surely not."

In February, U.S. President George Bush came to Beijing for a state visit, and another leader, Russian President Mikail Gorbachev, would be arriving in May for the first formal meeting in thirty years between the two powerful Communist countries. China was suddenly on the world stage. It seemed a good time for dissidents to speak out on democracy and human rights issues in the new, opened-up, liberal thinking China ... or so they hoped.

The unexpected death of Hu Yao Bang, a lesser member of the Politburo, on April 15, presented an avenue for them to voice their grievances. The funeral was scheduled for Saturday, April 22 and people began memorial activities the day before, laying wreaths at the monument to The People's Heroes in Tiananmen Square. Over a hundred thousand students gathered, singing and chanting slogans, ready to spend the night in the open, waiting for the morning funeral. Thousands of ordinary Beijingers came, not so much for the funeral, but curious about what was happening with the students.

Precisely at 9a.m. Saturday morning, loudspeakers announced the beginning of the ceremony. The students crowded toward the Great Hall of the People and a sea of 5,000 soldiers positioned themselves in front of the massive stone steps, standing eye to eye with the chanting, singing students. Three young men were allowed to kneel on the steps, holding up a petition for the leaders, Deng Xiaoping in particular, but in the end they were ignored.

The funeral was over in forty-five minutes. The cortege and some of the leaders, including Deng Xiaoping, slipped out a side door and no one in the Square had a chance to say their farewells to Hu Yao Bang, let alone have their petitions received by the government.

Dissension was bubbling to the surface. On the campuses of Beijing University and Qinghua University, as well as the colleges, an alliance of protesting voices rose simultaneously. Lessons were suspended, mass rallies were organized and everyone began marching. Out came the banners and posters criticizing the government for corruption, incompetence and turning a deaf ear to the people. Slogans were barked through bullhorns and by April 29, the crowds in Tiananmen Square swelled to over 150,000.

Big Character posters shouted out the words:

"Cry for the people"
"Demand democracy"
"Save our country with blood"
"Freedom of the press"
"The news should tell the truth"

The government labeled the whole outburst as no more than student turmoil, further enraging the people.

Two weeks later, on May 13, thousands of students went on a hunger strike and within the next few days over three thousand needed medical care after fainting from heat exhaustion. People came, encouraging the sit-ins, offering them food, water, blankets and money. Did these charitable people think it was a worthwhile cause or did they just feel sympathy for young students sleeping in the cold every night? Chen Yu Hua tried to understand the students' patriotic feelings but she did not agree with this form of protest.

Gorbachev came and went. His three-day visit had been disastrous and he was never taken to Tiananmen Square. The streets were choked with marchers, bicycles and vehicles. Celebrations and some public appearances for the Russian President had to be cancelled, proving to be a major embarrassment for the Chinese government. They were reluctant to admit they had lost control over events happening in the city.

On May 19, the students called off their hunger strike and probably the whole Tiananmen affair, given time, might have dissolved in the hot summer sun. Too late. The next morning, May 20, Premier Li Peng proclaimed martial law and 100,000 soldiers were positioned around Beijing.

Chen Yu Hua worried about the students, the future of China and her future. It reminded her of the Anti-Rightist Movement in the 1950s and the Cultural Revolution in the 1960s. The slogans, the Big Character Letter posters, the flying couplets, the parades ... it was all so familiar. There were too many movements. It made China weak.

Chen Yu Hua received many letters from Qinghai imploring her not to go near the demonstrations and to stay at the university. Liu Hao and the Chen family, including relatives she hadn't seen for years, begged her not to get involved. They watched TV everyday, they said, hoping never to see her face amongst the countless demonstrators.

After martial law was imposed, Chen Yu Hua stayed close to the university. Teachers warned students about going to Tiananmen Square and tried to keep them interested in their studies, but no one cared about studies in these hectic days.

Duojie brought an urgent message to Chen Yu Hua. "Sixteen of us are taking the train back home to Qinghai. I think you should come with us. We all feel something terrible is about to happen in the city."

"I'm not sure ..."

"Please, think about it," he pleaded, "you must come."

The uneasy morning of May 23 began hot and muggy. Chen Yu Hua joined the other sixteen students from Beiwai. They packed their bags and took the bus to the railway station where they found a scene of mass confusion and noise beyond belief, panic-stricken crowds desperate to leave the explosive political situation in Beijing. It reminded her of the old black and white newsreels she had seen in school of the 1949 Liberation. It was too awful. These people wore the same expressions of fear and worry. Chen Yu Hua was overcome with anxiety and the terrible thought that she could lose her life on this trip. They could all die. Oh, China ... what have we done to ourselves again?

Frantically she tried to keep up with her friends. Duojie

grabbed her thin jacket and yanked her up the stairs fighting the flood of people rushing to the trains. They came to a stop on the platform and counted themselves, "15—16—17!"

"It's impossible to get tickets to Xining," shouted one of the students, who had pushed his way to the madhouse ticket window, "I bought ones for Ningxia on Train 43 … from there we'll have to try somehow to get to Lanzhou."

"I heard that students along the way are demonstrating in sympathy with the ones in Beijing," called Duojie, his high-pitched voice reaching to be heard over the terrible noise. "In the countryside they're lying across the tracks … slowing all the trains."

It was unbearably hot and Chen Yu Hua was exhausted. Her clothes clung to her body in the thick humid air and she could hardly breathe. She gulped at the smoky fumes and worried about fainting. Suddenly, from nowhere a hysterical woman grabbed her sleeve. Small fingers wound around her arm in a vice-grip. "I've lost my child … my little boy," the woman shrieked, digging hard nails through the soft material. "He's gone … my boy … he was holding my hand … you have to help me find my little boy. Please … please, I beg you."

"Chen Yu Hua we can't wait," howled Duojie and he roughly wrenched the mother's hand from Chen Yu Hua's arm. She heard the woman scream, then felt herself being pulled hard along the platform, running through the hissing steam, past the huge iron wheels that were shunting dangerously. When she looked back the woman was gone, swallowed by the crowd and the smoke but she was sure she could hear her screams again and again.

"Why didn't we help? We should have tried." But no one listened and her voice was lost like the woman's child. She had to keep going. Her arms ached. Her head ached and still they had to squeeze themselves on to Train 43.

When they finally spotted their train it was jam-packed. Duojie and another young man shouted over the clamor for everyone to stay together. "Do not get separated. Stay together! We all have to get on this train … we can't leave anyone behind."

They pulled and pushed one another, shoved and heaved, and scrambled to get through the open windows. Duojie swung his lithe body into the coach and stretched down for Chen Yu Hua, dragging her up. In all the manhandling the strap on her right shoe broke and it tumbled to the ground. A quick-thinking young woman tossed it into the coach before Chen Yu Hua realized what had happened.

Chen Yu Hua and her mates had nowhere to sit but at least they were all together ... head count again ... 15—16—17. She put her broken shoe back on and leaned with the others against the coach wall, shoving her feet in-between the feet and legs of the people sitting on the floor opposite her. The heat. The raw smells. The constant shouting. She was sick to her stomach and had to focus her mind somewhere else or she could never get through this day. She stared blankly into space and wondered if the pitiful mother had found her child, then closed her eyes, trying to erase the troubling image of the screaming gaping mouth and the feverish eyes.

Iron scraped iron; squealing, discordant. The train jerked, pitching students into one another ... once, twice, several more times before slowly crawling along the track.

She turned her thoughts to Liu Hao and Si Xian.

They stood all the way through Hebei Province, with its open skies and mountain ranges, medieval villages and mud huts, and on to Inner Mongolia. They stood and they stood. The splendid grasslands of Inner Mongolia gave way to the coalmines of Shanxi Province. The local people had coal dust on their faces, their clothes were black and the land itself was black with the dust. Still they stood, feeling the endless hypnotic motion of the train beneath their feet as it swayed along uneven rails across Northwest China. Some students were lucky; if they were small enough they squeezed into the overhead wire luggage racks or crammed under the seats. Chen Yu Hua could stand no more. She was so tired and famished that she crawled under a seat and lay on the filthy floor where fits of sleep were measured in moments.

Going to the over-used toilet was a major excursion. She had to step carefully across legs attached to sleeping bodies ... at least they got to sleep. One time when she was coming out of the toilet she decided to go to the dining coach to find some water and perhaps a little food. People had been getting off the train at every station along the way, making it easier for her to move around.

She found the dining coach attendants friendly, and when she told them she was a student from Beijing, they wouldn't take any money for food. She was offered buns and hot water and they asked questions about her university and the student protests.

"They are heroes," said a conductor with admiration in his voice.

Chen Yu Hua did not know what to say, except, "thank you for being so kind." It was confusing to her that students who caused all this chaos could be called heroes.

Just when the people were letting go of their fears and living with more freedom, just when they, and she, didn't have to worry about starving or fleeing for their lives, just when she was going to university ... this upheaval had to happen.

She sighed and made her way back to the coach where Duojie had somehow wangled seats for most of the seventeen. His sleepy head collapsed on her shoulder when she curled in beside him. Poor Duojie ... young Tibetan Duojie from the high plains. Poor me. Why should you and I have all these unwanted interruptions in our lives?

And she fell into her first deep sleep.

Graduation day was here. No more trips up the high mountain passes, no more freezing classrooms, no more smiling midwife students. I was sad it was over.

"Does Mr. Cheng have a truck for all these kits?" asked Bill.

The front hall of our little house was stacked on both sides with heavy royal blue satchels imprinted with the flags of China and Canada, and the words "Midwife Project of Qinghai 1996" spelled out in English and Mandarin.

"Yes, yes," assured Miss Chen, "they said they have a big vehicle."

Just then an ambulance pulled up at the bottom of the lane. Driver Zhang, Mr. Cheng and others from our office leaped out and began loading the four hundred bags. So our procession to Datong, over the road to hell, began with an ambulance, followed by our little white station wagon and various other cars carrying the necessary officials for the graduation ceremony.

The theatre in Datong was almost full. Four hundred midwives, many in traditional costume, and their children were waiting for us to arrive. On the stage Vice Governor A (pronounced "R") headed the group of dignitaries ready to give their opening speeches. They sat at long tables with embroidered white cloth coverings, bowls of fresh flowers, and flags of Canada and China. The TV cameras rolled and the show began.

The people of Canada were thanked for their generous contribution. The municipal and provincial governments were thanked. Doctors, nurses and the teachers were thanked as well as the women who took part in the project.

It was time to hand out the kits. The teachers, including the young girl I had lectured about soap and water, brought their students on stage: Tibetan women, their long thick hair carefully braided; Hui Muslims with dark green or black embossed lace scarves covering their hair; Tu women, who believed their peoples were created from feathers left floating in the air by a flock of white cranes; and Mongolians, who descended from the time before Genghis Khan.

It was a moving and emotional ceremony and it was an honor to present each midwife the first birthing kit they ever owned, and an honor when a young Muslim woman said sincerely to Bill and me "God bless Canada. We will never forget tonight."

The three cars filled with staff and leaders, including the Vice Governor, began our trip back to Xining. I felt depressed. Although the project was going smoothly and the ceremony ended with immense dignity, I had this terrible letdown, a guilt feeling that our efforts in Qinghai meant little. There was so much left to do and the project was like a drop of water in the sea.

We squeezed together in our little white car and Mr. Cheng led the singing ... "xiao he wan wan xiang nan li" ... a popular song about the imminent return of Hong Kong to China. We sang on every one of our trips. Bill and I learned to hum along to familiar Chinese songs and now and then we all belted out "Edelweiss" or "Red River Valley", not knowing all the words to either song.

"Cheer up, Jeri," said Miss Chen interrupting her singing to tell me the Vice Governor had a surprise for us. Not another restaurant, I thought selfishly. I just wanted to go home. But she said we were going to the county of Huzhu, one of several closed regions in Qinghai, to visit the home of Li Fa Xiu. "Do you remember her? The Tu Lady?"

"Great," I perked up. "But don't we need special permission?"

"Of course," said Miss Chen, and when she translated my question, everyone in the car laughed, "the special permission is given by the Vice Governor ... she is with us ... in the other car."

Bill and I laughed too. Chen Yu Hua always knew how to cheer us.

We first met Li Fa Xiu when she came to our house bringing a beautiful collection of embroidery pieces so fine it is called Blind Stitching. The loss of sight is very possible after years creating this miniscule needlework. Not only were Tu people famous for embroidery, but also for beautiful paintings of local scenes called Farmers' Art. This type of painting had great detail and vibrant colors unlike traditional Chinese art with its birds-eye view of the landscape and monochromatic colors.

The Tu lady, her husband and children welcomed us to their home. I'm sure they had never entertained a Vice Governor before, let alone a couple of Canadians. The concrete floor, freshly washed in our honor, was still wet, ceramic pots of fuchsia plants blossomed in the porch and tea was ready to be served, steaming in glasses too hot to handle.

Li Fa Xiu was dressed in her traditional clothes, a rich patchwork of colors. Her unique hat, with its turned up broad brim, perched like a gold flying saucer on the center part of her jet-black hair.

We sipped our tea and ate cashews. I wasn't unhappy anymore, not in this peaceful spotless house adorned with original art and amazing needlework, in the company of the Tu family.

twenty-nine

中国

Chen Yu Hua arrived home in Xining late on the evening of May 25.

"I was so worried," Liu Hao said, "we have had no news about Beijing. What happened?"

Chen Yu Hua related the story of the student protests, the parades, the martial law, the panic in the city, and how she and sixteen of her colleagues managed to push themselves onto a crowded train to Ningxia. They had arrived at Yinchuan on the morning of May 24 exhausted, dirty and hungry, to find that all trains had stopped running and were delayed at Yinchuan until further notice. "Apparently down the line hundreds of students from Lanzhou University and regional colleges were lying across the tracks and were refusing to budge," she said, "and the protests were now as far west as Ganzu Province. We were starving. We found a small shop, devoured hot noodles and discussed the sit-ins and disruptions of the train schedules. The situation was uncertain and no news was coming out of Beijing. We didn't know what was happening. We could do nothing but wait."

Chen Yu Hua told Liu Hao that Yinchuan was divided into two parts: the New City where the railway station was situated, and the Old City with its much more interesting ancient architecture. She had persuaded her friends to explore the streets of the Old City.

The students found themselves in a small, almost derelict museum where they read the history of Yinchuan, the capital of Ningxia Autonomous Region. It was the home of a large population of Hui Muslims who were descended from Arab traders arriving in China around the first century B.C. It was also the fabled home of the Western Xia.

They were fascinated when they read the legend about the Xia people being responsible for the death, but not the defeat, of Genghis Khan; and how the Xia Kingdom could have joined Khan in his period of unification, saving thousands of Muslim lives, but instead decided fatefully to fight to the death. After repulsing Khan in six furious battles, one of the Xia archers drove a poison tipped arrow into the great leader. Although Genghis Khan was on his deathbed he was able to issue one last villainous decree ... "Destroy the Xia Kingdom," and it was done with catastrophic results.

Leaving the museum they strolled along a pleasant tree-lined street which opened up into a small square, and were surprised to see that the surrounding buildings and tower were exact replicas of Tiananmen Square. They were told that some students held a demonstration the day before but there were no real public disturbances.

"They asked if anyone heard about Beijing."

No ... nothing.

They made their way back through the narrow streets to the bustling market at South Gate and were fascinated by new, strange foods. In this remote parched land the people of Ningxia had mastered irrigation to its highest level and row upon row of greenhouses attested to their hard work and creativity.

"Since the students were still protesting along the tracks, we spent a cold night on the hard benches in the railway station but it was still better than sleeping under the seats," Chen Yu Hua said. She shuddered, thinking of the train floor, sticky with grime. "When we woke the next morning there was no guarantee that the train would be moving in the next day or two, so all seventeen of us boarded the long distance bus to Lanzhou."

She described the eight-hour trip following the Yellow River, with the imposing Helanshan Range towering to the west, passing the giant Qingtongxia Reservoir and on to Jingyeran. Her eyes had seen cruel sights: barren wasteland, the wretched mud huts of impoverished farmers, and dead and starving animals, hides pulled tight across their skeletons, in one of the poorest, sorriest parts of the country. Eventually, during the long afternoon, the sad dry landscape melted away and a scattering of poplars came into view; tall straight white poplars with leaves of spring-green pushing out from every branch. And she knew they were close to Lanzhou.

"It took four more hours by train to reach Xining from Lanzhou ... everyone breathed a sigh of relief to know we had made it."

"What an adventure," said Liu Hao when she finished her story.

"I'm so happy to be here with you."

She would sleep in her own warm bed that night beside her loving husband and tomorrow she would see her daughter Si Xian.

Chen Yu Hua's visit with her family was marred by her uneasiness about the Foreign Studies University. She was worried. It did not help that a news blackout was imposed from Beijing and she was unable to contact any other students, not even Duojie or any of her friends from the group of seventeen.

She tried to be happy at home. She cooked all of Liu Hao's favorite foods, took Si Xian to see her relatives. "How perfect she is," they cooed. She was also invited to her father's impressive new house in Xunhua, but she had neither time nor inclination to go. "It is so large and beautiful," gushed her favorite aunt, "it's very modern with big windows. The floors are light brown brick and it has new fashionable blonde wood cabinets and a new tapestry sofa in blues and pale green ... and many other new things."

"It sounds very nice," Chen Yu Hua said, with little enthusiasm. Although she was ashamed of the way she felt about the house, knowing it was the traditional Chinese way, she always harbored some resentment that her father built a new house for himself, and gave his sons the old houses, but none to his daughters.

Her favorite aunt also gave her a homecoming banquet and her friends pleaded for stories of Beijing, but nothing seemed to quiet her fears and she worried incessantly about her studies. She wondered if the classes had yet begun. Was the protest over? She assumed that after martial law was brought into effect, the students would calm down and go back to their colleges and universities. But she couldn't be sure and could not wait any longer.

Nine days later, on June 3, she kissed her husband and little girl goodbye and boarded the train for the return trip to Beijing, optimistic that the insanity she had left behind was now spent and the city was back to normal.

Chen Yu Hua arrived in Beijing in the afternoon of June 5. She noticed there were fewer people than usual at the station. The subway was closed down, there were no buses on the streets, and she wondered where were the hoards of bicycles? The streets had never been empty of bicycles before. She was petrified when she saw the number of soldiers carrying rifles, pacing back and forth. Back and forth. She felt their eyes watching her. She stood still, her head bowed and her two packs hanging from limp arms. Her room at the university was miles away from the station and she had not a clue which way to start walking.

"Are you all right?" A middle-aged man was speaking to her in a Beijing accent. "Where are you going? There is no transportation today ... is someone meeting you?"

Chen Yu Hua was suspicious of strangers but this afternoon she was lost and needed help. She smiled feebly. The man sensed she was too frightened to answer. "I just arrived on the train from Shanxi," he said in a reassuring voice, "I'm a mechanic there ... I've been away for six months. I'm coming home to visit my wife and children."

"I went home, too ... to Xining for awhile," answered Chen Yu Hua in a halting soft voice. "I'm a student at Beiwai. I hoped everything would be back to normal by now." She looked around, "but ... the guns?"

A young man had been eavesdropping on their conversation. He introduced himself as a soldier who had been on leave to Hainan Island and had just arrived home. He, too, was shocked to find armed soldiers at the railway station.

"Come, we can all start out towards Beiwai together," said the Beijing man confidently, taking the heaviest bag from Chen Yu Hua. "I live about a two hour walk from here. We can have some noodles at my house then you can go on to your university. I'm sure there will be people on the streets going that way ... you can join them."

"You must not walk by yourself," cautioned the soldier, "you being a student ... it wouldn't be safe."

Chen Yu Hua relaxed. Like it or not, she had no choice but to trust her two companions. "Thank you very much for helping me," she said.

Three people in a row, the Beijing man, the student, and the soldier, bent their heads and hustled along the twisting back lanes of the stricken city. The Beijing man knew all the shortcuts. Turning into a main thoroughfare, they passed the blackened skeletons of five burned-out buses. It was a foreign world; not the city she knew. Armed soldiers stood on the rooftops of buildings watching them, tracing their every move. A strange silence hovered on the thick hot air. No children's voices. No loitering groups of gossiping neighbors, only the soft shuffling of frightened feet. The few people who were on the streets, scurried by like ghosts, trying to be as inconspicuous as possible.

In some places Chen Yu Hua was aware of walking over shattered glass. Window glass. Bits of placards and charred cloth were strewn about. To her sick amazement she saw bullet holes in the brick walls and the lampposts. Overturned vehicles and chunks of broken concrete blocked parts of the road, and she stumbled and almost fell over a tire that had spun away from a farm tractor lying on its side. Piled against it were boards from old wooden fences that had been ripped from the earth: posts, staves from barrels, pieces of canvas, curls of wire and broken furniture ... a barricade? She felt queasy. It was a war zone.

"Hurry," urged the Beijing man. His voice, harsh and commanding, startled her, but she was too frightened to raise her head. In the awful silence she just walked on with the men, sometimes tripping and sending loose rocks spinning in front of her echoing through the empty streets. The Beijing man had set the pace; it was fast and steady.

When they reached his home in a place called Xisi, near Tiananmen, it was getting dusk. His wife opened the gate when she heard him call. Excited at seeing her husband she blurted the dreadful news about Tiananmen Square and the students. She had not been outside her siheyuan in days, she told them, too afraid of what was happening on the streets. Minutes later the three thirsty and fatigued comrade marchers slumped onto stools at the kitchen table while the tattling wife spewed words so fast she hardly stopped to inhale. She handed each of them a glass of tea and poured hot water over dried noodles.

"I'm sorry ... I have no fresh noodles," she apologized, "all the stores are closed, and anyway, I didn't want to go out. They say it's too dangerous."

She related more gossip she had heard from friends and neighbors about the pro-democracy protest by the students, the tanks in the Square. It was rumored, she said, that Li Peng, with Deng Xiaoping's blessing ... had ordered the soldiers to open fire on the students. Many of them died, hundreds of them. She knew people who were there and saw it all.

The four of them were horrified to think that Chinese soldiers could kill Chinese people in this New Open China. It was unimaginable and all too tragic. No one had expected the government to be so harsh.

"I don't think it's safe for you to go out on the streets tonight," said the Beijing man's wife, "it's a long way to the university and you could be all alone."

"I have to go," said Chen Yu Hua, pulling some cakes from her bag and laying them on the table. "I'll be fine."

She thanked the woman for the noodles and tea, and the man for helping her get across Beijing, and left with the young soldier. They had given each other their home addresses, promising to keep in touch and always to remember this unexpected experience and the few tense hours they had shared together.

The soldier walked with her for several blocks then said goodbye, wishing her a safe journey, and turned towards his own home.

Chen Yu Hua went on alone carrying her two packs. There were more people on the streets the further she got from the center of Beijing, but she was still apprehensive. Passersby talked in low voices. She met a young man a few blocks from where he was studying at the National Minorities Institute. He told her several students belonging to the Institute had died the day before when tanks opened fire on the people on Tiananmen Square. His voice was so sorrowful and quavering that he could hardy tell the story.

"Also this morning," he said, "a student placed himself in great danger by standing in front of a moving tank."

"What happened to him?"

"It was a miracle. The tank stopped. No one knows who the man was ... he disappeared into the crowd." Chen Yu Hua heard the admiration in his emotional voice as they stood staring through the wrought iron gates at the National Minorities Institute. The front doors were draped in black crepe and large photos of the dead students were posted on the walls.

"I wonder what happened to Duojie," she mused softly.

"Who?" Asked the young student.

"I was just thinking of a friend of mine from Xining," she answered. "I haven't heard from him lately."

The student didn't answer. He was too sad and despondent.

"Goodbye," he said quietly as he turned towards the Institute, "I hope you find your friend."

She remembered the last time she said goodbye to Duojie. To endure such an ordeal was a great trauma for all of them and she wondered if perhaps he would decide not to come back to Beijing. She wouldn't blame him.

It was late and very dark when she finally reached her room. She had walked two and a half hours in oppressive humid heat from the Beijing man's home, dragging her exhausted body through the gates, down the last remaining stretch of the lane, under the shadowy trees and up to the wooden doors of her dormitory in the Foreign Studies University. It was only eight months ago when she first walked down this lane. Was it really only eight months? She dropped like a stone on the bed, her feverish mind unable to analyze the numbing events happening around her.

The students at the university were grim and subdued. They tried to find out details about Tiananmen but there were no TV or press reports as yet. Even if they searched for the truth would they find it? Would they be afraid to find it? Would the newspapers tell them the real truth? Chen Yu Hua and some of her classmates went to Fuchengmen Bridge where the mutilated body of a young soldier was hanging, burned beyond recognition, his genitals cut out. Chen Yu Hua threw up on the roadside. They were told that students committed the grisly murder. Was this the truth?

It was several days before lessons resumed in the classes. Chinese newspapers reported that between three and four hundred people had died in the Tiananmen Incident. What the rest of the world witnessed on TV became known as the Tiananmen Massacre. No exact numbers were ever published about the deaths on June 4, 1989. Whatever sparked the protest; a democracy movement, a radical group in the universities, a political struggle, hatred towards the Party or whatever it was, many lives were lost in Beijing that fearsome night. Not only did students die on Tiananmen Square, The Gate of Heavenly Peace, but also ordinary workers and citizens of Beijing perished in the volleys of gunfire on Chang'an Boulevard and Fuxingmen Avenue.

Chen Yu Hua often said, "I will never forget the parades, the train trip, and the horror stories about Tiananmen Square."

She thought about the poem in her father's book A Dream of Red Mansions:

> *A tale of grief is told,*
> *a fantasy most melancholy.*
> *Since all live in a dream,*
> *why laugh at others' folly?*

And sometimes she felt it was all a bad dream.

When we asked Miss Chen about her parents, all she would confide was, "My mother died in an accident." So we were surprised when one day she declared, "Tomorrow I am taking both of you and Si Xian to my hometown, to meet my father and family."

And so she did.

Driver Pei had driven us safely through Peace and Safe County, over Qingsha Pass, down into the green valleys of Hua Long, through Lamu Gorge, and past the suspension bridge over the Yellow River. Through Jiezi County, the ancestral home of the Salar people. Through Gandu Township, where her father had once been headmaster, to Xunhua to stand in the courtyard of the Chen home with the Chen family.

"This is my father," said Miss Chen proudly.

Chen Jian Pin was in his late sixties. He was not a tall man but had a commanding presence and there was no doubt his family held him in great respect. The house was an impressive residence, newly built. Carved designs on the bright yellow fascias followed the curves of the long sweeping rooflines, and over the front door, carved in red calligraphy by Chen Jian Pin, was the distinguished family name.

We were welcomed into the main room. The sun was incredibly bright streaming through the open windows and doors like something you could touch. During his lifetime, Jian Pin had built three homes, one for each son. This was the largest and most modern and, like the other two, would always remain in the family. Multihued rugs were scattered on the brick floors, and walls displayed calligraphy scrolls penned by his hand. An oblong French-style gold pendulum clock, looking very ornate and incongruous with the setting, hung above a black and white picture of Jian Pin as a young man.

There was a contemporary bookshelf and a large cabinet with glass doors, a tapestry sofa with a protective sheet thrown over it, two easy chairs and a coffee table. Rich satin comforters were folded on a kang bed along one wall and a round coal stove stood in the center of the room. On top of a bureau sat a small shrine surrounded by vases of calligraphy brushes, and another photo, this one of a young lady.

"This is my mother Jia Ying, when she was very young," said Miss Chen. She picked up the picture and gave it to Si Xian, who stared at the pretty girl with the serious face and short black hair pulled smoothly back behind her ears.

Bill and I sat next to a window in a peaceful alcove, the mountains towering above us, and lunched with Miss Chen and Jian Pin for two full hours on mouth-watering deep-fried chicken legs rolled in sesame seeds, pancakes made with beaten eggs, chopped green onions, tomatoes, and mashed potato, pressed thin and gently sautéed in rapeseed oil.

Father and daughter spoke of their scholarly family. "My parents retired from their teaching careers in 1985," Miss Chen told us, "They were admired for the excellent way they educated their seven children ... every one of us passed the entrance exams for secondary schools or colleges or universities. My extended family has fifty males and fifty-four females. The Chen family is so large we need name tags when we have a gathering."

After lunch we went to the first family home or, as Miss Chen said, "number one home where I grew up." It was still occupied by her father's relatives and they courteously invited us to see inside the old house. Miss Chen showed us the room where she and her sisters once slept, then suddenly scrambled up a ladder with Si Xian close on her heels. Leaning over the railing she called down to us, "You must come and see my secret room ... I used to play cards here with my sisters ... I loved this place, it was a sanctuary to get away from my troubles."

I managed to climb up a few rungs, just enough to peer over the top of the floor in time to see her bend down and disappear into another room. "It's so small ... I can't believe I ever fitted in here," she called in a muffled voice.

That day was the first time Si Xian had been to the house where her mother lived as a little girl, and to the room where she played. She saw for the first time the dusty lanes where her mother hauled water buckets on her thin young shoulders. She saw the fields where her mother foraged for food and carried her siblings on her back; looked at the apple trees and heard the Tibetan women singing as they gathered firewood to pile on their donkeys.

We walked back to the new house, past old men playing mahjong under the trees, and came to a small elaborate building with the same turned up sculptured roof as a temple, surrounded by ornamental gardens. It stood out like a jeweled palace on a street filled with timeworn homes and shops.

"What is this attractive building?" Bill asked.

"It's what you in the West call a funeral home. If a person dies in a hospital or somewhere other than their own home it is considered unlucky for the family to have the body returned to the home so it's brought here. The family will come to pay their respects." She stopped and waved her hands around, "but the day is too sunny and beautiful to talk about funerals."

Children followed us everywhere, silent and staring. I asked why the kids didn't greet us with a hello.

"I think they are just too overwhelmed to speak," she said. "They see very few foreign faces in Xunhua."

It had been a privilege to spend the day with this gracious family: Miss Chen's three sisters, three brothers, sisters-in-law, brothers-in-law, and the five grandchildren. "See you again," the young ones giggled, the only English words they knew after hello and bye-bye. Chen Jian Pin presented us with a long scroll of calligraphy painted by his own hand. "This is a very famous Chinese saying," said Miss Chen. She pointed to each character and read the words: A friend from afar brings a distant shore near.

As we said our farewells I sensed Jian Pin was reluctant to let his daughter go; there was a spiritual bond between them. He stood on the side of the road, not waving or moving, and we watched him for a long time until our car turned a corner and he was lost from sight.

We drove back through Gandu Township, past the stately old villa once owned by the warlord, Ma Bu Fang, and with the sun glowing crimson in the western sky, we went over the mountains to Xining.

thirty

中国

Chen Yu Hua had tears in her eyes as she hugged her husband and little daughter. It was mid-January, 1990, and she had returned to Xining from Beijing for the winter holiday.

"Si Xian is beautiful and she talks so well," she said proudly to Liu Hao, "and I can't believe how happy I am to be home. Soon I'll be finished with Beiwai and home to stay."

She hugged Liu Hao again.

Three days went by. Three glorious days for Chen Yu Hua. She busied herself around the small flat and never left the side of her little girl.

"I would like to see my mother and father before I go back to Beijing," she said to her husband, "I think we could all go to Xunhua next week providing the weather is good in the mountain pass."

He ignored her words and said matter-of-factly, "I heard today that Wang Zhu's mother was killed last Thursday in an accident."

Chen Yu Hua had never met Wang Zhu but knew she was a teacher at the school.

"How awful," she said, "what happened?"

"The old lady was actually shopping in her home village, walking near the market when a car knocked her to the ground and she struck her head. It was a bad death." Liu Hao's voice was so solemn it frightened her. "I think it must be terrible to have your mother die like that."

"Yes, of course it would," she agreed, wondering why he was so sad and concerned about an old mother in Hunan Province.

He put his hand on her arm. "Chen Yu Hua," he said, "do you think you and I would be mentally prepared if we lost one of our parents like Wang Zhu did?"

The sun was going down and it was getting cold in the flat, but the banging and clanking of the pipes in the radiators, and the bitter coal smell in the air hinted that warmth was on the way from the compound's heating plant.

She trembled slightly, not only from the cold but from a chilly sixth sense warning her. Of what? Was one of her parents ill? If so, why wouldn't Liu Hao just tell her? If there were a tragedy in the family she would most certainly have heard about it before now. Her brain shrugged off the thought.

"I don't know why you ask, I only know we are very strong people, Liu Hao," she said softly, "and in the future when one of us loses a parent we will be mentally prepared. I'm sure of that."

He was satisfied and smiled. "Good," he said, pushing his daughter's arms into her little padded jacket, "let's take Si Xian for a walk now."

It was the next evening when Liu Hao broke the dreadful news. Chen Yu Hua noticed how edgy and ill at ease he had been all day until he finally asked her to sit down; he had something important to say.

"Remember when we talked about losing a parent?"

Chen Yu Hua did not answer. She sat and reflected on what her husband had said the night before. If one of her parents had fallen ill or even died, would she be ready to accept it? Was he telling her now that one of them was gone? Was it her father? He was getting older. Did he have a heart attack? Was her husband about to tell her that her father had died and she would never see him again? Never have the chance to say, "No matter how many differences there were between us, I have always loved you." That would be too painful. Too unthinkable.

"My mother is dead?"

Chen Yu Hua sat stunned and motionless as Liu Hao recounted how her mother had been killed sixteen days earlier on a street very close to her home. It was on the twenty-ninth of December. Her father and mother had ridden their bicycles to the

County Hospital to visit a relative. On their way back Jian Pin asked his wife to come with him to see a friend. He wanted to return a borrowed book and it would only take a few minutes, but Jia Ying said no, she had too much work to do at home.

"I'm sure she had," said Chen Yu Hua, her voice reproachful, "she was always working."

"Your father told me he had a strange feeling ... almost a premonition as he watched your mother leave. He said he should have insisted she stay and wait for him."

Liu Hao continued the story. When Jia Ying was only a few minutes from her gate, a speeding van came out of nowhere and struck her with such force that she died instantly. She was wearing the black coat that Chen Yu Hua had given her.

"It was soaked in blood," said Liu Hao gently, "your poor mother."

Chen Yu Hua sat very still. The pressure in her head was agonizing. She remembered when she had given her mother the black cashmere wool coat. It was after Chen Yu Hua started teaching. She had saved her money for such a long time to buy Jia Ying something new.

Her mother had caressed the soft wool cloth and told her daughter, "I never thought I would ever own such a fine coat."

Tears of grief welled up and burned Chen Yu Hua's eyes.

"What else?" she asked.

"They had an investigation," said Liu Hao and told her that the van had no horn, and the driver, a young Muslim boy, was speeding too fast and could not stop in time. Jian Pin and his family had to deal with the accident. They could charge the driver and he would be sentenced to prison for three to four years. But the family decided that was not going to bring Jia Ying back to them, so they accepted an offer of 3,000 yuan from the family of the driver to drop any charges. Jian Pin was a cautious man. He believed what the Muslim people believed: it was fate that killed his wife, and he did not want to cause any controversy between the two peoples.

When Liu Hao was through talking he wiped the tears from Chen Yu Hua's cheeks with a warm cloth and held her hands in his.

She was heart broken. "Is that all my mother's life was worth

... 3,000 yuan?"

"Chen Yu Hua, please," Liu Hao tried to console her, "of course not, but your family decided it was the best way."

"She should have lived to be old and die in her sleep. Not on a dirty road where donkeys walk ... she should have had a good death ... a five blossom death ... marriage, a son, being respected, a grandson." She took a deep breath, "But my mother died on the street ... a very bad death," she said softly.

"I know."

"Why didn't you tell me?" she sobbed. "Why did you wait until I came home?"

"Your father forbade us to tell you because you were preparing for final term exams and he had no wish to upset you."

The next day Chen Yu Hua, her husband and her little girl took the long distance bus to Xunhua, where her oldest brother met them. Chen Yu Hua did not go with the others to the house but walked alone to the Chen family graves and there, in the shadow of the giant treeless mountains, she found the new mound of turned soil. She wept and wept, and fell on her knees to the icy ground, calling for her mother.

Through her tears she saw him standing near the Chen ancestral headstones.

Her father had come to meet her. His face was drawn and haggard, but he still had an elegant, commanding presence, straight and firm, and for a moment she was reminded of Professor Li. They were both gentlemen from the same era; both educated the same way; both scholars. She began to understand him for the man he really was. How fortunate she and her family had been to have this proud, strong-minded and courageous father to protect them, guide them and educate them through the painful and dangerous years of their youth.

She looked at him truly for the first time. All her anger and resentment melted away.

She ran to him, threw her arms around him and they both wept. Jian Pin told his daughter how sorry he was for making her life miserable. He only wanted the best for her. He regretted the years of isolation, the wasted years of silence, his unbending pride and the anger he felt when she disobeyed him. He had tried to ignore her, to punish her, but secretly he admired her strength and determination. Could she ever forgive him?

"I love you," he said, "you are my favorite child and I am very proud of you."

She answered simply that she had always loved and respected him, and together they walked back to the new house.

The night before we were to leave for Beijing, a farewell dinner and dance was held in our honor at the Xining Dasha; the last thing we ever expected. An impressive brass plaque was presented to us by the mayor ... "you are now honorary citizens of Xining," he said. Vice Governor Bai Ma placed Tibetan Hadas, long white-fringed scarves around our necks and proposed the farewell toast. Halfway through the party the lights went out and, while the men clicked on their lighters, someone called for candles. The candles came. They were small, two-inch birthday candles. So we all held flickering two-inch birthday candles and carried on laughing and talking as if the room was bathed in light.

At the Xining airport the next day we said our goodbyes to the mayors and some of the staff. It was hard to say goodbye to Miss Wei, knowing we may never see her again. And little Si Xian, who told us the best present she ever got was our toaster, and she would look after it forever and would always miss her gramma and grampa. Driver Zhang was honestly sad to see us go. "Miss you," he said in real English, and Mr. Cheng added "come back."

Miss Chen and Boss Liu accompanied us to Beijing and we were now sitting in the Cherry Blossom Hotel in Chaoyang District waiting for Driver Wong and the cars needed to transport our six large suitcases, the usual carry-ons and a heavy royal blue wool Tibetan rug to the airport.

This day Bill and I were going home to Canada.

We hated to leave Miss Chen. She sat staring out the window, her eyes half closed. Who was this Chinese woman? Do I really know you Miss Chen, Chen Yu Hua, Jade Flower, Scarlett? Intelligent, frustrating, caring, loving. Before we came to China we understood nothing about the Chinese people. Nothing. A lot of misinformation. How naïve we were.

Suddenly she turned to me. "Jeri, I know how you like to write ... would you tell my life story in a book?"

I was surprised.

"I'll send you lots of letters ... all about me, about my family and my life.

"I'll try."

I suppose I was secretly thrilled. Now I would get to know Miss Chen.

"Promise?"

"Yes, I promise."

The teeming Beijing airport was loud and crazy. We said goodbye to Driver Wong and Boss Liu. I was crying. Miss Chen was crying.

"They won't let us go any further to help you," Miss Chen said anxiously, "Can you manage?"

We struggled awkwardly with our cases, though they were not quite as heavy as when we arrived the year before. Then suddenly we were wrenched along by the persistent crowds. No time to say goodbye properly.

She stood at the barrier, calling and waving. We couldn't hear her and could barely see her, and then she was gone from us.

We left China and Miss Chen.

Our great adventure was over and our lives changed forever. We never looked at China in the same way again, or Canada, or the world, or poverty and wealth.

Never looked at life in the same way again.

Ten Years Later

In the past ten years much has changed in Qinghai.

Since 1996, the Central Government of China has pumped billions of yuan into Qinghai in the effort to improve its fragile economy and modernize living conditions. When we visited Xining in 1998, old buildings were being demolished and new ones erected. A casualty of progress was our little Canadian house, which had escaped the wrecker's ball and survived as a Tourist Office for a short time. Surprisingly, our green apple tree was still standing, lonely and leaning to one side, on a brick paved square in front of the new Qinghai TV office tower.

A recent letter from Chen Yu Hua tells us she has a new position with the Qinghai Provincial Government. Prior to this, she served three years as Second Secretary in the Chinese Embassy in Amman, Jordan.

She and Mr. Liu have purchased a large new two-bedroom apartment. It has a long sunny porch, a full bathroom and a modern kitchen with a stainless steel sink and stove. Their daughter, Si Xian, has taken the English name Susan and now studies at the prestigious Sun Yat-Sen University in Guangzhou.

In her letter, Chen Yu Hua described the changes in the Foreign Trade & Economic Development Commission. Mr. Cheng and Boss Liu have retired, Young Liu has moved on to head another department and Miss Wei continues her career with the Commission. She and Young Zhan, married in 1996, have a little boy.

Madam Ding has retired from the Women's Bureau. Madam Yang has transferred to another department in Datong. Mayor Yang, Mayor Liu and Ms. Chen Jing Jun have also retired. Number One Mayor Liu has been promoted to a higher office with the Provincial Government.

The expectant women of Datong and other counties are now

required to go to district hospitals and clinics to deliver their babies. This will dramatically decrease the mortality rate in childbirth.

Chen Yu Hua also writes that the One Child Policy has been changed. Since the elderly population of China is enormous and becoming a burden on the young generation, the government deems it necessary to increase the birthrate. If couples are both from one-child families, they are allowed to have two children; in the countryside, farmers enjoy more favorable policies.

Infrastructure has been greatly improved in Qinghai, including three new expressways and two ring roads around the city. The Qinghai-Tibet railway, scheduled to be officially opened on June 1, 2006, will connect southern China with the western region. Trains from Beijing, Guangzhou and other major coastal cities will pass through Xining on the way to Lhasa, bringing tourists and economic development.

New hotels have been built in Xining, including the first five-star Yinlong Hotel. There are two grand public squares and a new gymnasium.

Miss Chen assures us that living standards of the people are improving. "They are buying fashionable clothes and furniture," she says, "and moving into new houses and flats in garden-like residential areas."

Introduced in 2002, the Tour of Qinghai Lake Bicycle Race (a world class race in the same category as the Tour De France) has brought an international dimension to tourism, highlighting the wild and beautiful Tibetan Plateau. The race is a major influence in the drive to renovate all hotels and tourist facilities, including the Qinghai Lake Hotel (Birds Island Hotel), improving standards for foreign and domestic tourists. In 1995, foreign tourists to Qinghai numbered only 5,000; in 2005, foreign tourists reached 38,000 and domestic visitors totaled over 3 million.

Miss Chen ends her letter with these words, "The most important change is that people are more open-minded than before. We now hold international exhibitions, concerts, conferences, festivals and business activities attracting much attention from outside Qinghai. Life is getting better all the time."

ISBN 141208125-4